EUSEBIUS
AS CHURCH
HISTORIAN

EUSEBIUS
AS CHURCH
HISTORIAN

ROBERT M. GRANT

CLARENDON PRESS · OXFORD
1980

Oxford University Press, Walton Street, Oxford OX2 6DP

OXFORD LONDON GLASGOW
NEW YORK TORONTO MELBOURNE WELLINGTON
KUALA LUMPUR SINGAPORE JAKARTA HONG KONG TOKYO
DELHI BOMBAY CALCUTTA MADRAS KARACHI
NAIROBI DAR ES SALAAM CAPE TOWN

Published in the United States
by Oxford University Press, New York

British Library Cataloguing in Publication Data

Grant, Robert McQueen
Eusebius as church historian.
1. Eusebius, *Bp of Caesarea*. Ecclesiastical
history
2. Church history — Primitive and early church,
ca. 30–600
I. Title
270.1   BR160.E55   80–40342
ISBN 0–19–826441–0

Set by Hope Services, Abingdon
and printed in Great Britain by
Billing & Sons Limited,
Guildford, London and Worcester

PREFACE

About ten years ago, when I began intensive studies in the *Church History*, conclusions seemed easier to draw than they do now. For patience and/or criticism my thanks are due to students and colleagues at the University of Chicago, the Catholic University of America, Haverford College, the University of London (King's College), and McMaster University, as well as to fellow members of various Patristic Conferences at Oxford and the Lyons Conference of 1977. My thanks are also due to the editors of various collections of essays in which earlier versions of my interpretations were published.

Professor T. D. Barnes deserves special mention because his comments on the topics discussed have usually proved right. Professor R. L. Wilken deserves special mention because he has corrected contradictions and deleted repetitions, though he may not have found them all. I am grateful to Professor Arnaldo Momigliano for his criticism after I read part of the study in his seminar at Chicago.

As for details, citations with a Roman numeral and one or two Arabic ones refer to the *Church History* of Eusebius. The Latin *Chronicle* is cited by pages in the edition of Helm. Translations are usually taken from or based on Lawlor and Oulton.

R. M. G.

CONTENTS

ABBREVIATIONS

AE	*L'Année épigraphique*
BGU	*Ägyptische Urkunden aus den Königlichen Stättlichen Museen zu Berlin. Griechische Urkunden*
Chrest.	See Bibliography under Mitteis, L.
CHSB	*Corpus Scriptorum Historiae Byzantinae*
CIL	*Corpus Inscriptionum Latinarum*
CSCO	*Corpus Scriptorum Christianorum Orientalium*
CSEL	*Corpus Scriptorum Ecclesiasticorum Latinorum*
ETL	*Ephemerides Theologicae Lovanienses*
FGrHist	*Die Fragmente der griechischen Historiker*
HTR	*Harvard Theological Review*
ILS	*Inscriptiones Latinae Selectae*
JAOI	*Jahreshefte des Oesterreichischen Archäologischen Institutes*
JEH	*Journal of Ecclesiastical History*
JRS	*Journal of Roman Studies*
JTS	*Journal of Theological Studies*
OGI	*Orientis Graeci Inscriptiones selectae*
P	Papyrus (conventional identifications)
PG	*Patrologia Graeca*
PL	*Patrologia Latina*
RB	*Revue biblique*
RE	*Realencyclopädie der classischen Altertumswissenschaft*
RSR	*Recherches de science religieuse*
TU	*Texte und Untersuchungen*
VC	*Vigiliae Christianae*
ZKG	*Zeitschrift für Kirchengeschichte*
ZNW	*Zeitschrift für die Neutestamentliche Wissenschaft*

I

EUSEBIUS AND HIS CHURCH HISTORY:
INTRODUCTION

Scholars have criticized the *Church History* of Eusebius for many centuries, though not always for the right reasons. As early as the fifth century the historian Socrates Scholasticus criticized Eusebius' account of the Manichees. Unfortunately he relied on the apocryphal *Acta Archelai*.[1] While Eusebius' account is thoroughly inadequate, the vivid details offered by the *Acta* are not much better. In more recent times, scholars have noted the gaps and contradictions to be found in Eusebius' text. They had no sound basis for their theories, however, until Eduard Schwartz published his magisterial edition in 1903 to 1909, as well as his own analysis of the textual, literary, and historical problems. Other important works include *Eusebiana* by H. J. Lawlor, the translation and commentary by Lawlor and J. E. L. Oulton, the study of *Eusebius als Historiker seiner Zeit* by R. Laqueur (often excessively ingenious), and the analysis of *Les Vues historiques d'Eusèbe de Césarée durant la période prénicéenne* by J. Sirinelli. One should also mention the studies of T. D. Barnes, published chiefly in the *Journal of Theological Studies* but including his report at the Eighth Patristic Conference on 'The First Edition of Eusebius' *Ecclesiastical History*'.

My own concern is somewhat different from those of all these scholars. They have tended to accept and endorse the presence of radical changes during the composition of Eusebius' last three books, dealing with contemporary events, but (with the exception of Barnes) have treated the first seven as handed down virtually unaltered. The purpose of this book is to show how Eusebius' mind changed (a point stressed by Sirinelli) and how the fact that 'he is very *desultory* in his treatment' — a charge levied by Lightfoot and Westcott in 1880 — sometimes makes it possible to detect various 'strata' in the *Church History*.[2]

When we look for evidence to show that Eusebius' mind changed as he was writing, we naturally investigate his earliest historical effort, the

---

[1] Socrates, *H. E.* i. 22; Eusebius, *H. E.* vii. 31; *Acta Archelai*, pp. 62–4 Beeson.
[2] J. B. Lightfoot (and B. F. Westcott), 'Eusebius of Caesarea', *Dictionary of Christian Biography*, II (London, 1880), 326.

Chronicle. Unfortunately this work survives only in a Latin version by Jerome, an Armenian version often influenced by the Latin, and incomplete quotations in Byzantine chronographers. Jerome tells us that Eusebius carried his *Chronicle* as far as the year 326 (*Chron.*, p. 231, 12 Helm), but it is hard to see how Eusebius could have written the *Church History* without benefit of the chronological structure provided by an earlier work./At the very least, he must have had the main outlines of the *Chronicle* available as he began the *History*. This is what he says he had, in a passage almost certainly derived from his first edition (I. 1. 6). To be sure, not everything in Jerome's version comes from Eusebius. Jerome explicitly stated in his preface that he added materials on Roman history, with which Eusebius as a Greek writer was not especially concerned. In tracing Eusebius' thought we must subtract everything Roman from Jerome's version of the *Chronicle*. Enough remains, however, for us to follow certain ideas and interpretations from the *Chronicle* to one aspect, presumably early, of the *History* and then on to a reinterpretation. The importance of this kind of study lies in a new picture of Eusebius and his historical work and, in addition, a new picture of certain aspects of the history of theology (especially but not exclusively in relation to politics) in the early fourth century.

II

THE CHRONICLE OF EUSEBIUS

The *Chronicle* of Eusebius consisted of two books, of which only the second concerns us. The first was a 'chronography' with excerpts from older historians and chroniclers. Its goal was the synchronization of biblical and extra-biblical history. As Eusebius pointed out in his preface as translated by Jerome, for dating Moses in the time of Inachus, fifty years before the Trojan war, he relied on the Christian writers Clement, Africanus, and Tatian, as well as the Jewish authors Josephus and Justus (of Tiberias). He noted that Porphyry when writing against the Christians placed Moses even earlier.[1] Such points, characteristic of Jewish and Christian apologetics, clearly indicate the apologetic goal of the *Chronicle*. The second book consisted of 'chronological lists' arranged in tabular form and attempting to provide precise dates for persons and events.[2] As a framework Eusebius used years beginning with the birth of Abraham.

We do not possess these 'chronological lists' in their original language or form, though excerpts in later Byzantine chronographies often use Eusebius' words. The whole work exists in two translations. The Armenian version is often highly regarded. It breaks off at the end of the 270th Olympiad after referring to the twenty-year reign of Diocletian which ended a year later, and scholars have sometimes thought that it reflects an edition ending with the year 303. Using it presents a problem, however, for it includes almost all the additions made by Jerome in his Latin version, along with many errors. The most reliable version is the one made by Jerome (with a note that Eusebius carried his work to 325) and expanded to cover events as far as 379.

---

[1] Eusebius–Jerome, *Chron. Lat.* (ed. R. Helm; hereafter cited as *Chron.*), 7–8; cf. R. Helm, 'De Eusebii in Chronicorum libro auctoribus', *Eranos*, 22 (1924), 1–40.

[2] J. K. Fotheringham, *The Bodleian Manuscript of Jerome's Version of the Chronicle of Eusebius* (Oxford, 1905), 7–16; R. Helm, 'Eusebius' Chronik und ihre Tabellenform', *Abhandlungen Berl. Akad.* 1923, *Philol.-hist. Kl.* 4, 3–56. For a lucid discussion of these problems cf. A. A. Mosshammer, *The Chronicle of Eusebius and Greek Chronographic Tradition* (Lewisburg, N. J. – London, 1979), 29–83; on Eusebius' sources, 128–68. Unfortunately (for our purposes) the author is primarily concerned with early Greek chronology.

In his preface Jerome spoke of 'many' additions that he made from Suetonius and other illustrious historians (*Chron.*, p. 6 Helm).[3] In a letter of the year 374 (*Ep.* 10. 3) he asked a friend to send him the 'history' of Aurelius Victor. This proves that he was acquainted with at least one of the annalists of the late fourth century, though many of his comments are exactly paralleled in Eutropius, not Aurelius Victor.[4] In recovering Eusebius' work we must subtract discussions of Roman history, in which as Jerome noted, Eusebius took little interest. We must delete anything related to the city of Rome, to Roman philosophers, or to philosophers at Rome.

On the other hand, the list of Greek philosophers for years between 68 and 176 (none later) is almost certainly derived from a Greek Middle Platonist source like the one recently discussed by H. D. Saffrey.[5] Jerome took no interest in such matters. And the philosopher for 176 is Atticus 'of the Platonic sect',[6] presumably given recognition in the year when Marcus Aurelius endowed chairs at Athens (Lucian, *Eun.* 3) and Herodes Atticus selected the holders (Philostratus, *Vit. soph.* p. 566). There is no mention of Numenius, Plotinus, or Porphyry, all utilized in Eusebius' later *Gospel Preparation*, and we therefore assume that the list used in the *Chronicle* was earlier than Plotinus.

Eusebius was not primarily concerned with philosophy. What he needed was a chronological skeleton to support the structure of his literary history of Christianity. He certainly possessed the *Chronographies* of Julius Africanus, which carried events up to the year 221, and the later *Chronicle* of the philosopher Porphyry, which ran from the capture of Troy to the reign of the Emperor Claudius Gothicus (268-270).[7] Both Africanus and Porphyry left him a free hand in dealing with events in the Christian era. As Photius long ago noted, Africanus dealt only cursorily with events from the time of Christ to the reign of the Emperor Macrinus (217-218). Indeed, Byzantine chronographers cite his work for only two items in the two

---

[3] T. Mommsen, 'Ueber die Quellen der Chronik des Hieronymus', *Abhandlungen der philol.-hist. Cl. der Königlichen Sächsischen Gesellschaft der Wissenschaften*, 1 (1850), 669-93; cf. A. Reifferscheid, *C. Suetoni Tranquilli ... Reliquiae* (Leipzig, 1860), 94-7.

[4] R. Helm, 'Hieronymus und Eutrop', *Rheinisches Museum*, 76 (1927), 138-70; 254-306.

[5] 'Un lecteur antique de œuvres de Numénius', *Forma Futuri: Studi in onore del cardinale Michele Pellegrino* (Torino, 1975), 145-53.

[6] Cf. J. Dillon, *The Middle Platonists* (London, 1977), 247-51.

[7] References to Africanus in the Armenian *Chronicle*, pp. 34, 47, 48, 61 Karst; to Porphyry, p. 125, 24-5.

centuries: the teaching of Clement at Alexandria under Commodus (180-192) and the reign of the 'holy man' Abgar at Edessa in the early third century. Eusebius himself supplies a third notice: Africanus journeyed to Alexandria because of the fame of Heraclas, who was teaching there (VI. 31. 2).[8] As for Porphyry, this opponent of Christianity had no interest in Christian history, even though he once met Origen (VI. 19. 5). Eusebius might have relied on Porphyry for the dates of emperors between 218 and 268, but he did not do so. His own discussions of regnal years include errors from about 244 onward. More important, then, was Africanus, whose work he presumably could use for bishops, at least in the principal sees, as well as emperors. He may have used the *Chronicle* by Hippolytus of Rome, but it is surprising that in discussing Hippolytus' works (VI. 22) he does not mention it.

For events in the earliest Christian period, Eusebius relied on the New Testament (chiefly Acts) and the historical writings of Josephus.[9] This pattern in the *Chronicle* thus anticipated the one in the *Church History*. For the whole of the first century the primary sources, apart from succession lists, were Josephus, Philo, Tertullian, and Clement of Alexandria. Eusebius used a Greek translation of Tertullian's *Apology* for information about Tiberius, Nero, and Domitian, as well as the Pliny–Trajan correspondence.[10] Without Tertullian's work Eusebius could have said little about first-century emperors and Christians. What he took from Clement of Alexandria (mostly from the lost *Outlines*) consisted of legends about the apostolic succession, chiefly at Jerusalem.

It is surprising how little content would remain in the *Chronicle* if one were to remove the lists of emperors and bishops and, up to the end of the first century, the contributions of Josephus. After that point much of the material comes from martyr-acts such as those of Polycarp, Pionius, and the Gallicans, from collections of the writings of various authors, and from dossiers already available on particular heresies or schisms. A very rough calculation suggests that apart from succession lists Eusebius has fewer than a hundred historical items for

---

[8] H. Gelzer, *Sextus Julius Africanus und die byzantinische Chronographie*, I (Leipzig, 1898), 280.
[9] Cf. E. Schürer, 'Zur Chronologie des Lebens Pauli zugleich ein Beitrag zur Kritik der Chronik des Eusebius', *Zeitschrift für Wissenschaftliche Theologie*, 21 (1898), 21–42.
[10] Comparison of the Latin *Chronicle* with Tertullian, Pliny, and Eusebius' Greek reveals that Jerome used Pliny directly.

the period from the birth of Christ to the beginning of the persecution under Diocletian — and nothing not imperial or episcopal from that point to 325.

If we compare the Christian (Eusebian) content of the *Chronicle* with the first seven books of the *Church History*, we find that — apart from the basic imperial–episcopal framework — there is not a strong correlation. In what corresponds to Book I, the *Chronicle* mentions only the birth of Christ, the death of Herod, the banishment of Archelaus, and the death of Christ. The parallels to Book II are more extensive and they suggest that the note in the table of contents for that book must refer to its earliest version. 'We compiled the book from the writings of Clement, Tertullian, Josephus, and Philo.' These are precisely the sources of this section of the *Chronicle*. Only a few others are added in what is parallel to Book III, but Hegesippus must have been used for Domitian's attack on the family of David and Trajan's crucifixion of Simon of Jerusalem.

The *Chronicle* contains a good deal that does not appear in Book IV. There is a detailed account of the Jewish revolts under Trajan and Hadrian (different from IV. 2 and 6), considerable information on the history of philosophy, and a definite notice about the death of Lucius Verus in the ninth year of his reign. (We shall later see why this was omitted.) In IV. 19–21 Eusebius lists bishops and orthodox authors of the time of Marcus Aurelius and Lucius Verus. Two of them were merely correspondents of Dionysius of Corinth; two others were minor anti-heretical authors. None of these appears in the *Chronicle*. More significantly, Hegesippus is also absent. Presumably this writer became more important to Eusebius as he wrote (various editions of) the *Church History*.

In the *Chronicle* the martyrdoms of Polycarp (and Pionius) and the Gallicans were put together and placed two years before the death of Lucius Verus, presumably so that he could somehow be blamed for them. Eusebius explicitly indicated his enthusiasm for the philospher-emperor Marcus Aurelius by minimizing his responsibility for killing Christians, pointing to God's favour shown him by the rain-miracle, and noting the importance of those who taught him philosophy: Sextus of Chaeroneia, Claudius Maximus, and the Stoic Apollonius.

The parallels to Book V are important because they are so limited. There is nothing but the rain-miracle at the Danube under Marcus Aurelius, the mention of Atticus as head of the Platonic school (the last notice about a philosopher in the *Chronicle*), references to Irenaeus ,

Clement, and Pantaenus, and an allusion to the Quartodeciman controversy, presumably based on a dossier as in *Church History* V. 23–5.
For chronological reasons the account of the Gallican martyrs, so
significant in the *Church History*, is absent. Similarly there is no use
of the dossier on Montanism (V. 16–19), for the beginning· of the
movement has been set in an earlier period.

Like Book VI, the corresponding section of the *Chronicle* begins
with the death of Origen's father Leonides. Later on we learn that
Origen studied at Alexandria, became famous, and soon afterward
moved to Caesarea. Only a few other authors are named. In the
Chronicle we learn about Abgar, the 'holy king' at Edessa and about
Africanus' mission on behalf of Nicopolis; these two items obviously
come from the end of his *Chronographies* (cf. VI. 31. 2), and in the
Church History Eusebius passed them by. The *Chronicle* also included
notes about the Christian Emperor Philip and the anti-Christians
Maximinus Thrax and Decius.

The parallels to Book VII are insignificant except for bishop lists.
Persecution under Valerian comes from Dionysius of Alexandria. Next
comes the dossier on the trial of Paul of Samosata. The destruction of
the Bruchium quarter at Alexandria must have been mentioned in
relation to the famous Bishop Anatolius of Laodicea, involved in the
siege. The story of the Emperor Aurelian and his hope to persecute
must have been almost contemporary gossip. Then comes an odd
reference to 'the beginning of the 86th jubilee according to the
Hebrews'. The second year of Probus is identified with years according
to the calendars of Antioch, Tyre, Laodicea, Edessa, and Ascalon.
Earlier in the *Chronicle* there had been notes on the origins of the years
used at Antioch (p. 156, 6) and Edessa (p. 124, 24), while in the
Paschal Chronicle which sometimes relies on Eusebius we find the
origins of the years at Antioch (I. 355. 14), Laodicea (356. 3), and
Ascalon (346. 6). Why does this careful synchronism exist?

R. Helm, in a passage to which T. D. Barnes drew my attention,
suggested that the synchronism means that the *Chronicle* originally
ended (or a source ended?) at this point.[11] Helm does not seem to have
observed that what ends is a series of 'jubilees' calculated 'according to
the Hebrews'. These are the jubilee years from the 45th year of
Abraham up to this second year of Probus, obviously including whatever jubilees (counting every tenth one or, at the end, the fifth) lay

[11] 'Eusebius' Chronik und ihre Tabellenform', 42–3.

between the birth of Abraham — with which the *Chronicle* begins — and the year 325, with which in its last version it ended. A passage in the Babylonian Talmud confirms this picture of the jubilees. Elijah told Rabbi Judah, brother of Rabbi Salla the Pious, that the world has 'no fewer than 85 jubilees, and in the last the Son of David will come'.[12] To date this prediction we have another passage, cited by Jacob Neusner: 'Rabbi Judah, brother of Rabbi Salla the Pious . . . went to Abaye and asked him . . .'[13] Abaye was a younger contemporary of Eusebius and died in the year 338.[14] Therefore the importance of 85 or 86 jubilees was recognized among Jews in Eusebius' time and for this reason it was mentioned in the *Chronicle*. A subsidiary point seems to be that the beginning of the 81st jubilee coincided with the ministry of Jesus.[15]

Another kind of jubilee, observed by 'our ancestors', is provided with dates but no numbers. The first to be noted is set in the year of Abraham 2220, identified with the 12th year of Septimius Severus and the 251st year of Antioch. The second is placed in Abraham's 2,270th year, the third in his 2,320th, supposedly the first year of the Diocletianic persecution, and correlated with the 350th (351st?) year of Antioch. The last 'Christian' jubilee to be noted occurs in Abraham's 2,369th year. Since it is called 'Iobelaeus secundum Hebraeos' it looks like an incorrect gloss on Jerome's text and perhaps indicates that all the mentions of jubilees and 'our ancestors' are later additions. It is not clear whether or not Christians actually observed jubilees. In the *Apostolic Constitutions* (VII. 36. 4) the 'fiftieth year' can be symbolical or actual,[16] but Gelzer explicitly denied that the jubilees in the Byzantine chronographers were anything but arbitrary.[17]

Arbitrary or not, we conclude that the 'Hebrew' jubilees in Eusebius' *Chronicle* reflect an interest he himself felt and that this interest explains the synchronism in the second year of Probus. The synchronism does not necessarily indicate the end of an early *Chronicle*, even though

[12] Babylonian Talmud, Sanh. 97b (VII. 422 Goldschmidt; 303 Rodkinson).

[13] Shab. 112a, cited *A History of the Jews in Babylonia*, IV (Leiden, 1969), 177.

[14] W. Bacher, *Die Agada der babylonischen Amoräer* (repr. Hildesheim, 1967), 113 (148–51 on his birth date may be disregarded); H. L. Strack, *Introduction to the Talmud and Midrash* (Philadelphia, 1931), 132–3.

[15] Moses died at the end of the 50th Hebrew jubilee, and in the 51st Joshua = Jesus took over (p. 46a).

[16] See also Philo, *Dec.* 164; *Spec.* II. 110–17; *Virt.* 99–101; Josephus, *Ant.* III. 282–85; IV. 273; a 49-year cycle in the Book of Jubilees.

[17] op. cit., p. 276.

it is obvious that he has few materials for nearly forty years of his 'own times'. It may be that he said little about the bishops during these forty years because he was not impressed favourably by their behaviour.[18]

Whatever the precise date of the first edition of the *Chronicle* may have been, its importance for this study lies in the views which it contains that are different from those expressed in part or all of the *Church History*. Here we may briefly indicate what these items include. First, Eusebius takes a story which Josephus had told about the depart-ure of the divine presence from the Temple in Jerusalem, shortly before 66,[19] and sets it about forty years earlier (175. 13). Second, he rightly follows Josephus in setting the death of James the Just in about 61 and attributing it to stoning (182. 25).[20] Third, he held with Irenaeus that under Domitian the apostle John, banished to the island of Patmos, saw the apocalypse (192. 1). John's hearers at a later time were Papias of Hierapolis, Polycarp of Smyrna, and Ignatius of Antioch (193. 25).[21] Fourth, the heresiarch Basilides lived at Alexandria in 133 and founded the Gnostic movement (201. 1). (In the *Chronicle* there is no mention of any Gnostic except Basilides.) Fifth, the martyrdoms of Polycarp and Pionius, as well as those of the Gallicans, are dated in 167, two years before the death of Lucius Verus (205. 5).

All these points will prove significant when we endeavour to trace the development of some of Eusebius' ideas about early Church history.

---

[18] VIII. 1. 7–8; 2. 2; cf. the rhetorical conclusion of Book X (8–9) on the last ten years of Licinius' reign.
[19] Josephus, *Bell*. VI. 299.   [20] Josephus, *Ant*. XX. 200.
[21] Cf. Irenaeus, *Adv. haer.* V. 30. 3; for Papias and Polycarp, V. 33. 4.

III

EDITIONS OF THE CHURCH HISTORY

It has been customary to describe the *Church History* in relation to Eusebius' own statement about its contents (I. 1. 1–2). We shall be following the same course, not because the preface is early and shows what Eusebius had in mind at the beginning but because it is late and shows what he thought he had done. The only way to understand the *Church History* is to view it as a process, not a finished achievement. Even when we so view it we run into difficulties because of constant oscillations and alterations. Thus Eduard Schwartz pointed out that while the Greek manuscripts of X. 9 give high praise to Crispus, Constantine's son, the Syriac version refrains from mentioning his name, obviously since he had been killed by his father's order in 326. Eusebius presumably adjusted his text at that point, probably for the last time. In spite of this adjustment, the older Greek manuscripts remained in circulation, and Gelasius of Cyzicus, writing in the fifth century, used a text of the *Church History* in which Crispus' name was retained.[1]

In regard to Gelasius' text we may add that in his numerous quotations from the last three books of Eusebius' *Church History* the pattern of alteration already found within the manuscripts of Eusebius – as we shall see – is present. Eusebius as quoted by Gelasius more strenuously praises Constantine and demeans his adversary Licinius.[2] (Alterations favouring a higher Christology probably come from after Eusebius' time.)[3]

Such alterations are prominent in the *Church History* and especially in the last three books, thought it is the purpose of this study to show that they are fairly common in the first seven books as well. Modern research into the text of Eusebius began with Eduard Schwartz, whose edition remains indispensable. He showed that the many revisions evident in Books VIII–X are reflected in the two families of manuscripts, one represented primarily by the manuscripts BDM, the other by ATER or sometimes only AER.[4] BDM, along with the fifth-century

---

[1] Gelasius, *H. E.* I. 11. 16; II. 1. 4. [2] Ibid., I. 1. 4; 9. 1–2; 11, *passim.*
[3] Ibid., I. 7. 5; 10. 8; II. 1. 5.
[4] *Eusebius Werke*, II. *Die Kirchengeschichte*, 3 (Leipzig, 1909), xlvii–cxlvii.

Syriac version, reflects the edition of the *Church History* which Eusebius produced in the year 325, after Constantine's defeat of Licinius
but before the Council of Nicaea. On the other hand, ATER witnesses
to a text corrected from an earlier recension which included items not
to be found in BDM. Such items include the letter of Maximin's
praetorian prefect Sabinus (IX. 1. 3-6), the statement that God had
confirmed both Constantine and Licinius as rulers (IX. 11. 8), and the
imperial orders issued by both emperors (X. 5-7). They are obviously
related to the letter of Constantine to his own praetorian prefect on
December 16, 324: 'All men shall know that the constitutions and laws
of the tyrant Licinius are abolished and that the sanctions of ancient
law and of our statutes must be observed.'[5]

Manuscript evidence shows that Book VIII also underwent revision.
In the manuscripts AER there is an additional ending to the book. It
deals with the deaths of the tetrarchs (Diocletian, Maximian,
Constantius, Galerius) and points out that all but Constantius perished
miserably. The manuscript A notes that it was found 'as left out, in
some copies, in the eighth book'. E, on the other hand, describes it as
found 'at the end of Book VIII in some manuscripts – not as left out
but as found in some copies in relation to a different manner of style'.
R makes no comment. In this 'appendix' there are cross-references,
explicit or implicit, to VIII. 13. 11 (or *Mart. Pal.* 3. 5) and to VIII. 16.
2-5 and 17. 1-2. Obviously the section did provide the ending for Book
VIII at one time. But Book VIII was not what it now is, for statements
made in the 'appendix' clearly repeat what is now to be found in VIII.
4. 2-4 and 13. 10-15. Therefore these passages were not to be found in
Book VIII at the time when the 'appendix' was its conclusion. Since the
last tetrarch to die, Diocletian, perished in 313, it is obvious that the
'appendix' reflects an edition fairly soon after that point while the
edition involving appendectomy is later.[6] This later edition (ATER)
took from the 'appendix' the statement that Galerius was the architect
of the persecution (VIII. 16. 2-3) and included Licinius among those
who issued the edict of toleration in 311 (17. 5). It therefore appeared
before 324 and indeed, before 316, when war broke out between
Constantine and Licinius.[7] We thus possess evidence for three editions

[5] *Cod. Theod.* XV. 14. 1.
[6] This date was indicated (following Lactantius, *De mort. persec.* 42; Aurel.
Vict. *Epit.* 39. 6-7; Socrates, *H. E.* I. 2) by J. Moreau, *Lactance De la mort des
persécuteurs* (Paris, 1954), II, 420-23.
[7] For this date cf. C. Habicht, 'Zur Geschichte des Kaisers Konstantin',
Hermes, 86 (1958), 360-78.

of Book VIII.

Even more striking is the evidence in regard to Book VIII and the *Martyrs of Palestine*. ATE note that the *Martyrs* was once a part of Book VIII, as 'some copy' indicates; R expands the reference to the plural. Parallels and cross-references confirm the reliability of the comments. First the parallels, almost exact. These concern the beginning of the persecution (*Mart. Pal.* pr. = VIII. 2. 4-5), the behaviour of bishops during it (*Mart. Pal.* 1. 3-5 = VIII. 3. 1-4), and the 'palinode' of Galerius (*Mart. Pal.* 13. 11. 15 = VIII. 16. 1). They indicate that the beginning and the ending of the *Martyrs of Palestine* were virtually identical with comparable sections in Book VIII. One work provided the alternative version to the other. We might suppose, however, that these parallels supplied ATER with their only evidence for the notion that *Martyrs* was contained in Book VIII, were it not for the evidence of cross-references. *Mart. Pal.* 12 looks back to a passage written when Eusebius was beginning his discussion. In *Martyrs*, however, there is no such passage. It is to be found near the beginning of Book VIII (2. 2-3).[8] Another reference, this time in *Mart. Pal.* 13. 14, looks ahead to the quotation of the 'palinode' − found in VIII. 17. 3-10. These references indicate, as Laqueur pointed out, that at one time the *Martyrs of Palestine* was placed between VIII. 2. 3 and VIII. 17. 2.[9] Two further cross-references indicate what the time was. It was a time when Eusebius was about to write Book IX, in which he would discuss the restoration of peace to the Empire (*Mart. Pal.* 3. 7; IX. 1. 8-11) and the fall of Maximin (*Mart. Pal.* 7. 8; IX. 10. 13-11. 7).

The edition including *Mart. Pal.* presumably contained the following materials: VIII pr. − 2. 3; *Mart. Pal.*; VIII. 16. 1-17. 11a; 'appendix'. Later on, both *Martyrs* and 'appendix' were deleted, though material from *Martyrs* was kept in VIII. 2. 4-3. 4. Additions consisted of chapters 4-12 on persecution in various areas; 13. 1-7 on the rulers of famous churches and a cross-reference to *Martyrs* as a separate work; 13. 8 for an announcement of the 'palinode'; and, still later, 13. 9-15. 2 on the Roman Empire before and during the persecution.[10] Once more we find evidence for three editions of Book VIII. The first contained *Martyrs* and 'appendix'. The second contained neither but included

---

[8] With this we may compare the cross-reference in V.8. 1 (with III.3. 3).

[9] R. Laqueur, *Eusebius als Historiker seiner Zeit* (Berlin–Leipzig, 1929), 6-33. It is quite possible that against Laqueur we should follow T. D. Barnes (and others) in placing the longer *Mart. Pal.* before the shorter version.

[10] VIII. 13. 9-15. 2 breaks the continuity between 13. 8 and 16. 1.

some materials favouring Licinius. The third did not contain these favourable comments.

Apparently there were only two editions of Book X. The first, composed around 315 to go with the second edition of Book VIII (and IX), began with a doxology (ATERM), a discussion of the end of the persecution (1-3), Eusebius' sermon at Tyre for the rededication of the church (4), and imperial legislation up to the Synod of Arles (1 August 314). When Licinius was defeated and executed, Eusebius added chapters 8 and 9 on his madness, crimes, and 'lawless laws'. Obviously his pro-Christian legislation had to be deleted (X. 5-7, BDM). Both editions were dedicated to Paulinus, Bishop of Tyre and later of Antioch, who seems to have died just before the Council of Nicaea. The second edition therefore appeared at the end of 324 or the beginning of 325.

It is clear enough, then, that the last three books of the *Church History* have undergone numerous alterations as they were transformed from one edition to another. What of the first seven books? Schwartz believed that Eusebius' reference to 'the merciful and gracious help of our Saviour' (I. 1. 2) implied that he had in view VIII. 16. 1, where a similar phrase occurs.[11] Therefore the first edition contained eight books, not seven.[12] At the same time, Schwartz held that the first seven books were different from the others. 'One cannot find any gap or seam that would betray the presence of revisions, interpolations, or continuations.' Both Harnack and Laqueur, on the other hand, thought that in its first form Eusebius' work consisted of just seven books, though a few passages were added later when the persecution changed the situation. Laqueur held that the promise about 'the merciful and gracious help of our Saviour' was added later, as were the materials directed against the *Acts of Pilate*, composed in the time of Maximin (I. 9. 2-4; 11. 1-9).[13] To these materials T. D. Barnes has added all the references to the persecution of 303 to 311, the references to the *Apology for Origen* and the *Life of Pamphilus*, and the passage from Porphyry, *Against the Christians.*[14]

All these points require discussion before we enter upon our basic examination of Books I-VII. As for Laqueur, it may well be that the promise about merciful and gracious help was added later; but we shall

---

[11] Cf. also *Mart. Pal.* 13. 14.   [12] Schwartz, op. cit., lv–lvi.
[13] Laqueur, op. cit., 3-4; 121-3; cf. IX. 5. 1.
[14] Persecution. VII. 11. 26; 30. 22; 32. 1. 4. 22-3. 25. 28-9. 31; Origen and Pamphilus: VI. 23. 4; 32. 3; 33. 4; 36. 4; Porphyry: VI. 19. 2-8.

argue that Eusebius' whole preface, as it now stands, was produced for his edition of 315 and does not exactly correspond with what he had written earlier. As for Barnes, putting the reference to Porphyry late is based on his own special theory that Porphyry's work itself was composed early in the fourth century.[15] Normally one would suppose that Eusebius could refer to his own *Apology for Origen* and *Life of Pamphilus*, composed in 308 to 310 and perhaps in 311, but it cannot be proved that the *Church History* was actually written after these works. Finally, since Peter of Alexandria was martyred in November, 311, this reference (VII. 32. 31) must be late. Presumably the earliest reference to his martyrdom occurs in IX. 6. 2; later it appears here in VII and in VIII. 13. 7 (a list). If we look at Eusebius' three heroes described in VII. 32. 25-8, we find that Pamphilus was a martyr in 310, Pierius a scholar at Alexandria (no mention of his offering sacrifice before 307, as outlined in the *Apology of Phileas*), and Meletius of Pontus a refugee from persecution during 'seven whole years'. The silence about Pierius' misfortune may just be due to tact, not to composition before 307.

We conclude that there is no special reason to hold that Books I–VII came into existence as late as 311 or 312, or even in 303. On the other hand, there is no special reason to date them much earlier. The seventh book did not take long to produce, whenever it was written. Eusebius himself speaks of his reliance on letters by Dionysius 'the Great' of Alexandria (VII, pr.), the primary source of chapters 1–26. The next four chapters are based on a dossier related to Paul of Samosata and his heresy. Chapter 31 deals with the Manichees and uses language not unlike that found in Diocletian's rescript of 297 — or 302.[16] The last and very long chapter brings lists of bishops up to about 303, and the book ends with a conclusion on 'successions' and the 305-year period 'from the birth of our Saviour to the destruction of the places of prayer' in 303.

Barnes has argued that since an edition of the *Chronicle* may have ended around 280, the first edition of the *Church History* may have been completed about a decade later. He notes what a jumble the end of Book VII is. We agree, but in the chapter on the *Chronicle* we have suggested that the synchronism for 277 may not mark the end of an edition.

---

[15] T. D. Barnes, 'Porphyry Against the Christians', *JTS* 24 (1973), 424–42.
[16] See H. Chadwick, 'The Relativity of Moral Codes', in W. R. Schoedel– R. L. Wilken, *Early Christian Literature and the Classical Intellectual Tradition* (Paris, 1979), 141–3.

The question of a precise date for the first edition is not our main concern, however. Our own analysis of the first seven books does not depend on setting a particular year for the event, though in some respects an earlier date rather than a later one would allow adequate time for the changes within the first seven books which we hope to establish. In our view neither Schwartz nor Laqueur went far enough, and Schwartz's statement about the uniformity of the content of Books I–VII is not justified by the facts. There are at least six important points in regard to which Eusebius changed his mind between the first edition and the second. Presumably, then, these points reflect the attitudes present in Christian churches and among Christian leaders as the Church passed into persecution and then beyond it.

These points have to do with the death of the apostle James, the nature of the book of Revelation, the reliability of Papias of Hierapolis, the date of Hegesippus, the date of the Gallican martyrs, and the circumstances of the death of Origen. Beyond these points lies the question of the nature of the preface to the whole work (or to Books I–VII) as found in Book I. 1. 1–2.

It is interesting to observe that the first four points have to do with what is often called 'Jewish Christianity', and the movement of Eusebius' thought at this crucial time (say from 303 to 315) is away from the eschatological aspects of it but toward some rather legendary history.

In the *Chronicle* Eusebius sets the death of James the Just in the year 61 and follows Josephus in ascribing his martyrdom to stoning (p. 182, 25). Similarly in one form of the *History* he dies early in the reign of Nero (II. 22. 7–8), in fact before Nero's eighth year (II. 24). On the other hand, once Eusebius comes under the spell of Hegesippus he has Jerusalem besieged immediately after the martyrdom (II. 23. 18; III. 7. 8; 11). The first scheme is historical; the second seems to be related to anti-Jewish exegesis of the 'forty years' of Psalm 95.

Second, in the *Chronicle* we find that the apostle John wrote the book of Revelation (p. 192, 4); his leading pupil was Papias. These views are retained in the first edition of the *Church History*, but in the second the book of Revelation is treated as heretical, Papias as stupid (see Chapter XI).

Hegesippus is not mentioned in the *Chronicle*, and the death of James is ascribed to stoning, not to the complex causes which Hegesippus assigned. Presumably it was in the second edition of the *History* that Hegesippus came into his own.

In the *Chronicle* (p. 205, 9) the Gallican martyrs are set in the year 167, perhaps correctly, perhaps in order to give some excuse for representing the Emperor Lucius Verus as condemning them. In any case, Eusebius' desire to free Marcus Aurelius from blame results in confusion in the *Church History*. The martyrs are dated in the seventeenth year of the Emperor Antoninus Verus (V, pr. 1) but later their deaths are blamed on 'Antoninus', differentiated from his brother 'Marcus Aurelius Caesar' (V. 4. 3–5. 1). Here the date under Marcus Aurelius alone must be taken from the second edition, that under Lucius Verus (who died in 169) from the first.

Finally, the death of Origen, not dated in the *Chronicle*, was set under Decius in the *Apology for Origen*. Presumably this is when it was set in the first edition of the *Church History*, for the account of Origen's sufferings (VI. 39. 5) reads like a partly corrected account of his death. It would have been corrected for the second edition, in which the event was set somewhat later (VII. 2).

With points like these in mind, we can now turn to the preface and consider its structure in relation to the various editions of the *History*. It seems likely, as we have indicated, that in the first edition at the beginning there was a promise to discuss the canonical books of the New Testament. Eusebius says that this was the case (V. 8. 1). Such a promise is preserved in III. 3. 3, but it is a little late since usage of the New Testament has already been treated in II. 17. 12 and II. 23. 24-5 (see also II. 15). Presumably the promise in III. 3. 3 was an echo of one originally placed at the beginning, just as the promise about successions in a nearby context (III. 4. 11) echoes the original statement on the same subject (I. 1. 1). If we accept the notion of a seven-book first edition, the promise about the future aid to be given by the Saviour cannot have been a part of the preface.

On the other hand, we should suppose that Eusebius' claim to be a pioneer in the field (I. 1. 3), along with his description of his literary method (I. 1. 4), comes from the first edition. These remarks lead directly to an emphatic statement about successions and a reiteration of the claim to originality (I. 1. 5). If, as Thomas Halton has suggested, the preface as a whole — or at least the statement about subject-matter — comes out of Hegesippus, then we are not surprised to find it surfacing in the second edition. As we have already seen, Hegesippus' influence becomes stronger at that point. It is hard to imagine Eusebius as complimenting himself on his originality as he takes bits and pieces from his predecessor. It is easier to think that he simply retained the words even though he now knew that Hegesippus had anticipated some of his thoughts.

How did he work when he worked? According to his own statement he relied on his anthologies of Christian literature, then 'made into a body by historical treatment' (I. 1. 4),[17] or he could start from an 'epitome' or handbook of chronological information and move to full detail (I. 1. 6).[18] In either case the process could be called 'fleshing out'.

In Book II, according to a mysterious note at the end of the chapter headings, Eusebius used as sources 'the writings of Clement, Tertullian, Josephus, and Philo'. Certainly these are the sources for II. 1–12 and 14–22 and 26. They are also the sources for the whole of the parallel section in the *Chronicle* and therefore presumably underlay the first edition of the *History*. In Book II as it now stands, however, additional sources are employed in relation to three points: the heresy of Simon Magus (13), the death of James (23), and the deaths of Peter and Paul (25). In two out of the three cases the newly introduced authors are wrongly dated. Justin is placed 'not long after the apostles' (II. 13. 2), Hegesippus in 'the first succession of the apostles' (II. 23. 3). The early date explains the need for using their writings. In the other instance Eusebius cites brief passages from Gaius of Rome and Dionysius of Corinth and says that 'these points may serve to make the historical narratives more credible' (II. 25. 8).

Some justification for our emphasis on the list of sources can be found in the study of the *Natural History* of Pliny the Elder. The whole of his first book consists of lists of the authorities used in each of the subsequent books. In his long preface, addressed to the Emperor Vespasian, Pliny claims to have used a hundred authors (praef. 17). A. Klotz noted that since he actually names five hundred, the longer list must include authors cited by his sources.[19] This offers no parallel to Eusebius. On the other hand, W. Kroll argued that authors looked into later had their names added at the end of Pliny's lists.[20] This seems to fit our situation. Taking Kroll's suggestion we may assume that the names reflect the first state of Book II and that other names could have been added later.

---

[17] For 'body' cf. G. Avenarius, *Lukians Schrift zur Geschichtsschreibung* (Meisenheim/Glan, 1956), 107–8; also Artemidorus, *Onir.* IV, pr., p. 237, 12 Pack.

[18] For 'epitome' cf. F. Jacoby, *Apollodors Chronik* (*Philologische Untersuchungen*, 16, 1902), 20–1.

[19] 'Die Arbeitsweise der älteren Plinius und die Indices Auctorum', *Hermes*, 42 (1907), 323–9.

[20] 'Plinius der älterer', *RE* XXI (1951), 424–8.

Book III provides much evidence of Eusebius' rewriting, but we shall deal with his comments on the Johannine literature only when we discuss the canon of scripture (Chapter XI). As he begins his treatment of the post-apostolic age (III. 32–3) his handling of sources implies the existence of several phases. First, in chapter 32 he appeals to Hegesippus as his authority for information about the martyrdom of Simon or Symeon of Jerusalem under Trajan. He begins by paraphrasing and includes the statement that Symeon was accused of being a Christian. Next he quotes Hegesippus as saying that Symeon was accused of being a descendant of David and a Christian. In the third instance he quotes Hegesippus as saying that Symeon was accused 'on the same charge'. The same charge as what? If we look back to an earlier quotation from Hegesippus we find that the charge was that of being a descendant of David (III. 20. 1). It is hard to tell what has happened here, but we might guess that Eusebius first wrote the paraphrase from the first quotation (already Christianized). According to the *Chronicle* (p. 194, 19) Simon suffered as a Christian. For the second edition Eusebius looked back at Hegesippus' work, or got someone to look at it, and found the statement about 'the same charge'. The *Church History* seems to involve accumulation as well as correction. Thus after discussing Symeon and noting that he was accused by 'heretics', Eusebius says that Hegesippus stated that 'up to those times' (i.e. under Trajan) the Church remained a pure and uncorrupted virgin in respect of heresies (III. 32. 7). Only later (IV. 22. 4-5) does an explicit quotation let us know that the period in question was the reign of Vespasian, thirty years earlier. Eusebius should have corrected III. 32. 7, but the point was not important to him. Indeed, in the *Chronicle* we find that the heresiarch Basilides, 'from whom came the Gnostics', arrived at Alexandria in the year 132 (p. 201, 1).

In Book V Eusebius' new dating for the Gallican martyrs made difficulties for him. Originally he had placed Polycarp and the Gallicans under Lucius Verus, who died in 169. This is the date given in the *Chronicle* and implied in what must be the first edition of the *History* (V. 4. 3-5. 1). Further research had indicated the connection of the Gallicans with Eleutherus of Rome, bishop only in the seventeenth year of 'Antoninus Verus', or 177 (V, pr. 1). Eusebius was still able to ascribe their martyrdom to the evil Lucius by not saying anything about the date of his death, by indicating that 'Antoninus' was the brother of Marcus Aurelius, and by saying that the martyrdoms took place under Antoninus, while Marcus Aurelius favoured Christians (V. 5. 6).

Book VI presents many difficulties. One might suppose that its account of Origen was later than the *Apology for Origen* which Eusebius and Pamphilus jointly composed between 308 and 310. The references are ambiguous, however, as we shall see. At the beginning of the book Eusebius states that

there would be many things to say if one were attempting to set forth the man's life in a learned monograph, and indeed the narrative about him would require a work of its own; but for the present abridging most things as much as possible, we shall state a few of the facts about him, gathering our statements from certain letters and the account by his pupils whose lives were preserved into our times (VI. 2. 1).

This statement certainly points toward the 'life of Origen' in the *Apology*, but it may well reflect the time when Eusebius is revising his text in the light of the apologetic work, not the time when Book VI was first composed. In VI. 23. 4 he says that a full discussion of the controversies over Origen and his works would 'require a composition of its own, and we have described them at moderate length in the second volume of the *Apology* which we made for him.' The phrases are the same in substance as those in VI. 2, and give cross-references to the *Apology* in both instances. Again, Eusebius asks in VI. 32. 3, 'Why should one need to draw up an exact list of the man's works for the present, since it would require a treatise of its own?' There follows a cross-reference to the *Life of Pamphilus*. In VI. 33. 4 there is a reference to the sources for Origen's life ('handed down in memory by the older men of our times'). Eusebius is passing over some of their materials as irrelevant to 'the present work' and referring, for what 'it was necessary to know', to the *Apology* which he and Pamphilus had written. Finally, a cross-reference to the sixth book of the *Apology* (composed by Eusebius alone) is concerned with information about Origen's letters.[21] The combination of similar phrasing and cross-references clearly shows that the *Apology* preceded Book VI in its present form, though these items may well have been added for the second edition of the *Church History*.

Alternatively, Eusebius had not carried his *Church History* as far as Book VI before the persecution began, and the cross-references which we have cited belong to the one edition of that book. According to Eusebius, he himself collected Origen's letters, apparently in order to compose the *Apology* (VI. 36. 3-4), or at least the sixth book of it.

---

[21] Cf. P. Nautin, *Origène sa vie et son œuvre* (Paris, 1977), 100.

The account of Origen's sufferings in the time of Decius is based on the letters (VI. 39. 5), but Eusebius' account looks like the revision of a *martyrium*. Certainly Pamphilus, as we shall later see, believed that Origen was a martyr under Decius. We shall discuss this evidence in a later chapter. For the present it is enough to say that it looks as though in the *Apology* and the first edition of Book VI Origen was a martyr, while in the second edition, in VII. 2, and presumably in Eusebius' own Book VI of the *Apology* he was not. Does this show that Book VI was written after the *Apology*? No, it does not. Eusebius could have composed his works in the following sequence: first edition of Book VI (Origen a martyr), *Apology* with Pamphilus (Origen a martyr), *Apology* VI (Origen not a martyr), and second edition of Book VI (Origen not a martyr). This means that the passage in VII. 2 about Origen's death after the persecution (completely out of context) must be an interpolation into Book VII.

After composing his study of Origen, along with a few insertions concerning less important figures, Eusebius' interest in his subject seems to have declined. The last third of Book VI (40-6) consists of little more than quotations from or references to letters written from or to Dionysius of Alexandria. Book VII begins with the statement that 'Dionysius the great bishop of the Alexandrians will again assist us in our task by his own words.' We find just this, along with incidental additions, in the first two-thirds of the book (VII. 1-26). Next Eusebius makes use of a dossier concerning Paul of Samosata (VII. 27-30) and a fantasy about Mani, perhaps based on the official language of the late third century (VII. 31). All that remains to be done is to supply some information about the thirty-five years remaining before the persecution. Eusebius creates an inordinately long final chapter, about one-seventh of his book, beginning with the Bishops of Rome and Antioch (32, 1-4) and ending with Jerusalem and Alexandria (29-31). In between he sets local fables and reminiscences about Bishops of Laodicea in Syria and Caesarea in Palestine. It is a singular production and cannot have taken long to write.

Indeed, one could argue that Eusebius was substituting his lists and anecdotes for a history he had decided not to write. 'The rulers of this world would never find it easy to proceed against the churches of Christ unless the hand which fights for us were to permit this to be done, by a divine and heavenly judgment for our punishment and conversion, at whatever times it might find best.' (VII. 30. 21.) Punishment for what? Conversion from what? It is only at the beginning of Book VIII that we learn of the pride, sloth, envy, and railing among clerics and laymen alike during the years before 303.

IV

THE COMPOSITION OF THE CHURCH HISTORY

Our survey of the *Chronicle* in relation to the *Church History* suggested that it provided no more than the bare bones, plus a few joints, for the ultimate 'body' of the later work. Now we turn to the *History* itself to see what can be made of Eusebius' goals and attitudes as he constructed the work. What models influenced him? How and why did he produce various editions of the *History*? We must try to provide answers for such questions before we can consider the promises set forth at the beginning of the work, and the ways in which he kept them.

To judge from the opening paragraphs, Eusebius had a clear idea of how to begin the *History* and deal with various sections in it (I. 1. 2. 7). Since, however, we do not know that this part was written first, and since a reference backward in V. 8. 1 leads nowhere, we cannot lay much emphasis on this part of the work. He obviously knew that he had compiled chronological tables. The content of the work proves that he was an ecclesiastical author. He gives no reason for his readers to regard him as qualified to write about 'ecclesiastical history',[1] and we have no evidence for *Ecclesiastical History* as the title of his work before the beginning of Book VII.

It is odd that he does not name himself as the author or indicate what his qualifications were, beyond his references to earlier works[2] and to himself (without name) as one of the 'moderately capable' bishops, chosen to deliver a panegyric composed for the rededication of the church at Tyre (X. 4. 1). In other words, it was not an extempore address. He maintains the same silence in his other apologetic treatises. Presumably he expected his sources to speak for themselves (I. 1. 4) or, at any rate, through his summaries.

In his preface he explains what he means by 'history'. It involves the collection of useful materials out of what earlier authors mentioned sporadically, and then the unifying of these materials by means of 'historical arrangement'. It appears that a narrative is required. A story told by Clement deserves quoting 'both for the narrative and for its

[1] I. 1. 1; 5. 1; II, pr. 1.
[2] I. 1. 6; 2. 27; 6. 11; IV. 15. 47; V, pr. 2; 21. 5; VI (2); 23. 4; 32. 3; 33. 4; 36. 4.

utility to future readers' (III. 23. 19). The acts of the Gallican martyrs contain a narrative which is not only historical but didactic as well (V, pr. 2). Schwartz claimed that 'history' meant just a compilation of traditional material.[3] Sometimes this is the case, but in. Eusebius' *History* it involves something more. One can turn back to it after discussing something else (III. 4. 11; 26. 1; 31. 6). The importance of narrative is clear when we consider that one of Eusebius' favourite words in relation to history is διήγησις.[4] A διήγημα, wrote the rhetorician Hermogenes, is an account of just one event, whereas a διήγησις is concerned with many events, not just one. As examples of διήγησις he cited the history of Herodotus and the work of Thucydides.[5]

What a history needs to hold it together is a particular subject-matter, theme, or ὑπόθεσις. The term ὑπόθεσις sometimes bears just this meaning in Eusebius' work[6] as it does for example in Dionysius of Halicarnassus.[7] It comes to mean also the whole work (of which a part may be mentioned), or a work in process, or a work proposed.[8] The emphasis is laid on the whole rather than the parts. But the two meanings overlap.

Why write history? Following a long tradition, exemplified in Thucydides, Polybius, Dionysius of Halicarnassus, Diodorus, Josephus, and Lucian,[9] Eusebius insists on the utility of his history. At the very beginning he expresses the 'hope that it will be seen to be especially useful for those who place a high value on the utility of history' (I. 1. 5). Perhaps by coincidence, Eusebius also speaks of utility immediately after he has referred to his predecessors as raising beacons from afar (I. 1. 3–4). Just so, Polybius described real beacons and then insisted upon the great utility of systematic descriptions (X. 47. 13). Especially in Books III–V, where Eusebius is assembling scattered materials, he insists on the utility of virtually everything he quotes.[10] In Book VI he makes such a comment only on some letters of Origen (39. 5) and Dionysius (46. 5). In Book VII his point is different. He refers to materials cited for the sake of later generations (18. 1; 26. 3; 30. 1;

---

[3] E. Schwartz, 'Eusebios', *RE* VI (1907), 1395.
[4] I. 1. 3; 2. 1; 5. 1; II. 17. 13; III. 39. 12. 14; V, pr. 2; VI. 13. 9; 14. 1.
[5] Hermogenes, *Progymn.* 2 (4. 10–15 Rabe).
[6] I. 1. 3–5; V. 17. 5; VII. 26. 5; 32. 32.
[7] Dion. Hal. I. 1. 2. 4; 4. 1.
[8] E. Schwartz, *Eusebius: Kirchengeschichte*, iii (Leipzig, 1909), 205.
[9] Avenarius, op. cit., 22–6.
[10] I. 13. 22; III. 3. 1; 10. 6; 23. 5. 19; 39. 8; IV. 17. 1; 18. 1; 23. 1; 29. 7; V. 2. 8; 20. 3 (cf. V, pr. 1. 2. 4; 3. 1; 24. 14).

32. 32). Utility recurs in Book VIII (2. 3; 13. 8), in the first case along
with a mention of later readers.

Eusebius, like Polybius (II. 71. 2), can also refer to the 'necessity'
of discussing various matters. It was 'most necessary' for him to write
the *Church History* because no one else had dealt with the theme
(I. 1. 5). It was 'necessary' to begin with the pre-existent Christ because
he is the source of the name Christian (I. 1. 8). These historical and
theological explanations have literary implications, and in many other
instances the 'necessity' seems to explain why Eusebius has made use
of various source-materials.[11]

On the other hand, he is aware that he is leaving many matters out.
The discussions of utility and necessity clearly imply that he is willing
to omit whatever is not useful or not necessary. Certainly he is not
going to treat everything he has discussed elsewhere in his own works
(I. 1. 6; 2. 27; 6. 11). References to these works are not uncommon.
In Book I he refers to a summary he had provided in the *Chronological
Tables*, as compared with an account 'in full detail' to appear in the
History (1. 6).[12] Again, he refers to the *Prophetic Selections* as 'special
treatises' demonstrating predictions about Christ. In the *History* he will
be content with a shorter account (2. 27; cf. 6. 11). The preface to
Book II thus looks back to this shorter account and calls it a summary
(II, pr. 1). In Books IV and V there are references back to the 'ancient
martyrs' or 'martyrdoms of the ancients'.[13] Readers can consult the full
texts and therefore in the *History* Eusebius provides 'excerpts' (V, pr.
2). Book VI contains six cross-references, all apparently to works
written or compiled by Eusebius. First, if one were writing a biography
of Origen, 'the narrative concerning him would require a separate work'
(2. 1). It is not clear whether such a work already exists or not. Second,
discussion of various items in his career 'require a separate composition'.
Here Eusebius explicitly refers to the second book of the *Apology*
(23. 4). The third example is similar. A catalogue of Origen's works
'requires a separate study', and one can find it in the *Life of Pamphilus*
(32. 3). Other materials 'not relevant to the present work' can be found
in the *Apology* (33. 4), and Origen's letters in defence of his orthodoxy
are in a collection Eusebius made and used in the sixth book of the
Apology (36. 4). Such letters are mentioned again in the revised account

[11] I. 4. 1; 6. 11; II. 17. 14; III. 5. 5. 7; 23. 5; 25. 6; 39. 14. 17; IV. 15. 1;
26. 12; VI. 44. 1; VII. 32. 13.
[12] Cf. a reference back to the *Chronological Tables* in *Ecl. proph.* I. 1 (p. 1, 27).
[13] IV. 15. 47; V, pr. 2; 4. 3; 21. 5.

of Origen's death (39. 5). Other passages are concerned with Pamphilus and other martyrs. According to the *Martyrs of Palestine* (11. 3) Eusebius had recorded Pamphilus' biography in three books in a separate work. In VIII. 13. 6, however, he stated either that he would write this life or that he had already written it. The manuscripts vary. AT, perhaps reflecting the earliest version, look to the past; ERM, to the future. Again, in VIII. 13. 7 Eusebius says that witnesses of martyrdoms elsewhere should record what they have seen, while he will write his own record (presumably on Palestine).

Some things are left out because of their length. Eusebius does not intend to relate everything said by Philo (II. 5. 6; 17. 14) or Josephus (III. 5. 4. 7) or Justin (IV. 18. 1. 3. 10). He does not plan to give all the historical details about Nero (II. 25. 1-2). Other matters are passed over because of apologetic tradition. It was customary to say how evil the Gnostics were and to refrain from giving details. Eusebius takes the same line (II. 13. 5; III. 26. 2; 28. 6). He does not tell everything about the refutation of Montanist theology (V. 18. 14). As we have seen, he passes over Origen's thought. Though he does not say so, he follows the same practice when dealing with Paul of Samosata and other heretics. His omissions are especially conspicuous when he discusses the Manichees.

Other items are omitted because they would not be edifying. Eusebius explicitly states that it is not for him to describe the behaviour of bishops during the persecution (VIII. 2. 2; he has just done so without naming them, though he named one in VII. 32. 22) or their earlier dissensions and extraordinary behaviour. 'We resolved to tell nothing more about them than what we might use to vindicate the divine judgement.' Using a nautical metaphor based on I Timothy 1:19, Eusebius says he is not going to mention those who were attacked by 'pirates' in the persecution or lost their salvation in a shipwreck and chose to be plunged into the depths of the waves. Only what is 'useful' will be discussed (VIII. 2. 2-3). Similarly in the twelfth chapter of the *Martyrs of Palestine* he says he will not discuss what looks like the Meletian schism and its ill effects.

Along with the intentional omissions comes the need to generalize from relatively few instances. Eusebius' fondness for large numbers guides his thought on these matters. Thus he finds references to various provinces in the New Testament and wonders how one could tell 'how many and which' of the apostles' converts were genuinely zealous and able to be shepherds of the churches. Presumably one could list those mentioned by Paul, who had 'myriads of fellow-workers and, as he called them himself, fellow-soldiers, of whom the majority were judged worthy by him of everlasting remembrance'. The 'myriads', when counted, can be reduced to the actual figure of six (III. 4). The same subject recurs in III. 37. 4, where we learn that 'it is impossible for us to list all by name or to say how many there were in the first succession of the apostles who became shepherds or evangelists in the churches throughout the world.' Eusebius therefore recorded only those who wrote treatises on the apostolic teaching. This meant that he had in mind Polycarp, Papias, Ignatius (III. 36, with a fictitious reference to Ignatius' concern for tradition), Quadratus (37. 1; if he wrote, he must be the apologist of IV. 3. 2), and Clement (38). But he implies that there were multitudes.[14] Even when he is discussing the renegade bishops of the last persecution, he cannot refrain from adding 'myriads' as he reproduces a passage from the *Martyrs of Palestine* (1. 3; VIII. 3. 1).

Other inferences are drawn in regard to persecution and martyrdom. Eusebius claims that under Trajan there were sporadic persecutions in some cities because of popular uprisings (III. 32. 1). On the other hand, the persecution was so great in many places that Pliny was perturbed by the number of martyrs (33. 1). Even after Trajan mitigated the circumstances of Christians 'sometimes the populace, sometimes the local rulers contrived plots against us, so that without open persecution partial attacks broke out in various provinces and many of the faithful contested in various kinds of martyrdoms'. (33. 2.) These statements are based solely upon three pieces of evidence. First, Hegesippus' account of the martyrdom of the Bishop of Jerusalem, informed against by heretics; Eusebius paraphrases the evidence once and quotes it twice, perhaps to lend it greater weight (III. 32). Second, Pliny's correspondence with Trajan, paraphrased and then quoted from Tertullian (III. 33). Eusebius does not know that there actually was an anonymous, presumably 'popular' accusation against the Christians. Third, the letters of Ignatius (III. 36). These certainly show that Ignatius expected to be a martyr but do not prove that he was one. Eusebius therefore has to provide quotations from Irenaeus and Polycarp to prove that the bishop suffered martyrdom.

Inference also plays a part in Eusebius' discussion of the Gallican martyrs. In their time 'the persecution of us in some parts of the earth was ardently rekindled by popular violence in various cities and one can

---

[14] According to III. 24. 5 there were 12 apostles, 70 disciples, and 'myriads'.

make the conjecture from what happened in one nation that myriads of martyrs were prominent' (V, pr. 1). After describing the martyrdoms Eusebius concludes that from these examples 'it is possible to draw a logical inference as to what was done in the other provinces' (V. 2. 1). Actually, it is not possible to do so, for on the one hand Eusebius has not transcribed the list of no more than forty-eight martyrs which he had available (V. 4. 3), and on the other he did not use the apology of Theophilus, which refers to persecution around this time (though he knew of it, IV. 24), and did not know the contemporary apology of Athenagoras. The contemporary anti-Christian work by Celsus could have told him about widespread persecution, but he does not seem to have used it as a historical source. In this instance we see that Eusebius' inferences may have been partly right as to conclusions but thoroughly invalid as to reasoning.

When we get to Book VIII, then, where he is arguing from single examples to the universality and the intensity of the persecution, his method is completely inadequate.[15] Indeed, while it is likely that there were very many martyrdoms in Egypt, Eusebius' own *Martyrs of Palestine* shows that his generalizations exaggerate the number of martyrs. The effect is apologetic. He is trying to prove a case.

For this reason, the expressions marking the ends of sections or the beginnings of new ones or the transitions between the two echo the language of rhetoric and rhetorical philosophy. Eusebius is rather fond of using φέρε with the first person plural subjunctive verb in order to move on from one subject to another. Φέρε δὲ ἴδωμεν in *Ecl. proph.* III. 46 (p. 153, 13 Gaisford) comes directly from Plato. For Eusebius it marks the end of a long quotation from Africanus. It occurs eight times in the *History*, usually with the verb παραθώμεθα meaning 'Come, let us compare . . .'[16] Another expression simply involves the verbs for 'going' or 'going over' — from one subject to another. The reader will be transported from a narrative of the ancients to the divine scripture (II. 1. 8) or sometimes specifically to the continuing or subsequent narrative of events.[17] After a discussion of those whom he will not name, Eusebius urges us to 'go' with him to the sacred contests of the martyrs (VIII. 2. 3).

[15] Cf. VIII. 3. 4; 4. 1. 5; 6. 1. 10; 10. 12; 12. 1. 2. 10. 11; 13. 7; cf. 13. 9.
[16] I. 5. 1; 7. 1; II, pr. 2; 11. 1; V. 8. 1; VII. 26. 3; 32. 32; X. 5. 1; similar expressions in III. 5. 7; 24. 1. See also *Dem. Ev.* II, pr. 2; 3. 178; VI. 1. 2; VII, pr. 2; VIII, pr. 12; IX, pr. 2.
[17] III. 4. 11; 11. 1; 26. 1; 31. 6; V. 5. 7; VI. 32. 3.

Two connecting phrases are especially important. First, there is what sometimes precedes an exact quotation. 'There is nothing like hearing [whatever it may be] itself.'[18] This is an exact echo of the words of Demosthenes: 'There is nothing like hearing the law itself', obviously in a legal address. Second, there is the expression 'Take and read' — obviously aloud, since this was the method of reading in antiquity. K. Mras, editing the *Praeparatio Evangelica*, suggested that the phrase may reflect Eusebius' situation as he dictated (cf. VI. 23. 2; 36. 1; VII. 29. 2) the work and gave instructions for inserting quotations.[19] Gifford, on the other hand, had suggested that it was 'the formula by which an advocate called on the clerk or secretary to read ·the affidavit of a witness'.[20] Such a formula, attested in the papyri and the Acts of the martyrs,[21] may be more closely related to Eusebius' purpose; but both meanings could be involved. The second has an apologetic point.

We should also note the third-person imperatives that mark the end of quotations or discussions of particular authors or subjects. All of them[22] imply that the subject has been adequately discussed and Eusebius is about to turn to something else. The historian before Eusebius who seems most fully content with this kind of transition is Polybius. W. R. Paton translates Polybius I. 35. 10 as 'Well, on this subject I have said enough.'[23] The phrases are not necessarily apologetic, but they could reflect the idea that enough has been said to convince any reader. Similar expressions are 'this for that' and 'so much for this'.

Another apologetic feature of Eusebius' *History*, as every reader soon becomes aware, is its anthological character. It thus reminds us of such a predecessor as Clement of Alexandria and especially of his *Stromata*. Eusebius announced this aspect of his work when he started out (I. 1. 4). He was going to 'anthologize the words of the ancient writers as from spiritual meadows'. He liked to speak of anthologizing spiritual meadows and had used practically the same expression in his

---

[18] I. 13. 5; III. 7. 9; 32. 3; IV. 23. 9; VII. 23. 1; cf. *Praep. Ev. IV. 16. 14.*

[19] K. Mras, *Eusebius: Die Praeparatio Evangelica*, I (Berlin, 1956), lviii.

[20] E. H. Gifford, *Eusebii Pamphili Evangelicae Praeparationis Libri XV* (Oxford, 1903), IV. 104.

[21] In *Praeparatio* and in *H. E.* III. 8. 1; 23. 5; II. 23. 2 according to ATER. See also J. Geffcken, 'Augustins Tolle-lege-Erlebnis', *Archiv für Religionswissenschaft*, 31 (1934), 1–13; also *Acta Apollonii* 11; *Mart. Pionii* 20. 7.

[22] Δεδηλώσθω, εἰρήσθω, ἐπιτετηρήσθω, ἐχέτω, ἱστορήσθω, κείσθω, παρατεθείσθω, προτετηρήσθω, τιθέσθω.

[23] Ταῦτα μὲν οὖν ἡμῖν ἐπὶ τοσοῦτον εἰρήσθω; cf. Polybius XII. 4. 14. 22. 7; XVIII. 15. 17; cf. XXXI. 30. 4.

Eclogae propheticae (I. 1). Indeed, he had anthologized it himself.
Clement had described someone, probably his teacher Pantaenus,
as 'a truly Sicilian bee, picking the flowers of the prophetic and
apostolic meadow', who 'produced a pure kind of knowledge in the
souls of his disciples' (*Str.* I. 11. 2). Eusebius liked the whole passage
about Clement's teachers and quoted it in full (V. 11. 3–5) – except
for precisely these words about the Sicilian bee, left out of the middle
of the quotation. Evidently Eusebius had made it his own.[24]

We have still not discussed one basic difficulty in Eusebius'
composition. The *Praeparatio*, more than any other work, shows that
he knew how to plan a treatise and stick to his plan. The *Ecologae
propheticae* too follow a definite pattern and each book has a beginning
and an end. The *Church History* is not thus arranged, even though
historians and other authors were accustomed to pay attention to the
lengths of books and their beginnings and endings. Indeed, a comment
on length often served as a way of ending one book before beginning
another.

Some of the works which Eusebius certainly knew gave him
precedents for this kind of writing. In the first century BC Diodorus
Siculus broke off half-way through his first book to say that because of
its size this book, though remaining one, would be divided into two
parts for the sake of 'symmetry'. Size was an important consideration.
Diodorus believed that he could not have long prefaces for his several
books because he was going to deal with more than a millennium 'in
a few books' (actually forty). In addition, he thought that the 'acts'
of a city or a king should be told within the framework of a single
book. For this reason he was willing to devote a long Book XVI to
Philip of Macedon, a long Book XVII to Alexander the Great.[25]
Conceivably Eusebius derived from Diodorus the idea of having
prefaces – brief ones – only for his Books, I, II, VII, VIII, and X. He
paid no attention to Diodorus' idea of devoting one book to one hero,
for he spread his discussion of Dionysius 'the Great' over two books.

Perhaps he took Josephus more seriously, but the Jewish historian's
concern for length developed only gradually. Some books of the
Jewish War are twice as long as others. We find a comment on length
only in the late apologetic treatise *Against Apion*. Josephus thought
he ought to bring the first book to an end because it had already

---

[24] In addition, the reference to a Sicilian bee might have weakened his claim
that Clement's last teacher was from Egypt.
[25] Diodorus Siculus I. 29. 6; 41. 10; XIII. 1. 1–2.

achieved symmetrical size. In fact, it is almost the same length as the second book.[26]

The best precedents are to be found in the Alexandrian Christian writers. Clement said that the second book of his *Stromata* could not go beyond the proper size or number of chapters, and he feared that the third book had gone too far. Further evidence comes from late writings of Origen, composed at Caesarea and preserved in the library there. At the end of Book X of his *Commentary on John* he said that it was long enough. The next two books are lost, but at the beginning of Book XIII he wrote that he regretted having to discuss the Samaritan woman in Book XIII as well as in Book XII. The earlier book, however, had been long enough. At the end of Book XXXII — still nowhere near the end of the Gospel of John — Origen said that this tome too had reached sufficient size. The same comment is to be found in the treatise *Contra Celsum* at the ends of Books I, III, IV, VI, and VII. Since both Book IV and Book VII are described as long enough, and since Book IV is half as large again as Book VII,[27] it is obvious that the question of length was perhaps psychological, more certainly literary. It had nothing to do with the availability of papyrus.

Eusebius speaks of the length of his book(s) only in VIII. 6. 5, where he is arguing that readers can infer from the martyrdom of one imperial servant what the others were like. He claims that to include accounts of others would spoil the symmetry of Book VIII. Presumably he has symmetry in mind because he has removed the *Martyrs of Palestine* from the book. At the end of Book VII and the beginning of Book VIII he speaks of concluding the subject of successions and succession. Otherwise he does not explain why books end or begin where they do. The preface to Book II summarizes only certain aspects of Book I and states that Book II will be concerned with events 'after the ascension' of Christ. Actually it ends with the persecution of Christians under Nero and the impending Jewish catastrophe.

[26] We find further statements in second-century writers *not* used by Eusebius. Artemidorus, writing on dreams, explained that the preface to his work could not exceed the suitable length and said the same thing about his first book (*Onir.* pr., p. 3, 1 Pack; I. 82, p. 99, 13–16). Athenaeus ended his fourth and sixth books by pointing to their 'sufficient size'. Similarly the philosophical commentator Sextus Empiricus said that his seventh book *Against the astrologers* had reached sufficient size; he would therefore start from a new beginning (*Adv. math.* VII. 446). 'Another beginning' in Clement, *Str.* VII. 111. 4; Porphyry, *De abst.* I. 57 (p. 132 Nauck, ed. 2).

[27] T. Birt, *Das antike Buchwesen* (Berlin, 1882), 312–13; 332.

At the end of Book II Eusebius employs the 'resumptive' technique occasionally used by authors like Strabo. The last sentence of Book II, 'such was the condition of the Jews' (itself perhaps an echo of Josephus, *Antiquities* XVIII. 379), becomes the first sentence of ·Book III. Similarly at the end of Book IV we learn that 'at this time Soter, bishop of the Roman church, died.' If the sentence refers to some particular time, it must point to the eighth year of Marcus Aurelius and Lucius Verus, mentioned in IV. 19. But that was when Soter became bishop. At the beginning of Book V, then, we are told that 'Soter, bishop of the Roman church, ended his life in the eighth year of his rule' — the seventeenth year of 'Antoninus Verus'. The transition is resumptive but contains a correction of sorts.

Two other books may suggest that they end at the wrong points, or that originally they ended elsewhere. Eusebius' purpose becomes clear, however, when we examine the passages in question. First, at III. 31. 6 there is a summary of what has been discussed in regard to 'the apostles and apostolic times'. Book III could have ended here. It was already as long as either of the books before it. But Eusebius was eager to go on to those who 'held the first place in the succession from the apostles' (III. 37. 1). The last eight chapters of Book III hold the sub-apostolic age together with what came before it. Again, Book VI could have been brought to a suitable end with what Eusebius at first thought was the death of Origen (VI. 39. 5). He went on, however, with the letters of various bishops and especially of Dionysius of Alexandria (cf. VII, pr.). What he seems to be doing is holding generations together. 'Dionysius had been one of Origen's pupils' (VI. 29. 4).

The end of Book VII certainly reads like the end of a whole treatise. Eusebius has completed the ὑπόθεσις of the successions 'in these books' and has dealt with them from the birth of Christ to 'the destruction of the places of prayer — a period of three hundred and five years'. At the beginning of the book he named its number and referred to the whole as the *Ecclesiastical History*. Laqueur pointed out that Josephus too did not number his books in the text of the *Antiquities* until he got to the twentieth and last (XX. 267) and he inferred that Eusebius too originally stopped when he named a number.[28] One can add to this. As Eusebius spoke of the birth of Christ and the destruction of the churches, so Josephus had said that 'the present work contains

[28] R. Laqueur, 'Ephoros', *Hermes*, 46 (1911), 189–90.

the "tradition" from the first creation of man up to the twelfth year of the reign of Nero' (*Ant.* XX. 259). More than that, Josephus said that he had 'endeavoured to preserve the record of the line of the high priests who have served during two thousand years' in addition to 'the succession and conduct of the kings . . . for this is what I promised to do at the beginning of my history' (XX. 261). Still further, Josephus says that 'here will be the end of my *Antiquities*, following which begins my account of the war' (XX. 259). Just so, Eusebius proposes to go on in what presumably was once intended as a separate work, to the history of the final persecution or persecutions in Books VIII to X.

We have already discussed the various versions of these final books. Now we turn to examine the statements about content to be found at the beginning of the *Church History*.

V

PREFACE AND PROMISES

Now that we have seen something of Eusebius' methods of editing and of composition we are ready to turn to the preface with which his work now begins. At the very beginning of the *Church History* he provides four chapters which he calls a preface (προκατασκευή, I. 5. 1) or a prologue (προοίμιον, II, pr. 1). Such introductory sections are often the last to be composed. Quintilian condemned the practice just because it was common.[1] By examining a προκατασκευή one can sometimes obtain information about the way in which a historian has changed his mind. Thus Polybius at first planned to write a history of the League of Achaean states (II. 37; cf. IV. 1. 4-9). In later life he lived at Rome in the house of a Roman general and stood close to Roman leaders. He decided to write on the history of Rome and Carthage and set forth his new plan in a προκατασκευή (I. 3. 8-10).[2] In Origen's treatise *Contra Celsum* (pr. 6) we read that 'I decided to put this preface at the beginning after I had composed the reply to everything up to the point where Celsus puts the attack against Jesus into the mouth of a Jew.' Origen 'wrote the beginning of [his] answer to Celsus on one plan but after the first part followed a different one'. So it is that in *Contra Celsum*, I. 28 he says first that Celsus 'introduces a Jew' and then, repetitiously, that he 'impersonates a Jew'. Apparently he forgot that he had written 'introduces a Jew' when he turned back from dictating the prologue. Finally, there is the preface to Book II of the *Church History* by Socrates. There we find a frank statement about his earlier and injudicious confidence in Rufinus as an authority, necessarily shattered when he discovered the treatises of Athanasius as well as various contemporary letters. It became necessary for him to revise the first two books of his work.[3] We shall not look for such

[1] Quintilian, *Inst. orat.* III. 9. 8.

[2] Cf. M. Gelzer, 'Die hellenische προκατασκευή im 2. Buch des Polybius', *Hermes*, 75 (1940), 27-37; *Die Achaica im Geschichtswerk des Polybius* (*Abhandlungen der Preussischen Akademie der Wissenschaften*, 1940, *Philos. -hist. Kl.*, 2); *Ueber die Arbeitsweise des Polybius* (*Sitzungsberichte der Heidelberger Akademie der Wissenschaften*, 1956, 3).

[3] Cf. F. Geppert, *Die Quellen des Kirchenhistorikers Socrates Scholasticus* (Leipzig, 1898), 7.

frankness in Eusebius, but it may be that his prefaces will yield evidence of changes.

The preface to Book II of the *Church History* may suggest the presence of changes. According to this preface, Book I was a preface to the history of the Church, for it contained accounts of events before Christ's ascension. It dealt with 'the divinity of the saving Word and the antiquity of the doctrines of our teaching and the antiquity of the gospel way of life according to Christians' (I. 2-4). Then it discussed 'Items concerning his recent epiphany, those before he suffered and those related to the selection of the apostles'. Events before the passion, leading up to the selection of the apostles (and the seventy disciples), are discussed in I. 5-10 and continued in I. 12-13 after a discussion about John the Baptist and Jesus as attested in the *Antiquities* of Josephus (I. 11) which breaks the continuity and is related to the 'commentaries' on Pilate and Jesus, apparently forged about 312 (IX. 5. 1). It is at least possible, as Laqueur supposed, that I. 11 was added for Eusebius' second edition of 315.

We note that there is no reference to the promises made at the beginning of Book I. This may suggest, though it does not necessarily do so, that the promises too belong to the second edition.

Apart from the evidence of Book II, we should suggest that the whole collection of prefatory materials in Book I is a later addition, made for the edition of 315. These prefatory materials have been abridged, as Eusebius explicitly says (I. 2. 16; 4. 1; II, pr. 1). They begin with Old Testament proofs for the pre-existence of the divine Word and his manifestation in the theophanies (I. 2. 1-16). They are brief, but Eusebius provides a cross-reference to his *Eclogae propheticae* and adds that 'elsewhere' he has put together passages 'more cogently' (ἀποδεικτικώτερον, I. 2. 27). The *Eclogae* were written in 310 or 311, if we may rely on Schwartz's vision of a reference to the martyrdom of Pamphilus.[4] The book referred to 'elsewhere' may be the *Eclogae*. It may also be the *Demonstratio* (ἀπόδειξις) *Evangelica*, to be dated after Eusebius' *Praeparatio*, though not necessarily after the completion of the *Praeparatio*. Now the fourth book of the *Praeparatio* refers to the recent punishment of former persecutors at Antioch and Miletus (IV. 2. 10-11). Presumably this points to the investigations conducted by Licinius in 314 and described in *Church History*, IX. 11. 5-6. On the

---

[4] E. Schwartz, 'Eusebios', *RE* VI (1907), 1387; *Ecl. proph.* IV. 31 (230. 14-15, Gaisford); cf. D. S. Wallace-Hadrill in *HTR* 67 (1974), 55-63.

basis of this evidence we venture to set the prefatory materials in the edition of 315.

This is not to say that the *History* originally lacked a preface with promises. It is simply to say that the present preface was not there at first. This can be seen from the fact that in later books there are promises that imply the non-existence of this preface, as well as a reference back to a promise not found in the present preface First, in III. 4. 11 he says that 'as we go on our way, on occasion the points concerning the succession from the apostles at various times will be related.' Since in the present preface this promise is made twice (I. 1. 1. 4) it is odd to find it made again as if it had not been made at all. Second, in V. 8. 1 he writes thus: 'When we were beginning this work (πραγματεία) we made the promise to quote on occasion the sayings of the ancient ecclesiastical writers, in which they committed to writing the traditions about the canonical scriptures that came down to them.' This is a mixture of phrases now to be found in the first chapter of the *History* — 'sayings of the ancient authors', 'ecclesiastical authors', 'commit to writing' — with others from a promise about the canon actually to be found in III. 3. 3. (This promise says that he will discuss 'along with the successions' what it is that ecclesiastical writers have had to say about the canonical scriptures.) The word πραγματεία, as two other passages show (V, pr. 2; VI. 33. 4), refers to the whole *Church History*, i.e. to the beginning of Book I. But the promise of which he speaks is not to be found in our present text.

It is possible that Eusebius' memory failed him. It is more likely that at one time (in the first edition) the promise set forth at the beginning of Book I was different from what now stands there (from the second edition).

Does this deprive his statement of value as an index to his intentions? Perhaps it does, but it means that the statement about the promises is all the more valuable as an indication of what he thought he had achieved. Presumably it is much closer to the actual content than a statement of intentions would have been.

Before adding some observations about the historical promises, it will be worth while to quote them, noting the way in which Eusebius divides the materials. The numbers within parentheses refer to sections of I. 1. The translation is pedantically literal.

(1) The successions from the sacred apostles, along with the periods of time completed between our Saviour and ourselves [cf. VII. 32. 32]; how many and how great were the events which are said to have taken

place in ecclesiastical history, and how many were those who with distinction led and presided over the church in the most notable communities, and how many were those who in each generation were ambassadors of the divine Word orally or through written compositions; who and how many and when they were who, driving on to the extreme of error because of yearning for innovation, proclaimed themselves authors of 'knowledge falsely so-called' [I Tim. 6:20],[5] unsparingly ravaging the flock of Christ like fierce wolves [cf. Acts 20:29);

(2) in addition to these, the events which came upon the whole nation of the Jews immediately after the plot against our Saviour; and how many and of what sort and at what periods of time were the wars of the heathen against the divine Word, and how great the numbers of those who at various times endured the contest through blood and torture on his behalf; and the martyrdoms after these and in our own time, and the final merciful and gracious help of the Saviour — when proposing to commit all this to writing, I shall begin[6] from no other point than the first dispensation related to the Saviour and Lord Jesus, the Christ of God.

(3) But just here my work craves the indulgence of the considerate, since I acknowledge that it is beyond our power to keep the promise fully and without omission. We are the first to enter upon the subject, starting out as on some trackless desert way and praying that we may have God as guide and the power of the Lord as helper. We cannot find even the mere traces of any who went before us on the same way, except for a few indications by which in various ways various authors have left partial indications of the times in which they finished their course, raising their voices from a distance like beacons and calling and telling us as from a distant watch-tower, how we must walk and keep the course of the work straight without error or danger.

(4) As many items, then, as we consider useful for the proposed subject out of what they have occasionally mentioned, collecting them and anthologizing the appropriate sayings of earlier writers themselves as from intellectual meadows, we shall endeavour to organize through historical treatment, eager to preserve the successions from the especially distinguished apostles of our Saviour in the prominent churches that are still remembered even now.

(5) I regard the labour as especially necessary because I do not know any ecclesiastical author who has thus far been concerned with this kind of writing. I hope that it will be seen to be especially useful to those who set a high value on the utility of history.

---

[5] Irenaeus alludes to this verse in the title of his treatise Ἔλεγχος καὶ ἀνατροπὴ τῆς ψευδωνύμου γνώσεως and alludes to other verses from the Pastoral Epistles in his preface; similarly Theophilus of Antioch alludes to the Pastorals in *Ad Autol.* I. 1-2.

[6] Cf. G. Arnold, 'Mk 1 1 und Eröffnungswendungen', *ZNW* 68 (1977), 123-7.

(6) I have already made a summary of these matters in the *Chronological Lists* which I drew up, but in the present work I have proposed to make the narrative most complete.

One of the most striking features of this preface is the frequency with which correlative pronouns occur, especially toward the beginning ('how many', 'how much', etc.) It is unusual for a historian to employ them so often, but Eusebius used them intensively not only here but also at other points where he was introducing new kinds of materials or writing summaries. Similar terms recur in the preface to Book II, where he is summarizing Book I. In III. 5. 4 a very long sentence summarizes Josephus' account of the destruction of Jerusalem. It contains numerous examples of these pronouns and presumably was influenced by the presence of similar terms at the beginning of Josephus' own *Jewish War*.[7] The pronouns come to the fore again in a passage in VI. 39. 5 in which Eusebius must originally have introduced his account of the 'glorious martyrdom' of Origen. It was then a passage well worth introducing thus. As it stands now, it ends anticlimactically. Less intensive use of the terms is to be found in VII. 32. 32 (end of Book VII) and VIII. 1. 1 and 4. 5 (beginning of VIII), as well as toward the end of the *Martyrs of Palestine* (12. 12). A couple occur in the Tyrian sermon of X. 4 (21).

The main emphasis is on the quantitative. The pronouns also tend to sound alike and thus exemplify the rhetorical form called παρήχησις.[8] Beyond the rhetoric, they tend to imply that Eusebius is able to supply factual, even quantitative, answers to the problems of Church history. The most obvious answer to the question 'how many' — converts or martyrs — is 'a lot' or 'countless numbers' or 'myriads'. Walter Bauer criticized Eusebius for giving this kind of answer.[9] It seems likely, however, that readers were used to this kind of exaggeration. It is fairly common in Josephus and other historians.[10] A glance at Origen's *Commentary on John* reveals the presence of three large numbers on a single page.[11] Thus when Eusebius recounts the story of the persecution in his own day such numbers are accompanied by rhetorical inferences intended to maximize the number of martyrs, tortures,

---

[7] *Bell.* I. 21, 25, 27, 28.
[8] Cf. H. Diels, *Parmenides Lehrgedicht* (Berlin, 1897), 60–1.
[9] *Orthodoxy and Heresy in Earliest Christianity* (Philadelphia, 1971), 191–2.
[10] Cf. A. Byatt, 'Josephus and Population Numbers in First Century Palestine', *Palestine Exploration Quarterly*, 105 (1973), 51–60.
[11] *Ioh. comm.* X. 23 (p. 197, 16. 24. 31 Preuschen).

etc.[12] Evidently he had no accurate figures.

His emphasis on the quantitative in the prefaces might show that he was trying to write history in spite of his preoccupation with literary matters. All it actually indicates is one more way in which rhetoric influenced him.

Beyond this, we may expect to find allusions to predecessors in a preface of this sort. Perhaps we should note that the central section of the historical preface is devoted precisely to differentiating Eusebius' work from what went before. He insists that he is the first to deal with his subject-matter (I. 1. 3 and 5) and he criticizes his predecessors for having left a few indications and partial accounts, though of course they did serve as beacons. What he will do is use their sporadic efforts and produce a unified body of material through historical treatment. Obviously he thinks that they did not achieve a result like this.

We have already discussed Eusebius' use of the anthological figure used by Clement of Alexandria, with its mention of 'intellectual meadows'. Here we suggest that at this point he may be alluding to Clement's work and indicating that though it anthologized it made no use of 'historical treatment' and was therefore a source but not a model for the *Church History*.

T. Halton has argued that a more important predecessor in view was Hegesippus, since he dealt with the same themes and used similar language. He was obviously concerned with successions (III. 11–12; IV. 22), the activities of the rulers of the churches (IV. 22), heresies (III. 32. 7; IV. 22), the fate of the Jews (II. 23. 18), and the war of the Roman state against Christians (II. 23; III. 19–20. 32; IV. 8). In addition, both Hegesippus (IV. 22. 8–9) and Eusebius were concerned with canonical and uncanonical books.

Eusebius' claim to have arranged earlier materials through 'historical treatment' is significant, since in discussing his own use of Hegesippus he writes that he has 'arranged the narrative chronologically' (Lake).[13] Hegesippus was no historian (IV. 22. 8).

Eusebius was thus claiming that his account would be more complete than the partial treatments provided by Clement and Hegesippus, to mention only his major sources for the first two centuries. His work, at least for the eastern Roman provinces, would be universal as contrasted with their incompleteness. Perhaps he did not

---

[12] For example, VIII. 4. 4; 6. 1. 10; 12. 11.
[13] Oulton undertranslates: 'giving the accounts at suitable points'.

know the work of Polybius, in spite of occasional resemblances which we have noted. It would have told him that for a universal historian, 'partial' and 'special' histories dealing with particular and local events have no value at all (I. 4. 3-11). Just as Polybius claimed to be the first to write a general history of the rise of Rome, so Eusebius was claiming to be the first to write a general history of the rise of Christianity.[14]

We do not need to accept all that Eusebius claims for himself. His works contain much self-advertisement as well as 'self-plagiarization'. For instance, in the *Praeparatio Evangelica* he states that 'very many others have carefully laid down the evidence in their own writings, from which I shall presently make some few quotations.' The quotations are actually rather extensive. Then he goes on to say, 'I myself shall take a more innovative course than the said authors.' His course has very little novelty about it, for it follows traditional apologetic lines. As for 'self-plagiarization', the *Life of Constantine* (I. 33-II. 3) is filled with materials transferred from the last three books of the *Church History*, while the late works in praise of Constantine and *On the Theophany* echo not only the *Praeparatio* and *Demonstratio Evangelica* but also share many common materials.

Pioneering is obviously a matter of definition, at least in part. If ecclesiastical history is to be defined as Eusebius defines it at the beginning of the *Church History*, he was indeed the first person to collect just these materials and put them together in just this way. After all, he aimed at catholicity of interest and subject matter, and he followed the best models he could find in the Graeco-Roman world. Some problems remain in regard to his claims, however.

When Eusebius says he could not find even the traces of predecessors he is of course exaggerating. He is well aware of what he owes to Josephus, 'the most famous of the historians among the Hebrews' (I. 5. 3), especially since he frequently uses Josephus' accounts to confirm the historical truth of the scriptures. In addition, for the early period he found Luke, who wrote 'among us', especially valuable. Even though Eusebius refers to Luke-Acts as 'the divine scripture',[15] he views Luke as a historian. There is an echo of the preface to Acts in Eusebius' own

[14] Cf. the comments of A. Momigliano, 'Pagan and Christian Historiography in the Fourth Century A.D.', in *The Conflict Between Paganism and Christianity in the Fourth Century* (Oxford, 1963), 90; repr. in *Essays in Ancient and Modern Historiography* (Middletown, Conn., 1977), 116. On originality see Dionysius of Halicarnassus I. 5. 4; *De Thuc.* 9; Josephus, *Bell.* I. 15.

[15] I. 10. 2; II. 1. 8; 9. 4; 10. 10; cf. 18. 9.

preface to Book II. He frequently uses Acts as history and then provides additional information from 'tradition', presumably tradition as recorded in the *Hypotyposes* of Clement of Alexandria.[16] What Josephus confirms is generally the reliability of Acts.[17]

For the early days of Christianity Eusebius made use not only of Clement but also of Tertullian and Hegesippus. In his view these predecessors did not provide models for him. Clement's *Hypotyposes* contained scriptural exegesis, not history as such.[18] Tertullian was an apologist, as Eusebius pointed out (II. 2. 4). The mysterious Hegesippus, largely neglected in the *Chronicle*, later became more important in Eusebius' eyes and contributed a good deal of confusion to the *History* (see Chapter VII). Hegesippus gave him historical materials, but Hegesippus was no historian. Eusebius' word ὑπόμνημα does not imply 'history', and Hegesippus was concerned with problems of heresy and orthodoxy, not historical fact.[19]

The struggle with heresy was closely related to the rise of Church history, however, just as it was to the rise of systematic theology. When Hegesippus and Irenaeus attacked heretics as innovators or transmitters of merely secret traditions, they had to provide historical lists of orthodox authorities; similarly Eusebius himself gives lists of orthodox authors (IV. 21; V. 27). When Montanists defended spiritual gifts as traditional they needed a chain of tradition (V. 17. 4), just as Polycrates of Ephesus needed apostolic and episcopal warrant for his dating of Easter (V. 24. 2-7), and Roman adoptianists claimed that the Bishops of Rome before Zephyrinus had held their doctrine (V. 28. 3). When did heresy set in? In his *Chronicle* Eusebius placed the heresiarch Basilides in the year 133, mentioning no heretic earlier than him. In his first reading of Hegesippus (whom he wrongly supposed to belong to the first successors of the apostles, II. 23. 3) he reached the erroneous conclusion that Hegesippus dated the beginning of heresy in the time of Trajan (III. 32. 7). The passage when actually quoted showed that heresy began thirty or forty years earlier (IV. 22. 4). And in any event Eusebius had placed or was to place the beginning of heresy in the time of Claudius, when Simon Magus flourished (II. 13. 5). All these variations clearly show that there was no truly historical treatment of the problems before Eusebius or, at any rate, none known to him.

---

[16] I. 12. 1. 3; II. 1. 2-5; 9. 1-2; 22. 1-2; III. 4. 4-5.
[17] I. 5. 3; II. 10. 10; 11. 1; 12. 1-2; 21. 3.
[18] VI. 13. 2; 14. 1.
[19] N. Hyldahl, 'Hegesipps Hypomnemata', *Studia Theologica*, 14 (1960), 70-113.

One more author whose work verged on history should be mentioned among Eusebius' predecessors and sources. This was Julius Africanus, whose five books of *Chronographies* Eusebius calls reliable products of industry and effort (VI. 31. 2). They contributed practically nothing, however, to the *Chronicle* or the *Church History*, because Africanus included hardly any information about Church events. He mentioned Heraclas of Alexandria only because he himself went to Alexandria to see him.

As models, then, we can recognize only the Jewish historian Josephus and the Christian author of the book of Acts. With Josephus Eusebius would have shared ultimate recognition of the God-given character of Roman rule, in spite of persecution or war. Both authors firmly believed that the activities of the divine providence and the divine justice were clearly visible in historical events. Like Josephus, Eusebius liked to quote documents from earlier authors, though he did not share the enthusiasm of Josephus or Luke for composing speeches to be ascribed to various personages.[20] With Luke Eusebius shared 'the dramatic episode style' typical of Hellenistic authors.[21]

If we consider his sources in general, we find that they came from two ecclesiastical libraries. One had been created at Caesarea by Eusebius' teacher Pamphilus; it included the works of Origen 'and the other ecclesiastical authors' and had a catalogue apparently made by Eusebius himself (VI. 32. 3; 36. 3).[22] The other was the episcopal library at Jerusalem, founded by Alexander of Jerusalem, a pupil of Origen and other Alexandrian teachers (VI. 20. 1).[23] It certainly contained episcopal correspondence, perhaps more.[24] Conceivably the letters and other compositions by Beryllus of Bostra, the *Dialogue* of Gaius, and various works by Hippolytus were preserved there. We are tempted to suggest that Hegesippus was there, not at Caesarea

---

[20] Cf. H. St. J. Thackeray, *Josephus the Man and the Historian* (New York, 1929); H. W. Attridge, *The Interpretation of Biblical History in the Antiquitates Judaicae of Flavius Josephus* (Missoula, Mont., 1976).

[21] E. Plümacher, *Lukas als hellenistischer Schriftsteller* (Göttingen, 1972), 80–136; cf. H. J. Cadbury, *The Making of Luke-Acts* (New York, 1927).

[22] For the possible discovery of the library building cf. A. Negev, 'Inscriptions hébraïques, grecques et latines de Césarée Maritime', *RB* 78 (1971), 256–8; L. I. Levine, *Roman Caesarea* (Qedem 2, Jerusalem, 1975), 45–6.

[23] On the location of the library cf. J. T. Milik, 'La Topographie de Jérusalem vers la fin de l'époque byzantine', *Mélanges de l'Université Saint Joseph*, 37 (1960–1), 147–8. He claims that Julius Africanus also used it.

[24] On such correspondence cf. P. Nautin, *Lettres et écrivains chrétiens des iie et iiie siècles* (Paris, 1961).

(see pages 67–8). Presumably the collections at Caesarea and Jerusalem
were not completely different, however. After all, at Caesarea one
could find works by 'Origen and the other ecclesiastical authors' (VI.
32. 3).

Thus while Eusebius explicitly says that from the Jerusalem library
'we have been able ourselves to gather together the materials for the
subject in hand' (VI. 20. 1), we should not be justified in assuming that
works used in the *History* but not in the earlier *Chronicle* were to be
found only at Jerusalem.

The kind of literature he read in one library or the other (or both)
is described in the *Praeparatio* (I. 3. 4) as consisting of 'refutations and
contradictions of the arguments opposed to us', interpretations of
'the inspired and sacred scriptures in exegetical commentaries and in
homilies on particular points', and apologies expressed 'in a more
controversial manner'. In a later work against Marcellus (I. 4. 8) he
claimed to have read 'a great many ecclesiastical compositions by
men more ancient than Origen, various letters written by bishops
and synods long ago'. Here he probably refers to the controversies
over Montanism and Quartodecimanism as reflected in Book V of
the *Church History*.

If we ask how the librarians or the bishops decided what works
to include in the collections, it is obvious that friends of Origen would
value his writings. Alexander of Jerusalem was a pupil of Pantaenus,
Clement, and Origen (VI. 14. 9). And though Origen never referred to
Irenaeus, at least in his extant writings, Clement quoted from him
(VI. 13. 9), thus showing that there was a line of tradition that ran
back to Asia and indeed to Melito as well as Irenaeus (VI. 13. 9) and
beyond both to Polycarp and the apostle John (V. 24. 3–5). Irenaeus
certainly was a significant figure in the anti-Gnostic struggle in Egypt.
This point is proved by an Oxyrhynchus fragment of his work against
heresies. The papyrus (Oxy. III. 405) was written not more than
a generation after Irenaeus' original. The work itself, used in Rome by
Hippolytus, in Carthage by Tertullian, was authoritative. It deserved to
be in the library.

Irenaeus' work in turn could give leads to the orthodox literature
before his time. Eusebius cites instances where Irenaeus referred to
Clement of Rome (V. 6. 3), Hermas (V. 8. 7), Ignatius (III. 36. 12),
Polycarp (IV. 14. 3–8), Papias (III. 39. 1), Justin (IV. 8. 9), and,
when still at Rome with Justin, Tatian (IV. 29. 3). Eusebius came to
question Irenaeus' judgement about Papias (III. 39. 13) but not about

the others. He urged his own readers to study the works of Justin II. 13. 5; III. 26. 2) and Irenaeus (IV. 18. 1).

Eusebius himself collected more than a hundred letters of Origen for the library at Caesarea (VI. 36. 3–4). He also used earlier collections, such as the letters of Ignatius and, probably, Polycarp (III. 36). Certainly there was a collection of authors anti-heretical and chiefly anti-Marcionite; Eusebius made use of it in IV. 21–9. In V. 27–8 he deals with 'many works of the virtuous zeal of ancient and ecclesiastical men' still preserved 'by many' or at least by a library. First he lists undated works by names but unidentifiable authors. Next he turns to anonymous authors who are proved 'orthodox and ecclesiastical' by their exegesis of scripture. What he means by this expression, at least in regard to the anonymous anti-heretical work he proceeds to quote, is that such an author would speak of 'the simple faith of the divine scriptures' (V. 28. 15) and would use as authorities those whom Eusebius also recognized – Justin, Miltiades, Tatian, Clement, Irenaeus, and Melito (V. 28. 5). There are also records of synods in regard to Montanists (at any rate, a dossier, V. 16–19), Quartodecimans 23–5), Beryllus of Bostra (VI. 33), Novatianists (VI. 43–6), and Paul of Samosata (VII. 27–30). Letters of Dionysius of Alexandria on Novatianism (VI. 44–6), on re-baptism (VII. 2–9) and on other subjects existed in collections, and Eusebius himself collected letters by Origen, including many in defence of his orthodoxy (VI. 36. 3–4).

Orthodoxy was a primary concern of the collection in the library as in Eusebius' mind. Much of the discussion of Origen is devoted to showing how orthodox he was. Quotations from Dionysius of Alexandria show that this bishop was a militant traditionalist (e.g. VII. 7. 4-5), while from Eusebius' account (VII. 26. 1) one would never guess that he engaged in controversy with the Bishop of Rome. How strong Eusebius' emphasis on orthodox tradition could be appears from his description of the letters of Ignatius (III. 36. 4). Ignatius certainly warned the churches of Asia against heresy. But Eusebius adds that he 'urged them to hold fast to the tradition of the apostles; as he was already becoming a martyr, he thought it necessary to set it down in writing for security.' None of this comes from Ignatius.[25] It is simply what Eusebius believed he should have done.

---

[25] Though he tells the Ephesians (12. 1) that he is in danger while they are established (in security).

Conclusion

From this discussion we can see something of the ways in which Eusebius created his *Church History*. The preface was important to him because in it he set forth the most important themes he had tried to interpret. He was influenced by his predecessors, especially since their works were available in ecclesiastical libraries, and their influence explains some of the good and bad aspects of his work. In order to analyse the *History* more thoroughly we now turn to the individual themes.

VI

THE FIRST THEME: APOSTOLIC SUCCESSION

The very first words of the *Church History* mention 'the successions from the sacred apostles'. Then Eusebius goes on to speak of chronology, important events in ecclesiastical history, and significant leaders in the most famous communities (I. 1. 1). Only a few lines later he returns to the subject. He hopes to preserve 'the successions from the apostles of our Saviour, . . . at the least the most renowned of them, in the churches that are still significant and notable today' (I. 1. 4). His immediate model seems to be a passage at the beginning of the third book of Irenaeus' treatise *Adversus Haereses*, where this favourite bishop and theologian says that 'it would be too long, in a work such as this, to list the successions in all the churches'. Like Eusebius, the Bishop of Lyons had to make a selection, and he did so on the ground that the single example of Rome, doubly apostolic and scrupulously successive, could suffice (III. 3. 2). Eusebius refrains from quoting this passage but uses what immediately follows in Irenaeus' book. His reason for refraining is obvious: he wants to lay less emphasis on Rome than on the three eastern churches of Jerusalem, Alexandria, and Antioch, and on the Christian school of Origen, transferred from Alexandria to Caesarea.[1]

It should be noted that though the lists Eusebius is going to use are exclusively, indeed (in the case of Alexandria at least) excessively, episcopal, the promises to which we have just listened do not directly link apostolic succession with bishops. The first passage refers first to successions, next to events, only then to 'leaders and presidents'. The second speaks of making an anthology of early Christian literature and

---

[1] Much of the modern discussion can be found to begin with J. B. Lightfoot, *The Apostolic Fathers* I: *S. Clement of Rome*, i (London, 1890), 201–345; cf. A. Harnack, *Die Chronologie der altchristlichen Litteratur*, i (Leipzig, 1897), 70–230; C. H. Turner, 'The Early Episcopal Lists', *JTS*, 1 (1899–1900), 181–200; 529–53; 18 (1916–17), 103–34; 'Apostolic Succession: A. The Original Conception', H. B. Swete (ed.), *Essays on the Early History of the Church and the Ministry* (London, 1918), 95–142 (additional lexical notes, 197–206); E. Caspar, *Die älteste römische Bischofsliste* (Berlin, 1926), esp. 335–83; A. A. T. Ehrhardt, *The Apostolic Succession* London, 1953); A.-M. Javierre, 'Le Thème de la succession des apôtres dans la littérature chrétienne primitive', *Unam Sanctam*, 39 (1962), 171–221.

says that the anthologist will be happy if he preserves the successions. Certainly Eusebius thought that the episcopal successions had central importance. He did not think they had exclusive importance.

Presumably his attitude is partly due to the experience of his own times, when Donatists were active (X. 5. 18–6. 5), though he does not say so, and Meletian agitators (*Mart. Pal.* 12), not named as such, were rending the Church. Had he desired to criticize them, however, he could obviously have done so. It is more likely that his disaffection with the episcopate goes back farther, to the period before the last persecution, when bishop brawled with bishop (VIII. 1. 7–8) and during the persecution itself, when the shepherds hid and 'thousands' of other bishops offered pagan sacrifices (2. 1; 3. 1). Beyond that lies the time when Demetrius of Alexandria dared to slander Origen and attack the Bishops of Caesarea and Jerusalem (VI. 8. 4–5).

In addition, as a schoolman Eusebius was aware of the importance of legitimate succession, especially in the teaching of philosophy. He had made something of the idea in the *Chronicle* and would make more of it when he reproduced philosophical sources in his *Praeparatio Evangelica.*[2] The notion of succession was widespread in Hellenistic philosophy, and it achieved literary formulation in the book by Sotion (early second century BC) entitled *Successions of the Philosophers.* The basic idea, based on political history and testamentary law, was that the legitimacy of a philosopher was derived from his place in the school tradition. This is very close to the doctrine of Eusebius. In Eusebius' first sentence, he goes on from the successions to mention 'the times that have elapsed from the Saviour's day down to our own'. Such an emphasis as this was provided not by Sotion but by Sosicrates, who made use of Apollodorus' *Chronica* in order to get the years exactly right (Diog. Laert. I. 37–8). The parallel with Eusebius is even closer if we consider the fact that Eusebius next mentions events and uses the word πραγματευθῆναι. Just so, the title of the epitome of Sotion prepared by Heraclides Lembos was *Concerning the subject-matter (πραγματεία) of philosophical sects.*[3] (Eusebius will presently mention sects, αἱρέσεις, though without using the word.) We conclude that along with Eusebius' primary emphasis on episcopal succession there is a clearly identifiable emphasis on school succession, which actually existed, in his view, at Alexandria and Caesarea.

[2] See H. Diels, *Doxographi Graeci* (Berlin, 1879; repr. 1929), 169 n. 1.
[3] Ibid., 149 (cf. 152).

This school succession presented a more thoughtful approach to the meaning of tradition and succession than did the representatives of the episcopal succession before Dionysius 'the Great' of Alexandria. (Eusebius was to devote much space to him in Books VI and VII.) In fact, Origen vigorously insisted upon the importance of 'the tradition of the church and the apostles' as 'handed down in unbroken succession from the apostles' (*Princ.* praef. 2). Certainly Eusebius knew this passage; he quoted from the beginning of it in his treatise *Contra Marcellum* (I. 4. 26). But he did not quote from any of it in the *Church History* because Origen went on to differentiate the simple faith handed down for simple believers from the more complex explanations which the apostles left for schoolmen to investigate. Such a notion, hardly conciliatory when read by the successors of polemical bishops, was unsuited to the *Church History*, in which episcopal and school successions were understood as finally united, at least at Alexandria under Dionysius (Eusebius never mentions Theognostus) though not under Theonas (VII. 32. 30), and perhaps at Caesarea.

Like most early Christians, Eusebius had little use for successions other than his own. He had no sympathy with Gnostic claims to stand in succession from the apostles, though following Irenaeus he believed that one Gnostic might be the successor of another. Thus Menander was the successor of Simon Magus in the sense that he too was empowered by the Devil, was a Samaritan, and worked even greater magical tricks than those of his master (III. 26. 1). Marcion was Cerdo's successor in blasphemy (IV. 11. 2). Saturninus and Basilides were the successors of Menander just because a snake-like power, evidently diabolical, produced them from him (IV. 7. 3). But Eusebius makes no use of the idea of succession when he discusses the relations between Paul of Samosata or Mani and their predecessors.

There was also a succession of prophets. Eusebius knew that the Jews had not preserved 'an accurate succession of prophets' after the time of Artaxerxes (III. 10. 4, from Josephus), but this was not the kind of succession that made much difference to the Christian Church.[4] In Eusebius' opinion the problem arose when the Montanists claimed that their prophetesses were the successors of the daughters of Philip (III. 31. 4-5), of Quadratus (III. 37. 1), and of Ammia in Philadelphia

---

[4] The failure of the Jewish priestly succession, to which we shall return when speaking of the Bishops of Jerusalem, is discussed by Eusebius, usually after Josephus, in I. 6. 6. 8–10; 10. 2–5; II. 20. 1–3; 23. 21–4.

(V. 17. 3–4).[5] This kind of succession was to be rejected, for as the anonymous author against Montanism says, 'The apostle expects that the prophetic gift will be in every church until the final coming' (V. 17. 4; cf. 1 Cor. 1:7; Eph. 4:11–13).

Eusebius himself provided evidence to show that this was the case. He cited evidence from Justin to show that 'even up to his own time prophetic gifts shone upon the church' (IV. 18. 8), quoted a passage from the letter of the Gallican martyrs indicating that one of them 'had the Paraclete within him' (V. 1. 10), and quoted Irenaeus on the 'proofs of the divine and miraculous power in some churches up to his time' (V. 7).

We now turn to the episcopal successions in 'the most notable communities' known to Eusebius, those at Jerusalem, Alexandria, Antioch, and Rome. Beyond those, as we shall see, he knows something about a few local successions.

Jerusalem

Apart from the New Testament, Eusebius had five sources of information about the early Church in Jersalem. Four were authors and one was an anonymous list.

The first author was Aristo of Pella, who supplied information about the Jewish revolt under Bar Cochba (AD 132–5) and its consequences (IV. 6). Since Aristo came from Pella, to which some Jerusalem Christians fled before the first revolt (III. 5. 3), it is reasonable to assume that he was Eusebius' source for the story of their exodus.[6] In addition, given the rather detailed military information in the account of Bar Cochba's defeat, we should infer that similar information about the Jewish revolt under Trajan (IV. 2) also comes from Aristo. But there is nothing to show that he said anything about bishops.

The second author was the anti-heretical writer Hegesippus, who in the last book of his treatise discussed the martyrdom of James and the succession of bishops at Jerusalem. Hegesippus explained that there was a family succession or 'caliphate' in the Church there.[7] First 'James the Lord's brother succeeded to the rule of the church along with the

---

[5] He quotes the anti-Montanist Apollonius against the prophetesses but elsewhere is quite willing to mention the Old Testament prophetess Hulda without comment (*Chron.*, p. 96; *Praep. Ev.* X. 14. 6; cf. Clement, *Str.* I. 120. 2).

[6] The exodus to Pella cannot be reconciled with Hegesippus' notion that Vespasian besieged Jerusalem immediately after the death of James (II. 23. 18).

[7] E. Stauffer, 'Zum Kaliphat des Jacobus', *Zeitschrift für Religions- und Geistesgeschichte*, 4 (1952), 193–214.

apostles.' He was evidently superior to the Jewish high priest of his time, for 'to him alone it was permitted to enter the holy place' IV. 23. 4. 6; cf. Heb. 9:3). After his death Symeon, his cousin, was appointed bishop (IV. 22. 4). During the reign of Domitian two grandsons of the Lord's brother Jude were accused, not unreasonably, of being descendants of David. They were set free when they identified themselves as small farmers who expected a 'heavenly and angelic' kingdom of Christ at the end of the woild (III. 20. 1-5). They then 'ruled every church', presumably in Palestine, until the aged Simon oɪ Symeon was again accused of descent from David (III. 32. 6). He was a martyr under 'Trajan and the consular Atticus' (III. 32. 3; cf. 6). It may be that something has gone wrong with the text, where we find ὑπατικουαττικου or ἀττικουτουυπατικου. If there is anything to the story, it should probably be set around 115, when at least one 'king' arose among the Jewish rebels (IV. 2. 4), rather than a decade earlier.[8] In any case, Hegesippus tells us that Simon was aged 120. Here we definitely have episcopal succession, though in a special form which Hegesippus did not encounter at Rome (see below).

The third author was Clement of Alexandria, who in his lost *Hypotyposes* told how 'James the Just' was chosen as Bishop of Jerusalem by Peter, James, and John, and how after the resurrection the Lord delivered secret knowledge to James the Just, John, and Peter. In turn they delivered it to the other apostles, who passed it on to the seventy disciples (II. 1. 3-4). Clement also touched upon James's death (II. 1. 5). Obviously this is apostolic-episcopal succession.

The fourth author was the chronographer Julius Africanus, apparently a native of Jerusalem. In his letter to Aristides he spoke of how 'the human relatives of the Lord' handed on information about Jewish ideas on physical and legal descent (I. 7. 11). They kept genealogical records and were called 'desposyni', 'belonging to the Master'. They came from Nazareth and Kochaba (IV. 7. 14). Conceivably they supplied information to Hegesippus.

The anonymous list of Jerusalem bishops contains thirty names, beginning with James the Lord's brother and ending with Narcissus, who according to his coadjutor and successor, Alexander, reached the

---

[8] For the situation in Palestine cf. E. M. Smallwood, 'Palestine *c.* A. D. 115-118', *Historia*, 11 (1962), 500-10; for the earlier dating, Smallwood, 'Atticus, Legate of Judaea under Trajan', *JRS* 52 (1962), 131-3; *The Jews under Roman Rule* (Leiden, 1976), 421-7; 548.

age of 116 (VI. 11. 3).[9] This list definitely contained nothing but names. 'I have failed to find their dates preserved in writing; for indeed it is recorded that they were extremely short-lived', says Eusebius, about to set forth the first fifteen names (IV. 5. 1). The first fifteen have to be set before the revolt under Bar Cochba, for all of them were Jewish. All later bishops will be gentiles (V. 12). Perhaps Eusebius inferred this division from the fact that the fifteenth bishop was named Judas. The name seems unsuitable for a gentile.

The model for the list was probably given by the list of the high priests at Jerusalem, with fifteen names after the exile up to the Maccabees, seven (according to Eusebius' count in the *Chronicle*) from then to the time of Herod the Great, and twenty-eight (according to Josephus' count)[9a] until the destruction of the Temple. In such a list the dates were not all-important. What counted was the fact of succession.[10] Eusebius insisted that Jesus Christ was 'the true and only high priest of God' (I. 3. 19) and claimed that Hyrcanus was 'the last to whom the high-priestly succession belonged' (I. 6. 7). The Jewish high priesthood came to an end. 'Josephus explains . . . how Herod, when he was appointed king by the Romans, no longer appointed high priests of the ancient race.' In addition, he kept the sacred robe of the high priest 'under his own seal' (I. 6. 9–10). Thus the succession was no longer 'for life and by ancestral succession' (I. 10. 3).

Among Jewish Christians like Hegesippus' informants James the Lord's brother was somehow identified as the true high priest, or above the high priest because a Nazirite like Samson. Like the high priest he wore linen, alone entered the sanctuary, and constantly interceded for the people. Unlike the Aaronic high priest, he was not anointed with oil and did not use the bath.[11] In Hegesippus' time Polycrates of Ephesus, defender of traditional paschal observance in a Jewish–Christian setting, claimed that John the Lord's disciple had worn the *petalon* or high priest's mitre (V. 24. 3). The correlation of bishops with high priests was in the air.[12]

The list Eusebius possessed, whether from Hegesippus or not,

---

[9] For the situation cf. P. Nautin, *Lettres et écrivains chrétiens des iie et iiie siècles* (Paris, 1961), 105–21.

[9a] Josephus, *Ant.* XX. 250.

[10] Cf. E. Caspar, op. cit., 321–46; A. A. T. Ehrhardt, op. cit., 35–61.

[11] The passage (II. 23. 5–6) is probably an interpolation; for its content cf. E. Zuckschwerdt, 'Das Naziräat des Herrenbruders Jakobus nach Hegesipp', *ZNW* 68 (1977), 276–87.

[12] Cf. 1 Clem. 40–4; *Didascalia*, p. 86 Connolly; *Const. Apost.* II. 20. 1.

reflects at least two purposes. First, it must have been intended to show the continuity between the Jewish bishops of Jerusalem and their gentile successors. Second, it ended with Narcissus, 'still famous' and 'thirtieth from the apostles in consecutive succession' (V. 12. 1-2). For many years he was unable to function as bishop, and others filled his place. When he miraculously reappeared, he was counted as thirtieth and thirty-fourth bishop (*Chron.*, p. 209). Since the *History* list mentions him only as thirtieth, we must assume that it comes from early in his episcopate, or from circles in which his return was antici- pated.[13] To count him just as thirtieth is in harmony with the way in which Jewish high priests were counted.[14] Their high-priesthood was, so to speak, indelible.

The Jerusalem list, then, came into existence during the episcopate of Narcissus, apparently Bishop of Jerusalem from around 170.[15] If Hegesippus visited Rome around this time he may have persuaded the Romans of the importance of maintaining such lists. Eusebius does not draw any such conclusion, however.

Alexandria

According to a tradition at least as old as Clement of Alexandria, the evangelist Mark 'set out' after Peter's death for Alexandria, where he preached the Gospel and founded churches (II. 16. 1).[16] According to Eusebius, his source, presumably Clement, made Mark the first missionary to Egypt, but in the light of Acts 2:10 (Egyptians at Pentecost) this is probably wrong.[17] In V. 10. 1 Eusebius' reference to the Alexandrian school as 'filled with men of great learning and zeal for divine matters' seems to owe something to the description of the Alexandrian Apollos in Acts 18:24, though he certainly does not say so explicitly. In any case Mark was viewed as the founder of churches at Alexandria.

It may be that the early names in the episcopal list are the names of real persons, but as Caspar pointed out, the accession years for the early bishops tend to come at intervals of three Olympiads. He thought

---

[13] For such circles cf. the conjecture of Nautin, op. cit., 108-9.

[14] Josephus, *Ant.* XV. 40-1; cf. XVII. 339. 341; XVIII. 3.

[15] He was 116 years old (VI. 11. 3) approximately in the reign of Caracalla (VI. 8. 7). Presumably he did not become bishop when over 70.

[16] M. Smith, *Clement of Alexandria and a Secret Gospel of Mark* (Cambridge, Mass., 1973), 22-9; G. M. Lee, 'Eusebius on St. Mark and the Beginnings of Christianity in Egypt', *TU* 115 (1975), 422-31.

[17] Lee, op. cit., 430-1.

that this proved that Julius Africanus, who used Olympiads in his *Chronographies*, had artificially constructed the list.[18] The element of artifice seems more conspicuous in the work of a scholar who takes years dated in relation to emperors, converts them to Olympiads, and then claims that the intervals are regular.

The first Alexandrian bishop who was historically significant was Demetrius, famed for his relationship with Origen. During his episcopate Julius Africanus visited Alexandria (VI. 31. 2) and therefore must have known the date of his accession. Eusebius set it (V. 22) in the tenth year of Commodus (AD 189) and though it can be claimed that Julius Africanus was not so precise, the date can be defended on the ground that the dates in the *Chronographies* actually are precise and this one is historically probable.[19] On the other hand, when discussing the beginning of Origen's career Eusebius correctly synchronized the tenth year of Severus with the activity of Laetus as Prefect of Egypt and adds that Demetrius had 'recently' been made bishop (VI. 2. 2). But he had been bishop for thirteen years. Is 'recently' anything more than an attempt to vary verbal formulas?

What is especially interesting in Eusebius' account of the early Alexandrian bishops is the use he makes of Philo's *De vita contemplativa* with its account of the ascetic Jewish Therapeutae (II. 17). Though in V. 10. 1 he claims that 'from ancient custom' there had been a school among Alexandrian Christians, the point he makes in regard to the Therapeutae is not that they constituted such a school but that they were members of the Christian Church and were governed by a bishop (II. 17. 23). The two ideas can presumably be reconciled on the ground that the essence of Alexandrian Christianity was the union between school and Church.

Eusebius also insists on the existence of a school succession at Alexandria, since the school continued to exist into his own time (V. 10. 1). All he knows about early times is that Pantaenus taught Clement (V. 11. 2; cf. VI. 13. 2). 'Clement was the successor of Pantaenus and was in charge of instruction at Alexandria until the time when Origen was one of his pupils' (VI. 6). The links between these three may not have been quite so strong.[20] But Alexander of

---

[18] Caspar, op. cit., 406.

[19] P. Nautin, *Origène sa vie et son œuvre* (Paris, 1977), 65–70.

[20] Cf. G. Bardy, 'Aux origines de l'école d'Alexandrie', *RSR* 27 (1937), 65–90; 'Pour l'histoire de l'école d'Alexandrie', *Vivre et Penser*, 2 = *RB* 51 (1942), 80–109; M. Hornschuh, 'Das Leben des Origenes und die Entstehung der alexandrinischen Schule', *ZKG* 71 (1960), 1–25; 193–214.

Jerusalem wrote to Origen and mentioned that all three had taught him (VI. 14. 9). Heraclas succeeded Origen (VI. 26); Dionysius succeeded in turn (VI. 29. 4). Eusebius never mentions Theognostus and does not refer to Pierius as head of the school; he mentions only Achillas as 'entrusted with the school of the sacred faith' (VII. 32. 30).[21] The succession had somehow become less significant, especially in the light of the long episcopates of Maximus and Theonas.

Antioch

According to the *Chronicle*, soon after the beginning of the 205th Olympiad (AD 41) Peter left Antioch for Rome, Mark went to Alexandria, and Evodius became Bishop of Antioch. This is not Eusebius' view but Jerome's. Eusebius' own ideas about Peter and Mark are different. He followed Origen in holding that 'Peter seems to have preached to the Jews of the dispersion in Pontus and Galatia and Bithynia, Cappadocia and Asia [1 Pet. 1:1], finally came to Rome' (III. 1. 2). Mark was with Peter in Rome and wrote his Gospel there (II. 15. 2). In addition, he gives no date for Evodius but simply treats him as the predecessor of Ignatius (III. 22).

The way in which Eusebius dated Evodius' successor Ignatius in AD 107/8 must have been roughly as follows. Ignatius wrote to Polycarp as to a somewhat younger man. Polycarp was martyred at the age of eighty-six[22] in the year 166/167 (according to the *Chronicle*). Polycarp is not likely to have become a bishop under the age of thirty. Therefore the date of Ignatius' martyrdom could be set in about 110. What Eusebius gives is an approximation. In the *History* he sets the martyrdom of Polycarp soon after the accession of Marcus Aurelius (161) and thus is able to move the death of Ignatius back to about the third year of Trajan, or 100/1 (III. 36. 15). This point shows that the date for Ignatius depends on the date for Polycarp.

In the *Chronicle* Ignatius' accession is dated 69 to 70, while in the *Church History* we find the more correct statement that he 'was known' in the first year of Trajan (98-9). The exact dates of 128 and 141 for Cornelius and Eros are absent from the *History* and presumably come from Jerome.

Apart from Ignatius, the early Bishops of Antioch are ciphers,[23]

---

[21] Cf. L. B. Radford, *Three Teachers of Alexandria* (Cambridge, 1908).
[22] IV. 15. 20.
[23] The point was made a century ago by A. Harnack in *Die Zeit des Ignatius und die Chronologie der antiochenischen Bischöfe bis Tyrannus* (Leipzig, 1878).

since they wrote nothing before the time of Theophilus. The *Chronicle* assigns a date around 128 to Cornelius, around 141 to Eros, and about 168 to Theophilus himself. These dates are lacking in the *History*, where Theophilus 'was known' in 169 (IV. 20) and no date is assigned his successor Maximinus (177, according to the *Chronicle*). Similarly Serapion 'was known' in 189 according to the *History* but became bishop then according to the *Chronicle*. There is every reason to suppose that all this spurious accuracy is due to Jerome's revision of the *Chronicle*. Eusebius himself had little evidence for dating any of the second-century Bishops of Antioch.

It was Eusebius himself, however, who gave the impression that Theophilus wrote his treatise *Ad Autolycum* around the eighth year (IV. 19) of the previously mentioned reign (IV. 14. 10) of 'Marcus Aurelius Verus, also called Antoninus, with his brother Lucius'. Since Eusebius believed that Marcus Aurelius did not persecute Christians (see Chapter VII) he had to set a work which referred to persecution[24] under Lucius, who died in the ninth year of the joint reign. If Eusebius actually read *Ad Autolycum*, III. 27 he may have misunderstood Theophilus' statement that a freedman of Marcus Aurelius Verus prepared a chronicle which ran up to the death of his own patron the Emperor Verus. By 'Verus' Theophilus meant Marcus Aurelius, as the chronological notices prove.[25]

In regard to chronology, then, we have seen that 'the Church of Jerusalem, Alexandria, and Antioch have erred.' We now turn to see if 'so also the Church of Rome hath erred' (Article XIX) not in matters of faith but in dating the early bishops.

Rome

We have reserved this place for Rome not because we regard the eastern lists as superior but because we wanted to clear away their chronological inexactitude before turning to the Roman see. The Roman chronology, indeed, seems to lie at the base of the Antiochene one[26] (at least in Jerome's version) and possibly the Alexandrian one as well. In other words, if there is any chronologically reliable bishop list it is the one from Rome.

When we look at it closely, however, we find significant the basic

---

[24] *Ad Autolycum*, III. 30.   [25] Harnack, op. cit., 42; 62.
[26] Harnack, op. cit., 24.

point made by H. Boehmer[27] and seconded by Caspar:[28] Irenaeus, source for the Roman list, provided no dates whatever. He simply had a list of names from Peter and Paul to Eleutherus.[29] Irenaeus prefaces his list by explaining that it would take too long to list the successions of bishops in all the churches. He is therefore going to take one example from the church founded by Peter and Paul, the Roman church with which every other church must be in agreement.[30] We have already noted that Eusebius does not reproduce this preface, but he does provide the Greek text of what follows.[31] The list can be put in tabular form.

Linus	mentioned in 2 Timothy 4:21
Anencletus	(? mentioned in Titus 1:7)[32]
(3) Clement	witness to apostles; under Clement, church of Rome addressed dissent in Corinth (cf. III. 16)
Evarestus	
Alexander	
(6) Xystus	
Telesphorus	gloriously martyred (cf. IV. 10)
Hyginus	
Pius	
Anicetus	
Soter	
(12) Eleutherus	

Obviously there is no chronological information here. Indeed, we may wonder if Irenaeus could have provided any. On the one hand, he placed Jesus' birth around the forty-first year of Augustus,[33] gave him the age of thirty before a three-year ministry,[34] and set his crucifixion under Pontius Pilate, Procurator for Tiberius.[35] Unfortunately, he also

---

[27] 'Zur altrömischen Bischofsliste', *ZNW* 7 (1906), 333–9.
[28] *Die älteste römische Bischofsliste* (Berlin, 1926), 383; *Geschichte des Papsttums*, i (Tübingen, 1930), 569–70.
[29] *Adv. haer.* III. 3. 3 = *H. E.* V. 6. 1–4.
[30] *Adv. haer.* III. 3. 2.   [31] V. 6. 1–2 = *Adv. haer.* III. 3. 3.
[32] L. Abramowski in *JTS* 28 (1977), 104.
[33] *Adv. haer.* III. 21. 3.   [34] *Adv. haer.* II. 22. 3–4.
[35] *Adv. haer.* I. 27. 2.

accepted a 'tradition' (John 8:57) that Jesus nearly reached the age of fifty,[36] and in the *Epideixis* (74) Pontius Pilate had to become Procurator for Claudius.

Irenaeus did go so far as to relate the arrival of various heretics in Rome to the episcopates of Hyginus and his two successors,[37] but his purpose was not chronological. As Caspar pointed out, what he wanted to show was that orthodoxy always preceded heresy.[38]

In his time another list-maker visited Rome. This was Hegesippus, who described his efforts thus: 'When I was in Rome I made a succession-list[39] up to Anicetus, whose deacon was Eleutherus; Soter succeeded Anicetus, and after him came Eleutherus' (IV. 22. 3). As in Irenaeus' work, the emphasis is laid entirely on the fact of succession, not on chronology. If the list was included in the work Eusebius knew, Eusebius referred only to Irenaeus' list either because Hegesippus disagreed with it[40] or because he did not. We should not multiply hypothetical lists.

When Eusebius wanted to provide chronological anchorage for his list of Roman bishops he had no second-century authority whose work he could use. Apparently he relied on the *Chronographies* of Julius Africanus for the dating of Roman, and perhaps Alexandrian, bishops up to the year 221/222, the first year of the 250th Olympiad. Africanus provided a list synchronized with Olympiads, but from another chronographer Eusebius took a slightly divergent list which gave lengths of episcopates.[41] The last Roman bishop given a date by the year of an emperor's reign is Callistus, whose episcopate began in the first year of Antoninus (Elagabalus; VI. 21. 1-2), i.e. 222.

Africanus visited Alexandria 'because of the great fame of Heraclas' (VI. 31. 2). The bishop at the time (before 222) must have been Demetrius, and we can assume that Africanus found out when he took office, i.e. in the tenth year of Commodus.[42] He would have learned that Victor of Rome was his contemporary (V. 22). Perhaps he assumed that previous Bishops of Rome and Alexandria were also contemporaries. According to Eusebius, some of them were.[43] But the elaborate

---

[36] *Adv. haer.* II. 22. 5. Eusebius avoids reference to this (III. 23. 3).

[37] *Adv. haer.* I. 25. 6; 27. 1; III. 4. 3; cf. *H. E.* IV. 11. 1-2.

[38] Op. cit., 441.

[39] Διαδοχή (cf. V. 5. 9 for the same meaning).

[40] H. Kemler, 'Hegesipps römische Bischofsliste', *VC* 25 (1971), 182-96.

[41] Caspar, op. cit., 373-7; 393-406.   [42] Ibid., 398.

[43] The Romans Alexander, Xystus, and Telesphorus; the Alexandrians Primus, Justus, and (a little late, IV. 5. 5) Eumenes.

synchronizations produced by Caspar do not prove that Africanus was concerned with setting successions in Olympiads two or three apart. From the fragments of his *Chronographies* we know that he was concerned with precise years within Olympiads.

Whatever difficulties there may be with counting forward and backward are probably due to ancient difficulties with 'inclusive' and 'exclusive' modes of reckoning, and with the problem of adding years and portions of years. An ancient author could take Paul's expressions 'after three years' and 'through fourteen years' (Gal. 1:18; 2:1) to refer to 2 to 3 to 4 years and 13 to 14 to 15 years. Obviously sums of such periods were open to wide discrepancies. Difficulties also arose in regard to reigns or terms of office. H. St. J. Thackeray, following E. Schürer, notes that 'Josephus reckons the short portions of a Roman calendar year at the beginning and end of the reign as complete years.'[44] In Eusebius' reckoning, both in the *Chronicle* and in the *Church History*, we do not find that much consistency. And if the lengths of reigns are inconsistent, the lengths of episcopates must suffer similarly.

In regard to the Bishops of Rome, then, we conclude that Eusebius' dates are reliable only generally. That is to say that they fit in with what he knew and what we know about the Church history of the second and third centuries. The names before Clement are open to question, as is the nature of the episcopate itself. It can be added that while Polycrates of Ephesus may have heard of a Roman claim for primacy because of a promise made to Peter, he himself does not accept it but quotes (anonymously) 'Peter and the apostles' as 'men greater than I' who said, 'We must obey God rather than men' (V. 24. 7; Acts 5:29). Eusebius calls Peter 'the great and mighty leader of all the other apostles' and explains his position as due to his 'virtue' (II. 14. 5).

Other Churches

It is likely that Eusebius could have provided other episcopal lists had he wanted to do so. We should mention the two churches about which he seems best informed: his own Caesarea and another coastal city, Laodicea. From acts he knows that Caesarea was the city of the earliest gentile Christians (II. 3. 3). Origen had made a similar point.[45] Late in the second century the Bishop Theophilus jointly

---

[44] Josephus, ii (London, 1927), 317 n.
[45] *Num. hom.* XI. 3 (written at Caesarea).

headed a synod with Narcissus of Jerusalem (V. 23. 3). Theoctistus of Caesarea joined Alexander of Jerusalem in ordaining and defending Origen (VI. 8. 4; 19. 17). Theoctistus was succeeded by Domnus, Domnus by Theotecnus, an aggressive Origenist (VII. 15. 4; 28. 1; 30. 2). Agapius, Theotecnus' successor, was bishop in Eusebius' time (VII. 32. 24). Eusebius was also well informed about Laodicean bishops, partly from the letters of Dionysius of Alexandria,[46] partly from stories told about a coadjutor of Theotecnus of Caesarea,[47] and partly from his own memories of the renegade Stephanus and his own saintly friend Theodotus.[48] Given the existence of the four major lists, however, it was unnecessary to deal with successions in these sees. Continuity was already assured.

Conclusion

In Eusebius' mind there was no question about the historical reality of the apostolic succession. Christ himself called the twelve apostles and appointed the seventy discipes (I. 10. 7; cf. Luke 6:13–16; 10:1). The apostles appointed deacons (II. 1. 1; cf. Acts 6:1–6). Clement of Alexandria, an 'ambassador of orthodoxy' (III. 23. 2), told how three apostles appointed the first Bishop of Jerusalem (II. 1. 3); Irenaeus, another ambassador, told how the apostles who founded the Roman church selected its first bishop (V. 6. 1). After Mark went to Alexandria the ministry there included deacons and bishops (II. 16. 1; 17. 23). Many of Paul's converts became 'shepherds' (cf. Acts 20:28), as Eusebius knows from traditional exegesis of his epistles (III. 4. 3–10). In addition, Clement of Alexandria told how John appointed bishops in Asia (III. 23. 6) and Irenaeus described Polycarp's relation to John and other apostles (III. 36. 1; cf. V. 20. 6; 24. 16).

Eusebius therefore felt qualified to write a generalizing chapter on 'the first sequence in the succession from the apostles' (III. 37), with reliance on 1 Clement (42. 3–5) and Irenaeus for the ideas and on Pauline epistles for the language. The disciples of the apostles, he says, built on the Church foundations laid by their masters (1 Cor. 3:10; Eph. 2:20). They performed the 'work of evangelists' (2 Tim. 4:5; Eph. 4:11) in foreign parts and then passed on to other lands (Rom. 15:20–4), helped by the grace and co-operation of God (1 Cor. 3:9).

---

[46] Theymidres (VI. 46. 2); Heliodorus (VII. 5. 1).
[47] Socrates, Eusebius, Anatolius (VII. 32. 5–21).
[48] Stephanus, Theodotus (VII. 32. 22–3).

In each place they laid foundations and then appointed shepherds (Eph. 4:11).

He did not share the modern idea that the origins of the ministry present a historical problem. He may never have read 'the so-called Didachai of the Apostles' (III. 25. 4) with their instructions to congregations to 'appoint bishops and deacons'. If he did so he would undoubtedly have assumed that the ministry of apostles and prophets was being replaced in succession. He was well aware that there were apostles other than the Twelve (I. 12. 5). And the presbyter-bishops of the first two centuries certainly did not embarrass him, for he quoted Irenaeus to Victor on the subject of 'presiding presbyters' (cf. I Tim. 5:17) earlier than Soter at Rome (V. 24. 14–15). Like Irenaeus he regarded them as bishops whose line began with the apostles (V. 6. 1).[49]

His concern for the apostolic successions at Jerusalem, Alexandria, Antioch, and Rome was due first to his desire to broaden the base already laid by Irenaeus and Hegesippus with their emphasis on Rome alone. No doubt he could also have found lists related to Caesarea in Palestine and other cities, but he was laying emphasis on the two largest cities of the east and on the episcopal succession about which early writers had said the most, that in Jerusalem. These lists presented him with some chronological difficulties, especially because of the lack of dates at Jerusalem. Working partly by conjecture, partly from previous chronologists like Africanus, he solved the problems to his own satisfaction if not ours.

C. H. Turner, writing in H. B. Swete's *Essays on the Early History of the Church and the Ministry*, noted that Eusebius' picture of the apostolic succession was purely historical. He laid no emphasis on the transmission of correct doctrine, as in Irenaeus, or on the sacramental nature of episcopacy, as among some modern Christians.[50] We should add only this: while Eusebius knows quite a bit about the letters of Ignatius, he describes them in such a way as to neglect entirely their picture of the episcopal office. None of his other sources was likely to point toward high episcopal doctrine. What Eusebius means by 'apostolic succession' is essentially 'the historic episcopate'.

---

[49] Irenaeus, cited in V. 20. 7, also called Polycarp a presbyter, while Clement of Alexandria, cited in III. 23. 6–8, used 'bishop' and 'presbyter' interchangeably.

[50] H. B. Swete, *Essays on the Early History of the Church and the Ministry* (London, 1918), 132–42.

VII

THE SECOND THEME: EVENTS AND PERSONS

> How many and how great the events said to have
> taken place in ecclesiastical history, and how many
> those who with distinction led and presided over the
> church in the most notable communities, and how
> many those who in each generation were ambassadors
> of the divine Logos orally or through written
> compositions (I. 1. 1; p. 6, 2–6)

> As many items, then, as we consider useful for the
> proposed subject out of what they have what they
> have occasionally mentioned, collecting them and
> anthologizing the appropriate sayings of the earlier
> writers themselves as from intellectual meadows, we
> shall endeavour to organize through historical
> treatment, eager to preserve the successions from the
> especially distinguished apostles of our Saviour in the
> prominent churches that are still remembered even
> now (I. 1. 4; p. 8, 9–17)

The first theme of the *Church History* was easy enough to define. Eusebius' annalistic method was eminently suited for dealing with the successions from the apostles. For his second theme, however, he used more general language, using a verb (πραγματευθῆναι) pointed toward the 'pragmatic history' known to Greek writers after Polybius and apparently dividing the history of the Church into episcopal and non-episcopal segments, the non-episcopal into preachers/teachers and authors. In all likelihood, however, we cannot make too much of his sonorous language when he seems to make sharp distinctions. Bardy rightly criticized Grapin for such a procedure.[1] We must remember that his language is light or fluid. In a sentence of 167 words, not every pronoun counts. What Eusebius seems to have done is point generally to the content of his work and to the important people whom he was going to discuss.

The expression 'ambassadors of the divine Logos', actually based on the Greek verb πρεσβεύω, is important because it points to the divine origin of the gospel. Eusebius speaks of the persecutor Maximin as

---

[1] G. Bardy, *Eusèbe de Césarée Histoire Ecclésiastique* IV (Paris, 1960), 97 n. 1.

sending ambassadors to himself (IX. 2), but elsewhere the term refers to the apostles (III. 24. 3) and their successors, Justin (IV. 11. 8; 16. 1), Irenaeus, and Clement (III. 23. 2). Irenaeus and others in Gaul were ambassadors for peace to Eleutherus and Victor of Rome (V. 3. 4; 24. 18). Though the term is not used, Alexander of Jerusalem sent Clement to Antioch as an ambassador (VI. 11. 6). Finally, Origen (like Justin) was an ambassador for the truth, which Eusebius identifies as 'ecclesiastical orthodoxy' (VI. 18. 1), and he regarded a heretic as trying to be 'an ambassador of a godless and most impious opinion' (VI. 38). The term 'ambassador' for Eusebius, then, is related to orthodox and catholic tradition. It need not be differentiated from 'herald', used, for example, of Pantaenus (V. 10. 2).

Oral Tradition

Not all ambassadors wrote. Thus Mark had to record Peter's 'unwritten teaching of the divine proclamation' (II. 15. 1), but most of the first successors to the apostles did not write treatises on 'the apostolic teaching' (III. 37. 4). Papias of Hierapolis, who recorded the tradition about the Gospel of Mark, was not wrong in his enthusiasm for oral tradition or in making the statement that 'I did not suppose that information from books would help me as much as what came from a living voice still present' (III. 39. 4); unfortunately he was not discriminating in his choices. In the time of Hadrian 'champions of the truth' provided oral and written arguments (IV. 7. 15). Bishops opposed heretics in dialogues and by 'most accurate refutations through written treatises' (IV. 24). Indeed, much of our literature reflects prior oral disputations.[2] The point is obvious, but Eusebius deserves commendation for remaining alert to the non-literary aspects of Church life.

Oral tradition was also imporant for Eusebius when he dealt with the history of the church and school of Alexandria, especially since he had no really early source-materials (apart from Philo's account of the Therapeutae). Mark's mission as evangelist at Alexandria is described on the basis of what 'they say' (II. 16). What we learn about Pantaenus, head of the school in the late second century (V. 10), is ascribed to such sources as 'the story goes', 'they say', 'it is said', and 'the story is'.[3] On the other hand, Nautin believes that the expression 'the stories

---

[2] Cf. V. 10. 4; 16. 2; VI. 43. 2; VII. 24. 6–9; 29. 2.
[3] All such materials may, however, come from the *Hypotyposes* of Clement (VI. 13. 2).

people tell about Origen's boyhood' (VI. 2. 11) is an invention by Eusebius himself. From oral tradition, however, he derived the statement that Origen 'did not wear shoes or use wine and any food beyond the ordinary' (VI. 3. 12). Laudatory stories like this were presumably common in Origenist circles.[4]

When Eusebius describes Dionysius of Alexandria he never makes use of oral traditions. He is willing, however, to tell long and exotic stories, apparently based on tradition, about the Alexandrian activities of two Bishops of Laodicea, Anatolius and Eusebius (VII. 32. 5-12). The stories about them need not have come directly from Alexandria, since Anatolius, before succeeding Eusebius at Laodicea, was coadjutor to Theotecnus, Bishop of Caesarea (VII. 32. 21).

The account of the martyrdoms of the Alexandrians Potimiaena and Basilides, which Eusebius has clumsily appended to the martyrdoms of Origen's early pupils, also seems to come from oral sources. Eusebius states that 'the praise of this woman is still to this day loudly sung by her fellow-countrymen' (VI. 5. 1), and F. Augar noted that the story about her has hymnodic characteristics.[5] It may be that Eusebius was hinting at its source.

As for Rome, the story about how Fabian was selected as bishop because a dove settled on his head is clearly derived from hearsay (VI. 29. 2-4). Perhaps Eusebius also derived a story about the Emperor Philip as Christian from Rome. It contains expansions designed to make it credible: 'had he not done so . . . he would never . . .' (VI. 34).

Stories from Eusebius' own Caesarea are naturally prominent. There is a tale about martyrs under Valerian. No historical details are given, and we encounter the expressions 'they say' and 'the story goes' (VII. 12). Perhaps the story came from the group of informants whom Eusebius mentions a little later: friends of the Roman senator Astyrius 'who have survived to our day' (VII. 16). Certainly these friends told Eusebius about the martrydom of the Roman officer Marinus, given a splendid funeral by Astyrius himself. Marinus could have been promoted centurion had he not been accused of being a Christian. While he was meditating about his future course the Bishop Theotecnus took him into the church and asked him to choose between sword and book (of Gospels). This story, told in VII. 15, does not seem trustworthy, for Lieberman has shown that the choice is related to an

    [4] P. Nautin, *Origène sa vie et son œuvre* (Paris), 1977), 35; 41.
    [5] *Die Frau im römischen Christenprocess* (*TU* 28, 4, Leipzig, 1905), 16. I owe this reference to T. D. Barnes.

Aramaic play on words (*siifa, sifra*) a century earlier.[6] Presumably it was used for edification first by Jews and then by Christians. These same persons told a tale about the way in which Astyrius made a pagan sacrifice float to the surface, but we shall discuss the question in Chapter X, when we deal with miracles.

Of course Eusebius used oral tradition or gossip when discussing the persecutions of his own time, assigning motivations freely and falsely and combining gruesome accounts of the sufferings and deaths of martyrs with almost equally gruesome accounts of the deaths of Galerius (VIII. 16) and Maximin and his family (IX. 10. 14; 11. 7).[7] He could not, indeed, describe the death of Licinius since it had been brought about by his prospective patron Constantine. Maximian (not named) perished by strangling (VIII, App. 3) or 'a most shameful death' which he deserved because he too dared to plot against Constantine (VIII. 13. 15).

Written Materials

For the *Church History* as a whole, written materials were far more important than oral traditions. As one can see from Eusebius' other writings as well, he was a man of books and libraries. He illustrated his rhetorical skill not by making up speeches and ascribing them to the characters in his history but by setting forth the panegyric he himself had delivered, probably based on a written text, at Tyre (X. 4). He intended to create a Church history that would be a literary history at the same time.

We cannot deal with all the materials Eusebius employed for his *History*, but by considering those utilized in Book II we may be able to provide a fair sample. This is the book in which a prefatory note (in AEDM) states that 'the book has been compiled by us from the writings of Clement, Tertullian, Josephus, Philo.' These authors are, in fact, cited in the first four chapters and used frequently thereafter. Perhaps, however, the list is incomplete. Later on, Justin and Irenaeus appear as witnesses against Simonian heresy (13. 1-5). Hegesippus and (supposedly) Josephus are cited for the death of James (23. 3-20), and Gaius and Dionysius appear in regard to the deaths of Peter and Paul (25. 5-8). The names of these authors may have been omitted by

---

[6] S. Lieberman, 'The martyrs of Caesarea', *Annuaire de l'institut de philologie et d'histoire orientales et slaves*, 7 (1944), 445.

[7] There is an unacknowledged debt to Josephus' accounts of the death of Herod (cited in I. 8. 5-7. 9).

accident. On the other hand, they may not have been named because they were used only in editions after Eusebius' first draft.

First we should look at the use made of the authors named as sources.

The *Hypotyposes* or *Outlines* by Clement of Alexandria, in which one could find 'concise explanations of every canonical writing' (VI. 14. 1), gave Eusebius some information about early christianity in Jerusalem. 'After the ascension of the Saviour, Peter and James and John did not contend for glory on the ground that they had previously been honoured by the Saviour [presumably at the transfiguration] but chose James the Just as bishop of Jerusalem' (II. 1. 3). This appointment was important because James thus became a link in the tradition.

After the resurrection the Lord gave the *gnosis* to James the Just and John and Peter and they gave it to the other apostles and the other apostles gave it to the seventy, among whom was Barnabas. There were two Jameses, one the Just, who was thrown down from the pinnacle of the temple and beaten to death with a fuller's club, the other the one beheaded [Acts 12:2] (II. 1. 4-5).

Clement also identified Cephas, Sosthenes, and Matthias as among the seventy disciples (I. 12. 1-3), told a story about the death of James son of Zebedee (I. 9. 2-3), and discussed the origins of the Gospels and Hebrews (II. 15. 2; VI. 14. 2-7). Many centuries later, Photius found his treatise most unorthodox. For Eusebius, however, it was important because it linked the apostolic age with what followed.[8]

In addition, since Eusebius insists that Clement learned from Pantaenus (V. 11. 2; VI. 13. 2) it must have been through Pantaenus that 'he came very close to the succession of the apostles' (VI. 13. 8). This notion, further exaggerated by Photius so that Pantaenus even 'heard some of the apostles',[9] is actually based on Eusebius' own hypothesis about a passage in Clement's *Stromata*. This passage speaks of Clement's teachers, obviously including Pantaenus, as having 'preserved the true tradition of the blessed teaching which they received directly from Peter and James, John and Paul' (V. 11. 3-5), citing *Str.* I. 11. 3). Eusebius took 'directly' as a chronological statement, though this is really impossible.[10]

---

[8] On the *Hypotyposes* cf. T. Zahn, *Forschungen zur Geschichte des neutestamentlichen Kanons und der altchristlichen Literatur*, iii: *Supplementum Clementinum* (Erlangen, 1884), 64–93; 130–56; A. Méhat, *Étude sur les 'Stromates' de Clément d'Alexandrie* (Paris, 1966), 517–22.

[9] *PG* 103, 397A.

[10] On Mark at Alexandria (II. 16) cf. M. Smith, op. cit., 27.

Eusebius' second Christian source was Tertullian, not the Tertullian who became a Montanist (Eusebius knew nothing of this) or even the one whose treatise *Adversus Judaeos* is cited in the margin of the *Chronicle* (p. 169), for a date for the birth of Christ different from the one Eusebius supplies in the *Church History* — and in the *Chronicle* itself. The Tertullian of Eusebius was an imaginary figure expert in Roman law and famous at Rome.[11] He wrote an apology in Latin which Eusebius knew in a poor Greek translation. This translation underlies the discussion of Pilate's report to the Roman senate and Tiberius' reaction (*Chron.*, pp. 176-7), for the statement that Tiberius 'threatened accusers of the Christians with death' is found in Eusebius' quotation (II. 2. 6), not Tertullian's Latin. The textual situation in regard to Tertullian's paraphrase of Pliny in the *Chronicle* (p. 195) is more complicated. When we hear of the Christians that *ad confoederandam disciplinam vetari ab his homicidia furta adulteria latrocinia et his similia*, Tertullian himself supplies *homicidium, adulterium, fraudem, perfidiam et cetera scelera* (*Apol.* 2. 6) but not *furta* and *latrocinia*. These come from Pliny's letter to Trajan (X. 96. 7) and therefore were added by Jerome to the text of Eusebius' *Chronicle*.[12] Later in the *Chronicle* it is Jerome alone who gets Tertullian's ancestry mixed up.[13] The question has nothing to do with Eusebius.

In the *Church History* we find that when Eusebius provides a citation from Tertullian he almost always introduces it with a summary or a paraphrase. Thus in II. 2. 1-3 he paraphrases *Apol.* 21. 17-24 on Pilate's report about Christ to Tiberius and also *Apol.* 5. 1-2 on Tiberius' dealings with the senate. Given the context, he can now proceed to quote the Greek version of *Apol.* 5. 1-2 (II. 2. 5-6). The second summary is very brief and simply indicates that Nero was the first emperor to persecute Christians. He did so, according to the quotation, in Rome after he had subjugated the Orient (II. 25. 4): a disastrous mistranslation, based on Tertullian's words *cum maxime Romae orientem* (modifying *hanc sectam*) *Caesariano gladio ferocisse* (*Apol.* 5. 3). In the third case there is no summary. Eusebius simply quotes Tertullian (*Apol.* 5. 4) on Domitian's brief persecution and subsequent recall of exiles, not noticing that he will immediately contradict the statement about the recall by ascribing it to Nerva

---

[11] Cf. II. 2. 4; V. 5. 5; T. D. Barnes, *Tertullian* (Oxford, 1971), 25-6.
[12] In the light of this, correct Barnes, op. cit., 200-1.
[13] Ibid., 11-21.

(III. 20. 7-8).[14] The fourth case is especially interesting because before quoting Tertullian (*Apol.* 2. 6-7) on Pliny and Trajan Eusebius provides a very thorough paraphrase in which he makes the point, not found explicitly in either Pliny or Tertullian, that the Christians were doing nothing contrary to the laws but instead were doing everything in conformity to the laws (III. 33. 1-2. 3). This point seems to have drifted in from Hadrian's letter to the Proconsul of Asia, cited after Justin in IV. 9. 3. (The point is not made in the *Chronicle*.) Finally, Eusebius paraphrases *Apology* 5. 6 and indicates, unlike Tertullian, that pro-Christian letters of Marcus Aurelius were actually available. Then he quotes the next section of the *Apology* to show that the Emperors Vespasian, Trajan, Hadrian, and Pius did not actually persecute Christians (V. 5. 6-7). He leaves out the last three words of Tertullian's sentence: *nullus Verus impressit.* In his view Marcus Aurelius was not a persecutor and any persecutions in his time were due to Verus. This is why he suppresses these words.

We see, then, that Tertullian gave the kind of evidence Eusebius wanted in regard to early imperial attitudes toward Christians. Where the evidence did not go quite far enough, Eusebius amplified it. Where it went too far, he suppressed it. After he had finished moulding it, it was invaluable because it was ascribed to a prominent Roman lawyer who was also a Christian.

We shall discuss Eusebius' use of Josephus and Philo for both Jewish and Christian history when we reach Chapter IX on 'the fate of the Jews'. Here it is enough to say that he converts their pro-Jewish apologetic into materials useful for Christian propaganda. These two authors were peculiarly important, not only because the Alexandrian Christians had known their works but because in Eusebius' opinion both of them had been honoured by the Romans. Philo 'came to Rome in the time of Gaius', read his treatise *On virtues* to the senate under Claudius, and 'his works were so much admired as to be deemed worthy of accession to libraries' (II. 18. 8). Josephus 'was honoured by the erection of a statue in the city of Rome and his works were deemed worthy of place in the library' (III. 9. 2). It is easy enough to see why Eusebius wanted to quote the evidence of these authors.

In addition, however, he made some use in Book II of writings by Justin, Irenaeus, Hegesippus, Gaius of Rome, and Dionysius of Corinth.

---

[14] Dio too (LXVIII. 1. 2) says that Nerva restored the exiles; cf. Pliny, *Ep.* IV. 9. 2.

We now turn to these men. In dealing with the reign of Claudius, Eusebius had occasion to consider Simon Magus, the reputed father of heresy. He had already discussed him in relation to the history of Acts (II. 1. 10-12), but now he found that more information could be derived from Justin, Irenaeus (II. 13. 1-5), and what looks like an echo of the Gospel of Thomas[15] along with a framework somehow related to the pseudo-Clementine literature (II. 13. 6-7). The written sources were the best he could find. After quoting from Justin, he points out that Irenaeus agrees with him, and goes on to refer readers interested in heretical doctrine to Irenaeus' first book against heresies. This will remain Eusebius' attitude. He is not concerned with the history of doctrine either among the orthodox or among heretics.

Another writer whom Eusebius employs for early Christian traditions is Hegesippus. Unfortunately his treatment of this source leaves a great deal to be desired. He misunderstands it, misquotes it, and even misparaphrases it. By the time he finishes dealing with Hegesippus, Eusebius says that he has 'arranged the materials chronologically' (IV. 22. 8). What this must mean is that in the course of writing Books II-IV he has finally straightened a few things out. When he first mentioned Hegesippus he claimed that he belonged to 'the first succession of the apostles' and (therefore) gave a 'most accurate' account of the death of James the Just (II. 23. 3). Later on he tacitly corrected himself, setting Hegesippus first under Hadrian (IV. 8. 2), then under Antoninus Pius or even Marcus Aurelius (IV. 11. 7). The rise of heresy had to be moved from the reign of Trajan (III. 32. 7) back to that of Nero (IV. 22. 4-5).

In addition to a legendary narrative about the death of James, Hegesippus provided stories about early Christians chiefly at Jerusalem but also at Rome up to the early second century, as well as discussions of sects among the Jews and the rise of heresy among the Christians. Eusebius oscillates between quotation and paraphrase in a remarkable manner (notably in III. 32). It is hard to tell whether Hegesippus or our Church historian was confused and repetitious. Conceivably the two 'direct quotations' provided in III. 32 come from different parts of Hegesippus' work.[16] In any case, Eusebius has modified their meaning (see page 112).

We may suggest that Eusebius found Hegesippus' work, perhaps at

---

[15] See Chapter XI on 'the canon of scripture'.
[16] The second of them proves Eusebius' point; the first is irrelevant.

Jerusalem in view of its emphasis on that city, and inserted excerpts into the *History* at a time after he had set forth his own chronology and his own picture of the rise of heresy. Hegesippus presented a different view (as perhaps also about the Roman succession) but Eusebius aimed at completeness, not consistency.

The basic materials which Eusebius takes from Hegesippus are as follows.

A. IV. 22. 7, Jewish sects (back reference in II. 23. 8)

B. II. 23. 4-18, James and his martyrdom; the siege of Jerusalem (back allusion in III. 11)

C. IV. 22. 4-6. Simon of Jerusalem; Church a virgin before the rise of heresies (paraphrased in III. 11. 16; 32. 7)

D. Vespasian's search for family of David (III. 12, paraphrase)

E. III. 20. 1-2. Domitian's investigation of grandsons of Jude (paraphrased in III. 19 and 32. 5)

F. The grandsons of Jude and the kingdom of Christ (III. 20. 3-5, paraphrase)

G. III. 32. 6. Sectarians against Simon in the time of Trajan (paraphrased in III. 20. 6 and 32. 2. 3)

H. Trajan's search for family of David (III. 32. 4, paraphrase)

I. IV. 22. 2-3. Heresy and the church in Corinth and Rome (paraphrased in III. 16 and IV. 11. 7)

J. IV. 8. 2. Hadrian's favourite Antinous

The main differences between this reconstruction and that provided by Lawlor are due to his idea (not accepted here) that Epiphanius relied on Hegesippus rather than Eusebius, and our own notion that III. 32. 3 is really a paraphrase of III. 32. 6.[17]

Whatever Hegesippus' own purpose may have been as he composed his work, for Eusebius he has become the main source of information about the church of Jerusalem during its first century. His comments connect it with other evidence. thus Hegesippus agrees with Clement (II. 23. 3. 19), and the throne of James is still preserved at Jerusalem (VII. 19). Though Eusebius does not explicitly say so, both 1 Clement (III. 16) and Justin (IV. 8. 2-3) obviously agree with Hegesippus. By comment and context Eusebius has set Hegesippus in the framework

---

[17] H. J. Lawlor, *Eusebiana* (Oxford, 1912), 98-107. It looks as if III. 32. 6 was the source of III. 20. 6 and then of III. 32. 2 and 3. To be sure, III. 32. 3 is called an exact quotation, but so is II. 23. 20, actually derived not from Josephus but from Origen. Book II ends (26. 1-2) with two paraphrases of Josephus, called 'verbatim'.

of early Christian literature (IV. 21).

What did Hegesippus have to tell him about the early Bishops of Jerusalem?

First, that James, Simon, and the grandsons of Jude were all relatives of Jesus and therefore descendants of David and members of the tribe of Judah.

Second, that after the fall of Jerusalem Roman emperors or governors often searched for descendants of David because they did not want members of 'the royal tribe' to survive. Those who informed against the Bishops of Jerusalem even before the destruction of the Temple were members of seven Jewish sects hostile to 'the tribe of Judah and ⟨its⟩ Messiah' (IV. 22. 7).[18]

Third, these seven sects were apparently those named in the same passage as 'Essenes, Galilaeans, Hemerobaptists, Masbotheans, Samaritans, Sadducees, Pharisees'. The list makes no historical sense. Hegesippus also listed Masbotheans among Christian heretics (IV. 22. 5), while the groups hostile to James were 'scribes and Pharisees' (II. 23. 10. 12. 14).[19]

Something has certainly gone wrong in the account of the seven sects in II. 23. 8-9. There Hegesippus is quoted as saying that 'the aforementioned sects did not believe in resurrection or in ⟨one who would⟩ come to repay each in accordance with his works'. According to Luke (20:27)-Acts (23:8), the Sadducees denied that there would be a resurrection, and a fortiori a last judgement, but Pharisees and Essenes certainly believed in one. There must be something missing from the text, perhaps deleted to make room for the odd description of James as a Nazirite with high-priestly privileges (II. 23. 5-6).[20]

Fourth, when Simon was put to death some of his accusers were imprisoned because they belonged to 'the royal tribe of the Jews' (III. 32. 4), not to any of the seven sects. This point is related to Hegesippus' notion that the Romans were God's instruments against the persecutors. After the death of James, Vespasian besieged Jerusalem and later tracked down the descendants of David. Domitian released Christians. The judge of Simon admired his constancy — and searched for more descendants of David. All this is surely apologetic, as Hyldahl

---

[18] Cf. II. 23. 8; IV. 22. 5; III. 19; III. 32. 2. 3. 6.
[19] Scribes and Pharisees are often associated in Matthew.
[20] Cf. E. Zuckschwerdt, 'Das Naziräat des Herrenbruders Jakobus nach Hegesipp (Euseb. h. e. II. 23. 5-6)', ZNW 68 (1977), 276-87.

argued.[21] It is also useless for historical purposes.

We need to ask what effect Hegesippus had on Eusebius. There seem to have been several stages. First, in the *Chronicle* he did use Hegesippus but not at a crucial point. Eusebius maintained against Hegesippus that James was martyred by stoning and in the year 61/62, as in Josephus' account.[22] It is true that Eusebius identified Simon with Symeon, since apparently Hegesippus used one name, the Jerusalem bishop-list the other, and that with Hegesippus he ascribed the death of Simon to crucifixion. He blamed Trajan's persecution for the martyrdom, however, not Jewish sectarian plots.[23] Second, in an early edition of the *History* he also neglected Hegesippus. The earliest summary on the death of James (II. 23. 1-2) is based primarily on Clement and Josephus.[24] The statement that Christians left Jerusalem for Pella before the war (III. 5. 3) disagrees with Hegesippus' notion that Vespasian's siege began just after the death of James. Third, in a later version of the *History* Eusebius made more use of Hegesippus, and then he set him close in time to the apostles (II. 23. 3) – an error only gradually corrected. At this point he also referred to the martyrdom of James as immediately followed by the capture of Jerusalem (III. 11). He also wrongly supposed that Hegesippus had set the rise of heresy in or after the reign of Trajan (III. 32. 7). In spite of this new information, he did not correct the statements from Justin and Irenaeus according to which Simon Magus had been dated much earlier 13-14). Only later did he find out that Hegesippus actually dated the rise of heresy and the corruption of the Church under Vespasian (IV. 22. 5). He also realized that Hegesippus' own date was at least as late as Hadrian (IV. 8. 2), indeed later in the second century (IV. 11. 7). Finally he concluded that no matter what use he might have made of Hegesippus this man was no Church historian even though he was an 'ecclesiastical author' (I. 1. 5; cf. IV. 21).

Book II ends with two passages paraphrased from Josephus but defined as verbatim quotations. They are intended to point the way to the Jewish catastrophe to be described in Book III; indeed, the last sentence of Book II is repeated at the beginning of the next book.

---

[21] N. Hyldahl, 'Hegesipps Hypomnemata', *Studia Theologica*, 14 (1960), 70–113.

[22] *Chron.*, pp. 182–3.   [23] *Chron.*, p. 194.

[24] So is the summary in *Dem. Ev.* III. 5. 64 (question about Son of God is not in Hegesippus); but there are Hegesippan echoes in the description of James's superlative virtue.

Similarly the account of Paul and Peter to be found in II. 25. 5–8 is in essence repeated in the first chapter of the third book. Examination of II. 25 as a whole casts considerable light on Eusebius' way of writing history. First, he says that after Nero's eighth year (II. 24) 'the principate was now firmly secured for Nero' and he 'plunged into vile habits' (Oulton) including family murders. Eusebius' summary of these murders seems to be a paraphrase of a summary made by Josephus himself[25] while his idea that they took place late in the reign is due to the incorrect Greek version of Tertullian (see above). There follows a quotation from this version, and then comes the legendary statement that in Nero's time Paul was beheaded in Rome itself and Peter crucified (head-downwards, according to Origen in III. 1. 2).[26] In order to 'confirm the facts of the history' Eusebius adduces two witnesses. The first was an 'ecclesiastical man' named Gaius who at Rome wrote against the Montanist Proclus when Zephyrinus was Bishop of Rome; he mentioned the location of the 'trophies' of Peter and Paul.[27] As for the time when they were martyred, Eusebius invokes Dionysius of Corinth, who evidently relied on 1 Corinthians and 1 Clement to 'prove' that they taught and became martyrs together.

It is possible that these quotations belong to Eusebius' first draft of this book. His whole treatment of events and literature at this point is hard to follow, but such a difficulty does not prove the presence of interpolation. We might prefer to have the quotation from Dionysius connected with a discussion of 1 Clement (III. 16 or III. 38) or of Dionysius' letter to the Romans (IV. 23. 9–11). Eusebius preferred to place it here. On the other hand, at two other points Eusebius' quotations from Gaius compound or create confusion. First there is the discussion of the apostle or evangelist Philip. Eusebius quotes Clement of Alexandria to show that Philip 'gave his daughters in marriage to husbands' (III. 30. 1). Next he cites Polycrates of Ephesus on Philip's two daughters 'who grew old as virgins' and are buried at Hierapolis, while another 'lived in the Holy Spirit and rests at Ephesus'. Gaius 'agrees with what has been set forth' when he states that all four are buried at Hierapolis (III. 31. 3–4). But obviously Gaius does not agree. The second instance, to be discussed more fully in Chapter X on the canon, involves quoting Gaius' ascription of the Apocalypse of John to Cerinthus and also citing Dionysius of Alexandria as if he

---

[25] *Bell.* II. 250–1; cf. *Ant.* XX. 154–7.
[26] Cf. *Martyrium Pauli*, 5; *Acta Petri*, 37–8.
[27] Cf. J. Toynbee–J. B. Ward Perkins, *The Shrine of St. Peter* (New York, 1957).

agreed with Gaius (III. 28. 1-5). This contradicts Eusebius' earlier view and must have been added after his first version was written.

It looks as though beneath the surface of Eusebius' *History* we can dimly make out the shapes of earlier versions or drafts of versions in which various views were set forth. We have seen something of the ways in which he went about the construction of the end of Book II. When Eusebius has ended his discussion of Philip's daughters he says that he has finished with 'the apostles and the apostolic times' (III. 31. 6). He then goes on to the apostles' first successors (37. 4) — but he has already discussed this subject toward the beginning of Book III (4. 3-4). Indeed, it looks as though Books II-IV were the hardest to keep under control. At the end of Book III the chapter about Papias reflects the way in which Eusebius was changing his mind. At the end of Book IV we have been led to expect a discussion of authors ending with Irenaeus (IV. 21), but Eusebius actually concludes with Tatian and Bardesanes. His plan has changed, either as he writes or at a later time.

Book V was easier to write because so much of it could consist of materials on the Gallican martyrs, Irenaeus, the Montanists, and the Quartodecimans. Here the scribe or scribe could simply be told to copy out the materials. In Book VI Eusebius supplied accounts of men and events that were fully congenial. His heroes were Origen and Dionysius of Alexandria and he could use materials derived from both of them.

The School of Alexandria

Among Eusebius' primary concerns in the *Church History* was the school of Christian learning maintained in relation to the church of Alexandria. It was important to him not only because it had contributed to the development of a learned theology but also because Origen, its head in the early third century, had migrated to Caesarea in Palestine and established a similar school there. At Caesarea Eusebius' master Pamphilus had created a library of the works of 'Origen and other ecclesiastical authors' (VI. 32. 4). Without these schools Eusebius could not have written the *Church History*. Yet he tells us almost nothing about the school at Caesarea and, as we shall see, is the creator of the history of the school at Alexandria.

Unfortunately it is by no means clear where Eusebius found his materials for the early history of the Alexandrian church and school. The letter of Clement published by Morton Smith shows us that Eusebius almost certainly relied on Clement for his idea that 'Mark was the first to go to Egypt in order to preach the gospel which he had just written down' (II. 16. 1).[28] There is no way to tell where Clement himself got such an idea. As for Eusebius, he turns from Mark to emphasize the number of Mark's converts and to argue that he possesses a description of them in Philo's treatise *On the Contemplative Life*.

Eusebius sets the stage for his argument by claiming that, according to some tradition, Philo visited Peter at Rome during the reign of Claudius. The tradition is confirmed by the fact that the treatise, composed considerably later than the time of the visit, 'contains the rules of the church which are still observed in our time' (II. 17. 1). This confirmation obviously does not confirm. It depends on the prior assumption that the rules have always remained the same (a point not stated until IV. 7. 13). Philo's visit to Rome is actually mentioned in II. 18. 8. 'He is said to have read before the whole senate of the Romans his description of the impiety of Gaius, . . . and his works were so much admired as to be deemed worthy of being placed in libraries.' If Philo spoke at Rome about Gaius, he must have done so soon after the accession of Claudius, hence about the year 41. If he visited Peter, Peter must have been at Rome for about twenty-five years (see Chapter III). Mark must have gone to Alexandria well before Peter's death in order to gain converts and allow Philo to write about them. According to II. 24 Annianus, Mark's successor, became Bishop of Alexandria in the eighth year of Nero.

According to Eusebius, Philo gave a highly accurate account of the life of 'our ascetics'. His Therapeutae, like the Christian apostolic men, were of Hebrew origin. They were called Therapeutae because the name Christian was not yet in use everywhere. Like the Jerusalem Christians of Acts, they gave up their property. When Philo wrote they were to be found in a great many places but especially in Egypt and around Alexandria. (In other words, the Alexandrian Christians were the most conspicuous members of an almost universal society.) What Philo called their 'monasteries' were really churches, in which they combined study with liturgical worship. These points, says Eusebius, illustrate 'the characteristics of ecclesiastical life' (II. 17. 14). Doubts may still remain in the reader's mind, and Eusebius therefore gives further examples of the Therapeutic devotion to 'the gospel way of life' (continence and fasting, II. 17. 15-18), to 'gospel worship' (aged virgins, allegorical exegesis, paschal vigils,[29] the diaconate and the episcopate, II. 17.

[28] *Clement of Alexandria and a Secret Gospel of Mark* (Cambridge, Mass., 1973).
[29] For Eusebius' concern with the paschal vigil cf. V. 24. 12-13; VI. 34.

18-23). He concludes by claiming again that Philo described 'the first heralds of gospel teaching and the customs handed down by the apostles from the beginning' (II. 17. 24).

This is a Christian reinterpretation of what Philo actually wrote, even though it seemed historical to Jerome and Epiphanius.[30] Not so obvious, perhaps, is the fact that the principal motifs of the Philonic passages turn up again as the principal motifs in the early life of Origen. Is the similarity due to a continuing ideal? Or did Eusebius himself choose the Philonic passages since he already knew about Origen's youth? Or was it the other way round? In any case, there is strong emphasis on 'philosophy' and a 'philosophic life'.[31] The more practical concerns of the Therapeutae were much the same as Origen's. Both they and he were concerned with allegorical exegesis,[32] slept little,[33] and on the floor,[34] took no wine and only what food was necessary,[35] and gave up their property.[36] Eusebius, as we have seen, says that the Therapeutae were following the Gospel. He also says that Origen tried to observe 'the gospel sayings of the Saviour' (VI. 3. 10).[37]

Whatever the sources for Origen's early life may have been (see below), either Eusebius or a predecessor has conformed the account of this life to the ideal of the Therapeutae, one would suppose, and therefore we are as usual separated from Alexandrian actuality by several layers of tradition.

Eusebius must have been aware that for the earliest history of the Alexandrian church or school he had practically no materials other than those given him by Philo. He certainly was not going to use the odd story of an Alexandrian Christian would-be castrato naïvely recorded by Justin.[38] All that was left, then, was some information about the Gnostic teacher Basilides, chiefly derived from a certain Agrippa Castor (IV. 7. 6-8), but he had no desire to derive Church-historical information from anything concerning heretics. His account of Pantaenus is rather strange and seems to be taken from various sources (V. 10). He has just mentioned Julian as Bishop of Alexandria

---

[30] F. C. Conybeare, *Philo About the Contemplative Life* (Oxford, 1895), 318-20.
[31] II. 16. 2; 17. 5. 10. 16; VI. 3. 6. 9. 13.
[32] II. 17. 10-11. 20; VI. 2. 9-10.   [33] II. 17. 16; VI. 3. 9.
[34] II. 17. 22; VI. 3. 9.   [35] II. 17. 22. 17; VI. 3. 12.
[36] II. 17. 5-6; VI. 3. 9-10.
[37] Achillas, later head of the Alexandrian school, 'demonstrated a genuine mode of the gospel way of life' (VII. 32. 20).
[38] Justin, *Apol*. I. 29. 2-3. Eusebius cites *Apol*. I. 29. 4 (IV. 8. 3).

in 180. Now he says that Pantaenus 'was in charge of the school of the faithful there . . . since from ancient custom a school of the scriptures existed among them.' The 'ancient custom' is of course the one 'handed down by the apostles from the beginning' as discussed in relation to the Therapeutae. This school, Eusebius says, is still in existence, 'organized by men mighty in word and in zeal for divine matters' (V. 10. 1). Here we seem to find a dim echo of Eusebius' own investigation of the scriptures, for in Acts 18:24 we read that Apollos was a Jew, 'a native of Alexandria . . . an eloquent man, mighty in the scriptures'. Presumably someone at Alexandria (but not Eusebius?) regarded him as a member or a forerunner of the school. After this we find rather confused notices about Pantaenus and Stoics, Pantaenus and India (twice), and Pantaenus as head of the school at Alexandria until his death (V. 10. 2–4). Clement studied with him, for he said so in his *Hypotyposes* (V. 11. 2; VI. 13. 2).[39] According to Eusebius, eager to note or create an Alexandrian academic succession, Clement succeeded Pantaenus (VI. 6. 1) and somehow Origen succeeded him (VI. 8. 1. 3; cf. VI. 3. 3. 8). Origen made Heraclas his colleague (VI. 15) and when he left for Caesarea Heraclas took over the school, remaining in charge until he himself became bishop and Origen's pupil Dionysius succeeded him (VI. 29. 4). Of the later teachers Eusebius mentions only Pierius and Achillas (VII. 32. 27. 30).

The sections concerning the Therapeutae, Pantaenus, and Origen are not precisely the same, however. Whoever may have revised Philo's account of the Therapeutae (whether Eusebius or a predecessor) was concerned with 'our ascetics' who lived 'in accordance with the gospel' and in the church(es).[40] The ministry of the church was crowned by 'the supreme presidency of the episcopate' (II. 17. 23). This is quite unlike the picture given in the brief account of Pantaenus. We have just learned that a certain Julian 'was entrusted with the episcopate of the churches at Alexandria' (V. 9) when we are told that Pantaenus directed the school[41] of the faithful there — as we have already noted. In this section there is no mention of the church, only of the school, and it is the school that is traced back to the time of the apostles.

When we come to the early life of Origen, as the passage now stands in the *Church History* it contains primary emphasis on the life of the school (the word appears in VI. 3. 3) but, in addition, on an

[39] Cf. the comments of Origen (cited VI. 19. 13) and Alexander (VI. 14. 9).
[40] Church(es) in II. 17. 1. 9. 14. 23.
[41] For διατριβή as 'school' cf. P. Nautin, *Origène*, 36, n.2.

ecclesiastical rule (2. 14; cf. II. 17. 1) and on the bishop as ultimately in charge of the school (3. 2; 8. 3).

It thus seems likely that the account of the Therapeutae as Christians was constructed with the church, not the school, in mind. It might be better to say that it is not closely connected with any notions about school succession but that it may come from the Alexandrian school when concerned with a different point. Its purpose could be to show that ideally the church of Alexandria was a school and, of course, the school was a church.

Lives

At the beginning of Book VI Eusebius begins to employ a different approach to Church history. He has used two dossiers in Book V as well as a long account of martyrs and frequent discussions of Christian authors. The framework of the first thirty-nine (out of forty-six) chapters of Book VI, however, is given by a biographical sketch of Origen,[42] while the remainder of Book VI and most of Book VII is based on the letters of his pupil Dionysius, 'the great bishop of the Alexandrians'. There is nothing similar in the earlier books.

Had Eusebius read Hippolytus' *Refutation* he could have found an interesting account of Callistus and other Roman bishops, all from a hostile point of view, but there is no evidence that he had seen it (VI. 22). He actually knew Josephus' defensive autobiography, appended to the last book of the *Jewish Antiquities* (III. 10. 8), and he would use an autobiographical and apologetic letter by Origen (VI. 19. 11-14) as well as another by Dionysius (VI. 40; VII. 11. 1-19). In addition, from his account of the proceedings against Paul of Samosata we know that he emphasized personal behaviour more than theological doctrine (VII. 30. 6-17).

Eusebius did have a precedent for inserting biographical materials in the midst of a larger history. This was provided by Diodorus Siculus, whose universal history he cited both in the *Chronicle* and in the *Praeparatio Evangelica*. Diodorus had to face a problem not unlike the one Eusebius encountered when dealing with the two 'great' leaders of Alexandrian Christiantiy. He had to discuss the lives of two great leaders, Philip of Macedon and his son Alexander, like Dionysius, called 'the Great'. Diodorus described his procedure along the way. As he

---

[42] In VI. 9-11 we find fragments of a highly apologetic life of Narcissus of Jerusalem; but so much is suppressed that we cannot call it biography.

began to deal with the life of Philip in Book XVI he told his readers that 'in all historical treatises it is suitable for authors to include in their books the deeds of cities or kings that are complete in themselves from beginning to end.' For this reason, he said, he would try to include the deeds of Philip 'within this book'. At the beginning of Book XVII he summarized the basic points concerning Philip and then proposed to deal with the deeds of Alexander 'until his death' and to do so, as already intimated at the end of Book XVI, 'in one book'. Compared with the other books in Diodorus' history, however, Book XVII on Alexander is too long and a later editor (apparently) divided it into two parts, roughly equal, the first having to do with events in Europe, the second with events in Asia (63. 5). (On the lengths of books see Chapter II.)

Can we imagine that Eusebius faced a similar problem, though he solved it differently? Certainly Origen and Dionysius play a Church part comparable to that of Philip and Alexander in Diodorus. Like Diodorus, Eusebius changes his procedure when he comes to deal with these heroes. The difference is that the materials about Origen do not occupy all of one book and those dealing with Dionysius therefore have to be spread over two books.

A Life of Origen

Eusebius not only wrote the biographical sketch of Origen in Book VI of the *Church History* but also, partly in association with his teacher Pamphilus, composed an *Apology for Origen* in six books. 'The first five were composed by Pamphilus in prison, with the assistance of Eusebius; the sixth, when the martyr, deprived of life by the sword, departed toward the God whom he desired, was completed by Eusebius.'[43] This passage would be especially important if we could prove, not assume, that *History* followed *Apology*, for Pamphilus was in prison from 308 to 310.[44]

One might suppose that what we read in Photius' account of the *Apology* actually comes from the *Apology*, but Nautin has shown that such is not the case. The notice by Photius deals with the life of Origen in accordance with all the sources available and then provides some supplemental information on the audience and the author of the *Apology*. We shall set forth the materials on Origen along with Nautin's

---

[43] Photius, *PG* 103, 396C; cf. P. Nautin, *Origène sa vie et son œuvre* (Paris, 1977), 99–108.

[44] I owe this point to T.D. Barnes.

conclusions on their sources.

They say that during the persecutions under Severus Origen wrote
to his father Leonides, anointing him for the course of martyrdom;
by running well he gained the prizes (1 Cor. 9:24). Origen himself
was eager to strip himself for the contests in the stadium, but his
mother was able to check his impulse in spite of him. He indicates
this in a letter of his own.

According to Nautin, this narrative comes from Book VI of the
Apology, in which, as in VI. 2. 3-5, Eusebius made use of an autobiographical letter. Much of the language in Photius' account and in the
History is the same, but at a crucial point there is a difference.
According to the *Apology*, Origen was eager to strip (metaphorically);
according to the *History*, he wanted to keep his clothes on (literally).
In addition, in the *History* we read that Origen did not become a
martyr because of 'the divine and heavenly providence, acting for the
general good' (VI. 2. 4). Even allowing for Origen's self-esteem, we
must suppose that this comes from Eusebius. At this point it is hard to
say whether *Apology* or *History* came first, however.

Pamphilus the martyr and many others who inquired about Origen
from those who had seen him say that he departed from life with an
illustrious martyrdom at Caesarea itself when Decius was breathing
cruelty against the Christians. Others say that he survived until Gallus
and Volusianus and that in the 69th year of his age he died and was
buried at Tyre. The latter account is true, if indeed the letters ascribed
to him after the persecution of Decius do not contain fiction.

According to Nautin, the first version comes from what Pamphilus
wrote in the first five books of the *Apology*. The second could come
from the *History* (VII. 1) but the mention of Volusianus and Tyre
belongs to the Greek version of Jerome, *De viris inlustribus*. The
problem is even more complicated, however. In the *Church History*,
VI. 39. 5 Eusebius tells 'of what sort and how many' things happened
to Origen at the time of the persecution, 'of what sort and how many'
things he endured for the sake of Christ. The whole section is written
in a way intended to lead up to some highly significant event. At the
end, however, it peters out with statements about the judge's efforts
not to put Origen to death and about the letters Origen wrote. It
seems certain that this section originally contained an account of the
death of Origen, as the words τελευτή and τέλος indicate. Τελευτή

means 'death' in the *History*,[44] as τέλος sometimes does.[45] The point is confirmed by the chapter headings to Book VI. The majority of the manuscripts read 'Concerning events in the time of Decius' at this point. E and R, however, reflect what must be the earlier theme: 'Concerning the end (τέλος) of Origen'.

We conclude, then, that in the *Church History* we have evidence for an earlier account of Origen's death under Decius (VI. 39. 5 in its original form) and a later account set under Gallus (VI. 39. 5 as revised; VII. 1). The *Apology* obviously agreed with the earlier version, though we cannot tell which one came first.

They say that he passed through and taught every branch of learning. They say that this Origen (who they say was surnamed Adamantius because he bound his reasonings as with adamant chains) was a hearer of Clement, author of the *Stromata*, and his successor in the ecclesiastical school at Alexandria. Further they say that Clement was a hearer of Pantaenus and his successor in the school, and that Pantaenus heard those who had seen the apostles and even heard some of the apostles themselves.

Nautin suggests that where λέγουσι is used for 'they say' (in regard to Clement and Pantaenus) the materials come not from the *Apology* but from the *Church History*, in this case from VI. 13. 2 and V. 11. 5. We agree.

They say that the moves against Origen arose in this way. Demetrius was bishop of Alexandria; he treated Origen with praise and put him among his favourites. But when Origen was about to depart for Athens he was advanced to presbyter irregularly, without the agreement of his own bishop. Theotecnus, who was holding the archepiscopal authority in Caesarea of Palestine, performed the ordination of Origen, with the approval of Alexander of Jerusalem. For this reason the love of Demetrius turned into hate and his praises to censures.

Nautin traces most of this back to Jerome's treatise *De viris inlustribus*, apart from the confusion of Theoctistus with Theotecnus, easy to fall into. One wonders, however, about the relation of Demetrius' emotions in Photius to the analysis of his relations with Origen in the *History*.

In VI. 8. 4–5 we find two accounts, not one, of the attack Demetrius made on Origen. According to the first (8. 4), Demetrius at first encouraged Origen when we heard of his self-castration but later, when he saw that he was 'prospering and great and illustrious and universally

---

[44] I. 8. 4 (Josephus); 9. 2; II. 6. 1; 22. 4; 23. 3; III. 23. 1; 31. 1. 4; IV. 10; 15. 47; V. 16. 13; 17. 4. VI. 2. 15; 4. 1; VII. 1; 28. 3; VIII. 13. 5; IX. 10. 14.

[45] III. 32. 2. 8.

famous', he was overcome by 'something human' and proceeded to write to the bishops everywhere and tell them that the act was 'monstrous', He did so even though the most highly approved and distinguished bishops in Palestine, those of Caesarea and Jerusalem, honoured Origen and considered him worthy of the highest honour and ordained him to the presbyterate.

This version seems to be related to the *Apology*, in which Origen is described as endowed 'with the honour of the presbyterate'.[46] In the *Apology* as described by Photius we learn of Origen's (irregular) advancement to the presbyterate and the role of the Bishops of Caesarea and Jerusalem in his ordination. Second, the 'human emotion' of Demetrius seems to be an abbreviation of what is in the *Apology*. Because of Origen's ordination Demetrius' 'love turned into hate and his praises to censures'.[47] In the *Church History* Eusebius saw no reason for delving into Demetrius' emotional problems. On the basis of these parallels, and also because the account in VI. 8. 4 is so explicitly apologetic, we conclude that this *Church History* passage is based on the analogous section of the *Apology*.

In VI. 8. 5 the story is told over again. Here we learn that Origen 'had achieved great esteem and among all men everywhere had acquired no small repute for virtue and wisdom'. Then Demetrius, 'lacking any other accusation, spread grave slander about an act in his long past youth, venturing also to include in his accusations those who advanced him to the presbyterate'. There are echoes of the *Apology* here, but not so close as those in the preceding section. And it seems fairly clear that this version of the struggle is more closely related to what Eusebius is going on to say about Narcissus, Bishop of Jerusalem. In his case 'certain miserable creatures who could not endure his energy and the firmness of his conduct . . . devised an intrigue against him, spreading a certain grave slander to harm him.' They tried to confirm 'their accusations' by oaths, but his 'shining continence and all-virtuous behaviour' were more impressive.[48] It looks as though, in the construction of the *Church History*, Narcissus is being presented as another Origen, unjustly accused and finally vindicated. In other words,

[46] *PG* 17, 545B.

[47] For love turning to hate cf. *Didache*, 16. 3; Theophrastus in Plutarch, *Cato min.* 37. 2; Clement, *Paed.* II. 97. 3. Praises and censures are rhetorical terms; for hate as leading to falsehood cf. Avenarius, op. cit., 50–2. Licinius turned from friendship to envy of Constantine (X. 8. 2–3).

[48] VI. 9. 5; exact repetitions are underlined.

VI. 8. 5 anticipates VI. 9. 5 and was written for the *Church History*, whereas VI. 8. 4 summarizes the account in the *Apology*. The *Church History*, then, should be later than the *Apology*, at least in this part of it.

And a synod of bishops and some presbyters convenes against Origen. As Pamphilus says, it decrees that Origen is to leave Alexandria and is not to reside or teach there, but in no way is to be removed from the rank of the presbytery. But Demetrius, along with some Egyptian bishops, also deposed him from the priesthood; those who voted with him subscribed to the sentence with him. Theotecnus of Palestine cordially welcomed Origen to live in Caesarea when he had been banished from Alexandria and entrusted him with complete authority to teach. These are the causes, they say, from which the slanders against Origen broke forth.

Nautin has explained the probable origins of these materials. They come largely from Pamphilus in the *Apology* but have been reinterpreted and misinterpreted by Photius. The main point here for us is a cross-reference in VI. 23. 4 to the second book of the *Apology*. 'The agitations occasioned about him because of this [his ordination] and the decisions on the matters agitated made by those who presided over the churches . . . require a separate composition, and we have given a fairly full account in the second (book) of the *Apology* . . .' Presumably Eusebius could have provided an account of the controversy in the *History*, then could have written the *Apology*, then could have deleted the materials from the *History* and provided cross-references (cf. also VI. 32. 3). It seems more natural to suppose that he simply wrote the *Apology* and then gave references to it when writing the *History*.

The last section of Photius' comments explains that the *Apology* was sent to the confessors who were suffering in the mines; their leader was Patermythios, who soon after the death of Pamphilus was himself burned to death with others.[49] From Rufinus' translation of Book I we know that Pamphilus told them that Origen was a legitimate presbyter of the Church and that he led 'a most abstinent and truly philosophic life', observing 'the pure discipline of religion'.[50] Echoes of such claims recur in the *History*.

Whatever we may make of the sources of Eusebius' chapters on the early life of Origen (VI. 2–3; 8. 1–3), it is clear that they have apologetic purposes, and indeed they can be divided up in relation to four apologetic themes. The common vocabulary, with its special

---

[49] Patermythios, *Mart. Pal.* 13. 3; at Phaeno, VIII. 13. 5.
[50] *PG* 17, 545B.

emphasis on Origen as a παῖς[51] and his προθυμία,[52] shows that the four are interrelated. But the points are different, as Eusebius' conclusions explicitly state. He introduces his whole account by saying that 'the facts about Origen even from his swaddling-clothes are worth mentioning' (2. 2). Then comes the story of Origen's zeal for martyrdom, thwarted in his own case but carried out in his father's. Eusebius notes that this is 'the first proof of Origen's boyish readiness of mind and most genuine devotion to religion' (2. 6). More than that, it is actually a proof of his yearning for martyrdom, a subject on which Eusebius lays further emphasis later (3. 2-6; 13; above all, 39. 5). Second, we are told how from his childhood Origen was devoted to the study of the scriptures and was encouraged by his father. 'These are the stories, and others related to them, that they tell about Origen as a boy' (2. 11). This topic too, related to his concomitant studies of secular literature, will come up again (2. 15; 3. 8-9, etc.). The third point has to do with his youthful dislike of heresy and heretics and his observance of the Church's rule not to pray with heretics. He thus gave 'clear proofs of his orthodoxy in the faith at that age' (2. 14). This subject concerned him later as well (36. 4). Finally, he was renowned for his 'philosophical' and ascetic way of life (3. 6-7, 9-13; 8. 1-3). He exemplified devotion to religion (3. 6-7); he provided 'proofs of a philosophic life' (3. 13); and his self-castration proved 'not only his immature and youthful mind but also his faith and self-control' (8. 1).

Eusebius probably laid emphasis on these apologetic notes because he had just finished writing the *Apology for Origen*, either in its original five-book edition or with the sixth book by himself alone. Thus Book VI of the *Church History*, also in a revised form, would have been completed by 315. Its concentration on the theme of biography was due partly to Eusebius' discovery of an autobiographical-apologetic letter written by Origen (as Nautin has shown), partly to the apologetic theme present in Eusebius' mind and work at this time. Apparently no Christian before the third century had produced letters containing such vivid and usable autobiographical detail. (For some reason Eusebius did not like the Christ-centred person of Ignatius as reflected in his

---

[51] Martyrdom: 2. 3. 6 (twice); scripture study: 2. 7. 9. 10. 11 (twice); heresy: 2. 14 (ἐξ ἐκείνου); asceticism: 3. 11; 8. 1. 2 (twice); cf. 8. 4.

[52] Προθυμία, etc.: martyrdom: 2. 3. 3. 4. 6; 3. 3. 5. 13; scripture study: 2. 9; heresy: none; asceticism: 3. 11; 8. 3. Epiphanius picked up these points from Eusebius (*Haer.* LXIII 1. 1. 3. 5).

letters; perhaps this was due to a theological aversion.) Similarly in dealing with Dionysius of Alexandria Eusebius found a letter of defence directed against another bishop who had criticized his attitude toward martyrdom and his behaviour under persecution (VI. 40; VII. 11. 1–19). Autobiographical details were to be found in other letters by Dionysius, and since Eusebius was working rapidly he got some of the chronology mixed up. What is significant, however, is that simply by using such letters by Origen and Dionysius he was able to create a large part of the contents of Books VI and VII — as he was aware.

Conclusion

To a significant extent Eusebius' choice of materials about men and events depended on what he had heard in Palestine or found in the libraries, chiefly at Caesarea. Since the Caesarean library was Alexandrian in origin and the founder of the Jerusalem library had studied at Alexandria, the men and events tended to be Alexandrian too. In consequence the picture of Christians in general is unbalanced. It also lays undue emphasis on the life of Origen.

VIII

THE THIRD THEME: HERETICS

In the third place Eusebius intended to discuss the names, the numbers, and some of the doctrines of those who 'drove on to the end with a longing for misguided innovation'. Such men were introducing 'knowledge falsely so-called' (1 Tim. 6:20) and were like fierce wolves attacking the flock of Christ (Acts 20:29).

Since in Eusebius' view the doctrine of the Church was what Christ taught, and this teaching had been preserved in the apostolic succession 'always the same and always in similar fashion', doctrines expressed in 'manifold and polymorphous' modes were obviously false (IV. 7. 13). The word he uses for 'innovation' at the beginning (νεωτεροποιΐα) had been employed in regard to rebellion against the established order by Thucydides and Josephus. Eusebius himself would use it in later passages.[1] He was also fond of καινοτομία in spite of a bad precedent in Plato. According to the *Euthyphro* (3C), Socrates was accused of 'making innovations in religion' (καινοτομεῖν περὶ τὰ θεῖα). Eusebius does not hesitate to employ cognates when he speaks of heresy.[2]

When he wrote about heresies in the *Chronicle* he said little about them. Apparently he had not conducted research in the writing of Justin or Irenaeus and he did not mention any heretics before Basilides. 'Basilides, from whom the Gnostics are derived, stayed at Alexandria' in a year equivalent to 133.[3] The year might come from Clement of Alexandria, who set Basilides late in the reign of Hadrian,[4] or perhaps from the Agrippa Castor to be mentioned in IV. 7. 6–8. For such heretics as Valentinus, Cerdo, and Marcion, at Rome around 140 to 143, he relied on Irenaeus. We do not know how he knew that Montanism began about 170. Perhaps he found the information in an anti-Montanist dossier in the church library. His notice about Tatian comes from Irenaeus, and he set this in 172 for a reason we do not know, along with Bardesanes. The *Chronicle* sets the heresy of Paul of Samosata in the year 268 and that of the Manichees in 280. The

---

[1] Thucydides I. 102. 3; cf. *H. E.* IV. 6. 3; V. 15; 28. 2; VII. 4; *Mart. Pal.* 12.
[2] IV. 7. 13; 27; VII. 30. 4; 31. 1. Tatian uses the word of pagan comments about his conversion (*Or.* 35. 2), but neither Clement nor Eusebius quoted this.
[3] *Chron.*, p. 201 Helm.   [4] *Str.* VII. 106. 4.

latter date may reflect the arrival of missionaries in Eusebius' vicinity. More documentation would be needed for the *History*.

Perhaps Eusebius' major contribution to the study of heresy lies in his language. If one could take his rhetoric seriously, there was little need for discussion of the heretics, for their heresies were almost always 'extinguished', often immediately.[5] On the other hand, in a particular case Paul of Samosata 'tried to renew' the heresy of Artemon (V. 28. 1) and therefore some danger remained. Other heretics were really innovators, for no fewer than six of them are described as 'founders' of their own heresies.[6] Behind them all stood the Devil, often described as 'hating the good'.[7] Eusebius' language about the heretics, especially the early ones, is highly repetitive. The rites of the Simonians, he says, are full of marvel and frenzy and madness (II. 13. 7). Frenzy comes back with the Montanists (V. 17. 1–2), madness with the Manichees (VII. 31).

According to Lucian, bad historians began their works thus: 'For the most abominable and damnable scoundrel Vologesus began the war . . .'[8] The abusive language used of Vologesus comes from comedy (Aristophanes), where its setting is appropriate. It has no place in history. Eusebius did not see it that way. Heresy from Simon onward deserved to be called 'abominable', even with use of the comparative and the superlative.[9] Again, the word 'loathsome' occurs in comedy. Eusebius uses it and a compound in regard to heresies,[10] and of course speaks of 'unspeakable' or 'shameful' practices.[11]

Eusebius was not simply trying to use vulgar language when he spoke about heretics. He was concerned with the divine plan for the advance of the Church through the ages. As the Church advances, it overcomes impediments, heresy, or persecution, or both. The worse the heretics or persecutors are made to look, the more radiantly the light of the Church will shine. Moreover, he did not confine himself to abuse but, while rarely discussing heretical doctrines, often presented information about heretics. This information came to him — when he decided that he had to deal with the heretics — from Justin and Irenaeus. Usually he quoted Justin and backed him up with paraphrases of Irenaeus. For

---

[5] II. 14. 2; 15. 1; III. 29. 4; IV. 7. 14; VI. 38; VII. 31. 2.
[6] II. 13. 5; III. 28. 1; IV. 29. 1; V. 28. 6; VI. 43. 3; VII. 29. 1.
[7] II. 13. 1; 14. 1; III. 26. 1. 4; 27. 1; IV. 7. 1; V. 14; cf. G. J. M. Bartelink, 'Μισόκαλος', *VC* 12 (1958), 37–44.
[8] *Quom. hist. conscr.* 14.   [9] II. 13. 5. 8; cf. 1. 12.
[10] II. 13. 8; IV. 7. 9.   [11] II. 13. 7; IV. 7. 9.

heretics not discussed by Justin he generally relied on Irenaeus alone. We shall discuss the exceptions (Ebionites, Cerinthus, Nicolaitans) at a later point. In addition, Agrippa Castor is the source for an entirely untheological account of Basilides (IV. 7. 6-8).

The old heresies were not especially interesting to Eusebius and he had neither the means nor the inclination to investigate them thoroughly. He preferred not to say that Origen had been accused of heresy (cf. VI. 36. 4) and treated Dionysius of Alexandria as an opponent of heresy, not as a defender (VII. 26. 1). When he began writing the *Church History* or even produced his second edition he can hardly have imagined that anyone would ever make accusations against him.

It looks as if his views about ancient heresy were shaped partly by the accident of the materials he found available, partly by the accident of the way in which he used them. The primary example is Hegesippus. When Eusebius wrote the *Chronicle* he does not seem to have been acquainted, or at least well acquainted, with Hegesippus' work. He followed Josephus for the date when James was martyred by stoning and neglected the strange notions of Hegesippus (II. 23. 16-18). In the *History*, however, he accepted Hegesippus' peculiar chronology (cf. III. 11) even though it contradicted his more 'normal' ideas (III. 7. 8). Again, when he introduced a bit of Hegesippus (paraphrased) he understood that until the reign of Trajan 'the church remained a pure and uncorrupted virgin, for those who attempted to corrupt the healthful rule of the saving proclamation, if any such existed, lurked in obscure darkness' (III. 32. 7). For Eusebius this meant that heresy was never successful until after the death of the apostle John. What Hegesippus actually said, however, was that at the time of the death of James, a generation earlier, 'they called the church virgin, for it had not yet been corrupted . . .' He added that the corruption began when the unsuccessful candidate for the episcopate adhered to (one of) the seven sects among the (Jewish) people (IV. 22. 4-5). Though Hegesippus does not seem to have known much about Jewish sects, it looks as if Eusebius knew even less and therefore accepted these statements. There were obvious difficulties, however. In II. 23. 3 he had dated Hegesippus far too early, 'in the first succession from the apostles'. Later on he gave him a date toward the end of the second century (IV. 22. 3. 4).

Eusebius' accounts of the early heresies thus possess no value apart from that of the documents he quoted or paraphrased. He was no student of heresy and, of course, firmly believed that his own theology was orthodox. His ideas were controlled by the notion of a fixed deposit, held by himself and reliable colleagues and rejected by heretics early and late.

The relation of his ideas to the Church situation of his own time can best be illustrated from what he says about individual heresies.

Simon Magus and Menander

Because of his concern for annalistic history, with events carefully related to a year or short period of years, Eusebius splits up the narrative about early heresies which he got from Justin and Irenaeus. Simon first comes on the scene when he is discussed in relation to Philip's mission to Samaria as described in the book of Acts (II. 1. 10-12). Eusebius simply retells the story (as Irenaeus had done) and adds moralizing and rhetorical comments. Simon's successors attach themselves to the Church like a disease and they poison those who listen to them. When the history reaches the reign of Claudius it is time to deal with Simon again, for according to Justin he worked magical miracles during that reign. Relying on Justin and Irenaeus, Eusebius cloaks the story of Simon in rhetoric and ends with an account, presumably based on the Clementine romance (one form of which he rejects in III. 38. 4), of Simon's defeat by the apostle Peter and ultimate death (II. 13. 1-15. 1). Menander, Simon's successor, comes on the scene only when Eusebius 'returns to the historical narrative' after a discussion of the New Testament books and true orthodoxy. He promised immortality through magic and baptism. The Devil worked through him to slander 'the great mystery of godliness' (1 Tim. 3:16) and ridicule the ecclesiastical doctrines of the immortality of the soul and the resurrection of the dead (III. 26).

Probably the account of Menander is intended as a prelude to the attack on Cerinthus in III. 28 — itself an attack on apocalyptic eschatology or millenarianism, as we shall see later. Here it may suffice to quote what Eusebius himself wrote of Menander's promises to his followers: 'They would share in eternal immortality in this life, no longer mortal but remaining here to be endlessly ageless and immortal.' This looks like Eusebius' idea of the apocalyptic kingdom on earth.

From Saturninus to Bardesanes

In IV. 7 Eusebius returns to the brilliant situation of the churches and the concomitant rise of heresy. He writes that 'formerly the devil had used persecutions from outside as his weapon against the church, but now that he was excluded from this' he used heretics so that slander would be spread against Christians. This is an odd statement. What it means is that in Eusebius' opinion when Trajan wrote to Pliny ordering him not to search for Christians but to punish them if encountered, 'the imminent threat of persecution was extinguished to a certain extent' (III. 33. 2). Heresy had just begun (III. 32. 7-8).

How did heresy lead to slander? The next heretic mentioned by Irenaeus, Saturninus of Antioch, was an ascetic and cannot have been involved. Eusebius therefore paraphrases an injudicious summary by Irenaeus to the effect that Saturninus and Basilides taught approximately the same thing, and quickly passes on to Basilides, providing piquant details from Agrippa Castor (otherwise unknown). These points allow him to go ahead to Carpocrates, of whom 'Irenaeus writes that he was a contemporary of these' (IV. 7. 9). Actually Irenaeus did not say anything about Carpocrates' date, but Eusebius has to have it early so that the licentious Carpocratians can be responsible for the slanders about Christians which Justin knew before he was a Christian (IV. 8. 5).

Later comments about Valentinus and Cerdo, the teacher of Marcion, as well as about Valentinians and Marcionites, come entirely from Irenaeus and Justin (IV. 10-11). They serve only to fill in the meagre outlines of information about the episcopate of Hyginus of Rome. Later, under Anicetus, Polycarp came to Rome and opposed Valentinians and Marcionites just as the disciple John had opposed Cerinthus (IV. 14. 3-7). Still later, around 168, most of the authors who wrote on 'the orthodoxy of the sound faith of the apostolic tradition' (IV. 21) wrote against the Marcionites, though one wrote against Montanists (IV. 27), two against Encratites (IV. 28-9. 3). The discussion of Encratites serves as an introduction to the writings of Tatian, an author whom Eusebius sometimes admired.

According to the *Chronicle* (p. 206) Tatian was recognized as a heretic in the year 172 and led the Encratites. (In the same year Bardesanes became 'the founder of another heresy'.) But the materials Eusebius had at his disposal gave an ambiguous picture of Tatian. In his view the treatise *Adversus Graecos* was not only famous but also rhetorically effective and very useful (IV. 29. 7). He noted that Clement had used it in preparing a chronography, i.e. in *Stromata*, I (VI. 13. 7).[12] Though he certainly excerpted Clement's *Stromata*, III

---

[12] Cf. *Praep. Ev.* X. 11-12.

(III. 29. 2–4; 30. 1) he did not bother to observe that in that book Clement denounced Tatian's views.[13] In addition, he knew that an anonymous anti-heretical author referred to Tatian as a theological authority (V. 28. 4). Thus Eusebius could refer to Tatian as a witness to the martyrdom of Justin,[14] citing passages from *Adversus Graecos* and describing Tatian as 'a man who in early life was trained in the learning of the Greeks and gained no slight distinction in it' (IV. 16. 7–9). By implication Tatian was reliable, for at Rome he had a pupil who attacked the heresy of Marcion (V. 13. 1).

The ambiguity begins to appear when Eusebius repeats the statement about Tatian's pupil and adds that he proposed to provide the answers to a book by Tatian on 'problems' (V. 13. 8). In IV. 29 Eusebius followed Irenaeus in stating that Tatian adhered to the Encratites after the martyrdom of Justin and that he was the 'founder' of this heresy. Thus in the *Chronicle* Tatian 'was recognized' and Bardesanes 'founded', while in the *History* Tatian founded and Bardesanes left Valentinianism for the Church. More information? Simple confusion? Perhaps a mixture of the two.

At the very end of this section on anti-heretical writers, Eusebius has tacked on a mention of Bardesanes (IV. 30). As we have noted, in the *Chronicle* Bardesanes invented his own heresy. Here, with more information available, he has become a sometime Valentinian. Eusebius gives him a setting by referring to 'the same reign' (presumably that of Marcus Aurelius, IV. 14. 10), to the dialogue *To Antoninus*, to 'the persecution of that time', and to the death of Soter of Rome. The death of Soter, not dated in Book IV, is set in 177 at the beginning of Book V. The persecution is presumably the one in Gaul, which Eusebius thought was universal (V, pr. 1; 2. 1). But the basic connection with Bardesanes in given by the name Antoninus. Here Eusebius has simply made a mistake. The Antoninus associated with Bardesanes was either Caracalla or Elagabalus, as Holl and Drijvers have indicated.[15] Eusebius has dated Bardesanes nearly half a century too early.

---

[13] Clement, *Str.* III. 49. 81–2, 86.
[14] One need not accept the interpolation theory of R. Weijenborg, 'Die Berichte über Justin und Crescens bei Tatian', *Antonianum*, 47 (1972), 372–90, to see the difficulties.
[15] K. Holl, *Epiphanius Panarion* II (Berlin–Leipzig, 1922), 339; H. J. W. Drijvers, *Bardaisan of Edessa* (Assen, 1966), 63–4; 69.

The Montanists

At the beginning of Book V Eusebius says that the Christian brothers in Gaul wrote letters to the brothers in Asia and Phrygia[16] (presumably the account of the Gallican martyrs) and to Eleutherus of Rome. They were 'ambassadors for the sake of the peace of the churches' just as Irenaeus was (again) in the Quartodeciman controversy (V. 24. 17). The situation was one in which certain Phrygians were propagating their ideas about prophecy, 'for the many other miracles of the divine grace still being effected among various churches produced among many the belief that these persons too were prophesying' (V. 3. 4). Though Eusebius calls the judgement of the brothers in Gaul 'pious and most orthodox', we must infer that since it promoted peace it cannot have included denunciation of the Phrygians as heretics.

Later in Book V Eusebius presents quite a different picture. He introduces his discussion of the Phrygian heresy by ascribing it to 'the enemy of the church of God, who hates good and especially loves evil' and by comparing Montanists with poisonous snakes (V. 14). To balance his account, and to draw attention to what he is going to discuss beyond Montanism, he refers to Florinus and Blastus, deposed presbyters of the Roman church (V. 15). By mentioning them here and later showing that Irenaeus criticized both of them (V. 20) he can create the impression that Irenaeus also opposed Montanism — an impression for which there is no evidence whatever.

The anti-Montanist materials come from a dossier which included a lengthy anonymous treatise dedicated to Avircius or Abercius Marcellus, apparently Bishop of Hieropolis in Phrygia, another treatise by an ecclesiastical writer named Apollonius, and a letter by Serapion of Antioch to which was subjoined a document by Claudius Apollinarius, Bishop of Hierapolis (with an a, not an o). From these Eusebius picks out items derogatory to Montanists or, in his opinion, pointing toward chronological conclusions. Certainly the anonymous author wrote at the end of the reign of Commodus (V. 16. 19; cf. V. 9) and Serapion was bishop then (V. 22), but the date of Apollonius seems to be wrong if he wrote forty years after the movement began (V. 18. 12).

In regard to this 'heresy' the attitudes of Christians certainly changed. Tertullian says that a Roman bishop changed his mind (*Adv.*

---

[16] Phrygia is in the Roman province of Asia but is being given special emphasis as in Acts 16:6 and 18:23; cf. Justin, *Dial.* 1. 3.

Prax. 1. 5). What in Gaul under Irenaeus was not heresy was regarded as heresy in Asia, where synods stirred up the faithful (V. 16. 9-10). Eusebius is aware that Tertullian became a Montanist. He knows that Gaius of Rome, an ecclesiastical man, wrote against Proclus, head of the Phrygian sect (γνώμη not αἵρεσις, II. 25. 6), and he is willing to cite Proclus himself on the daughters of Philip (III. 31. 4). It may be that Eusebius' own attitude toward the Montanists gradually hardened. More probably, however, his various statements reflect various attitudes in his sources. In the *Chronicle* (p. 206) he referred to 'false prophecy' and to 'insane seers'.[17]

Ebionites — Artemon — Paul of Samosata; Sabellius; Novatian

After relying on Irenaeus and Justin for his account of Menander (III. 26) Eusebius turns to a different kind of group led astray by 'the evil demon'. These are the Ebionites (III. 27). He describes them almost exclusively in accordance with comments made by Origen,[18] though Irenaeus too noted that they rejected the apostle Paul.[19] As for their maintenance of both Sabbath and Sunday, this may have been observed by Eusebius himself. The two classes of Ebionites, those who deny the Virgin Birth and those who affirm it, come from Origen, but presumably Eusebius mentions the second class so that he can dissociate himself from 'mere man' Christology in which the Virgin Birth is accepted.[20]

Eusebius mentions Ebionites again when he is quoting Irenaeus on Greek version of the Old Testament (V. 8. 10). Both Theodotion and Aquila, according to Irenaeus, were 'Jewish proselytes'. When the Ebionites followed their version of Isaiah 7:14, with its prediction that a 'young woman', not a 'virgin', would bear a son, they used this translation to back up their view that Jesus was begotten by Joseph. We find further erudition in VI. 17, where Eusebius explains that Symmachus, another Old Testament translator, was also an Ebionite. He adds that the Ebionites consider the Christ to be 'a mere man' and keep the law 'in rather Jewish fashion'.

The last chapter of Book V brings us an anonymous treatise *Against the heresy of Artemon*. This book, to which Theodoret refers as 'the

---

[17] Eusebius also notes the continuance of prophetic and spiritual gifts in the second-century churches (IV. 18. 8; V. 7).
[18] *De princ.* IV. 3. 8; *Matt. comm.* XVI. 12; *C. Cels.* II. 1; V. 61. 65.
[19] *Adv. haer.* I. 26. 2.
[20] The discussion of Cerinthus (III. 28) belongs in Ch. IX (scripture).

little labyrinth',[21] is sometimes ascribed to Hippolytus but without cogent proof. In Eusebius' quotations there is no mention of Artemon. Instead, the heresy was inaugurated by a shoemaker named Theodotus, excommunicated by Victor of Rome (V. 28. 6, 9). Both Hippolytus and Pseudo-Tertullian definitely state that Theodotus regarded Jesus or Christ as an ordinary man, though born of a virgin.[22] His Christology was Ebionite in so far as Origen's second class of Ebionites were really Ebionites. We thus see that Eusebius is tracing a line of succession from Ebionites Class II to Artemon/Theodotus.

He is about to trace the line farther in order to reach Paul of Samosata. From his anonymous document he quotes a story showing how both angels and a bishop of Rome rebuked an Adoptianist bishop who was excessively concerned with rank and fond of filthy lucre (V. 28. 12). He therefore anticipated the attitude of the proud and avaricious Paul (VII. 30. 7-9). The logic-chopping exegesis of the earlier group[23] may be viewed as like the efforts of Paul to show that psalms addressed to Christ were 'modern and the compositions of modern men' (VII. 30. 10). Certainly the writer against Artemon insisted that 'all the psalms and hymns written by faithful brothers from the beginning praise Christ as the Word of God and speak of him as God' (V. 28. 6). One wonders if the anti-Artemonist is not writing in Paul's time, not earlier in the third century.

In the anti-Pauline dossier which Eusebius used, the Synod at Antioch delivered Paul to his predecessor Artemas (VII. 30. 16, 18), and Eusebius supposed that he was the same as Artemon (V. 28. 1). Epiphanius followed him in holding that Paul 'renewed the heresy of Artemon'.[24] Theodoret as usual favoured synthesis.[25] Perhaps the difference reflects no more that a personal preference. Eusebius preferred Artemon.[26] His opponents insisted on Artemas.[27]

What was wrong with Paul? When Eusebius introduces him in the *History* (VII. 27. 2) he simply repeats the first part of his discussion of the Ebionites (III. 27. 1-2). As he goes on with the story he argues that Paul tried to conceal his heterodoxy (VII. 28. 2), later called

---

[21] *Haer. fab.* II. 5 (*PG* 83, 392B).
[22] Hippolytus, *Ref.* VII. 35, 2; Pseudo-Tertullian, *Adv. omn. haer.* 8. 2.
[23] Cf. R. Walzer, *Galen on Jews and Christians* (Oxford, 1949), 75–86.
[24] *Haer.* LXV. 1. 4.   [25] *Haer. fab.* II. 4.
[26] *Ecl. proph.* (205. 12 Gaisford).
[27] Anti-Origenist in Pamphilus, *Apol. Orig.* I (*PG* 17, 578C–9A); Methodius, *Sympos.* VIII. 10; Alexander of Alexandria in Theodoret, *H. E.* 1. 4. 35.

'perverse' (30. 1). He describes the abilities of Paul's chief opponent and his use of stenographers to smoke out the heresy.[28] Quotations from the letter condemnatory lay emphasis on the personal problems involved, though there is one reference to notes taken on doctrinal matters. This is thoroughly characteristic of the *Church History*, in which one could glean only from VI. 36. 4 that Origen was accused of heresy. Here, it seems, Eusebius is simplifying and expects his readers to interpret Paul in the light of the Ebionites and Artemon/Artemas.

There was nothing novel about this sequence in Eusebius' time. Opponents of Origen had named Artemas and Paul. Methodius, in a passage perhaps not genuine,[28a] named errorists about the Son as like Artemas, about the Spirit, as Ebionites.[29] Alexander of Alexandria denounced Ebion, Artemas, and Paul of Samosata. Eusebius therefore fused his accounts of all three in his own effort to denounce 'mere man' Christologies[30] and differentiate his own Christology from such views. He could join his own opponents in attacking some of the dead.

Almost at the other extreme from 'mere man' Christology stood the theology of a certain Sabellius, whose views may be given the slogan 'mere God'. From Eusebius' *History* we learn absolutely nothing about them. From Dionysius of Alexandria he quotes just enough to show that the doctrine had spread recently and that it was irreligious and contained 'much blasphemy in regard to the almighty God, Father of our Lord Jesus Christ, much unbelief in regard to his only Child, the firstborn of all creation, the Word who became incarnate, as well as lack of perception in regard to the Holy Spirit' (VII. 6). This abusive language tells us little about what the Sabellians actually believed.

Dionysius also provided guidance for accusing opponents of implicit heresy. Novatian, he wrote, 'divided the church and drew some of the brethren to impieties and blasphemies [again!] and introduced most unholy teaching about God and falsely accuses our most compassionate Lord Jesus Christ of being without mercy'. Novatian also 'rejects the holy washing and overturns the faith and confession that precede it and absolutely puts the Holy Spirit to flight from among them'

---

[28] Cf. M. Richard, 'Malchion et Paul de Samosate: Le témoignage d'Eusèbe de Césarée', *ETL* 35 (1959), 325–38.

[28a] Methodius, *Sympos.* viii. 10.

[29] Cf. H. Musurillo, *St. Methodius: The Symposium* (Westminster, Md., 1958), 223–4.

[30] III. 27. 2; V. 8. 10; 28. 2, 6; VI. 17. 1; VII. 27. 2; cf. 30. 11.

(VII. 8). This chapter is entitled 'On the heterodoxy of Novatian', but it is clear that the heterodoxy was in the eye of the Alexandrian bishop who inferred heresy from schism. Eusebius followed this lead and accused Novatian of arrogance, hatred of the brethren, and inhumanity (VI. 43. 2). In addition, he was a 'founder of heresy' (see page 85). Eusebius believed it important to attack Novatian because of his rigorist attitude toward the lapsed in the persecution under Decius. Thus he praised Pionius for his 'correction and comfort to those who had fallen under temptation in the persecution' (IV. 15. 47) and contrasted the Gallicans' love for the brethren who had fallen with the 'inhuman and merciless attitude of those who after these events acted harshly to the members of Christ' (V. 2. 8). Eusebius says nothing about either the Melitians or the Donatists, successors of the rigorists during the last persecution. From his hints toward the end of the *Martyrs of Palestine* (ch. 12) it is evident that he shared Constantine's view of such persons, who 'even now do not stop perpetuating their private enmities' and 'are separate from one another in a disgraceful or, rather, abominable fashion'. If he could say that they were 'forgetful both of their own salvation and of the reverence they owe their most holy religion (αἵρεσις)', it is clear that Constantine or his translator did not have heresy in mind but that reference to it lay close by (X. 5. 22). It was hard for early Christians to differentiate heresy from schism.

The Manichees

The last heresy discussed in the *Church History* is that of the Manichees. Eusebius provides a minimum of information, a maximum of invective, perhaps because Jerusalem and Caesarea lay close to what had become the main route of westbound Manichaean missionaries in the late third century.[31] He tells us that the heresy is barbaric, demonic, and manic. Mani called himself the Christ, the Paraclete, and the Holy Spirit; like Jesus he had twelve disciples (VII. 31).

Eusebius' description of the Manichaean mission seems to contain echoes of phrases used by Diocletian in an imperial letter of 297.[32] Eusebius' 'from the land of the Persians' recalls Diocletian's 'from the

---

[31] Cf. E. de Stoop, *Essai sur la diffusion du manichéisme dans l'empire romain* (Ghent, 1909), 57–72.

[32] *Coll. leg. mos. et rom.* XV. 3. For the date as possibly 302 cf. H. Chadwick, 'The Relativity of Moral Codes: Rome and Persia in Late Antiquity', in W. R. Schoedel–R. L. Wilken, *Early Christian Literature and the Classical Intellectual Tradition* (Paris, 1979), 135–53, esp. 142.

Persian race hostile to us'. The ecclesiastic writes that it came 'into our whole world like some deadly poison'. The emperor refers to 'our whole world' and says 'like the poison of some deadly snake'. To be sure, Eusebius thought that Montanists too moved like some poisonous reptile (V. 14). But the ensemble of his remarks suggests that he may have had one eye on an official document, or at least on an official attitude. He assisted the imperial effort to repress a foreign religion by condemning it as a Christian heresy. Non-Christian readers of his book would become aware that orthodox Christianity was responsibly Roman.[33]

Other Christians shared Eusebius' view of the Manichees. Some Alexandrian bishop, perhaps Theonas, denounced them in a letter still extant on papyrus.[34] The hermit Anthony refused to be in communion with Manichees or any other heretics.[35] And in his later *Theophany* (IV. 30. 3–5; cf. 34) Eusebius listed important heretics as Marcionites, Valentinians and Basilidians, Bardesanes, and the sect of the Manichees. Athanasius took the same line. In his treatise *De synodis* he denounced Valentinians, Phrygians, and Manichees.[36]

Ecclesiastics thus viewed Manichaeism as a Christian heresy. This was not the opinion of the Manichees themselves or of the Roman emperors of the early fourth century. When Constantine condemned various Christian heretics he listed Valentinians, Marcionites, the followers of Paul of Samosata, and Phrygians.[37] Originally he thought that Novatianists were heretics too, but probably because of personal contacts with a Novatianist observer-bishop at Nicaea he changed his mind.[38] Responsible imperial ideas about heresy were thus rather different from those of the orthodox bishops. Constantine himself actually took the trouble to look into 'the sects of the superstitions, of the Manichees and the like', and acquired the services of a translator to help him with Greek books. The translator did a good job and was eventually promoted to the rank of praetorian prefect in the diocese of Oriens.[39]

[33] Cf. 'Manichees and Christians in the third and early fourth centuries', in *Ex orbe religionum: Studia Geo Widengren* (Leiden, 1972), I, 430–9.

[34] P. Ryl. iii. 469, where we find four references to 'mania'.

[35] Athanasius, *Vit. Ant.* 68 (*PG* 26, 940B).

[36] *De syn.* 13. 4 (241. 10 Opitz). Athanasius names only the heretics noted by Eusebius (*PG* 26, 16C–17A; 800A; 804A) except, of course, for Arians (1165A).

[37] Eusebius, *Vit. Const.* III. 64. 1.

[38] *Cod. Theod.* XVI. 5. 2; Socrates, *H. E.* I. 10.

[39] Ammianus Marcellinus, XV. 13. 2.

Conclusion

In the opinion of Eusebius and his anti-heretical predecessors there was nothing good about heresy or heretics. The Devil worked through heresy in order to darken 'the radiance of the universal and only true church' which 'always holds the same doctrines in the same way' (IV. 7. 13). Heresy is evil not only because of its falsity but because it leads to division. Eusebius obviously shared the view quoted from Dionysius of Alexandria (VI. 45): 'One ought to suffer anything for the sake of not cutting apart the church of God. It would not be less glorious to suffer martyrdom to avoid schism than to avoid idolatry. In my opinion, it would be more glorious.' Long-dead heresies disturbed the unity of the Church and Eusebius is eager to criticize them. Both Montanism and Novatianism have led to schism. And by treating Manichaeism as a Christian heresy Eusebius can point to a foe against whom Christians can unite. By severely criticizing Paul of Samosata he can dissociate his own doctrine from Paul's theology and his own person from Paul's questionable behaviour.

After discussing enemies of the Church who at one time or another dwelt inside it, Eusebius turns to two outside groups which he also regards as enemies: first the Jews and then the Graeco-Roman persecutors of Christianity.

IX

THE FOURTH THEME: THE FATE OF THE JEWS

At the beginning of the *Church History* Eusebius explicitly promised to discuss 'the consequences which came upon the whole nation of the Jews for the plot against our Saviour'. He apparently derived the notion of Jewish plots, along with the word ἐπιβουλή, from the Acts of the Apostles.[1] Others had spoken of plots; indeed, the *Church History* itself is full of them. Eusebius mentions plots against his hero Origen, and Origen mentions them himself.[2] The idea of consequences falling upon 'the whole nation of the Jews', however, clearly involves an interpretation of the fall of Jerusalem in the year 70, and in the course of the *Church History* it becomes clear that Eusebius connects this event with the crucifixion of Jesus.

Other attempts had been made to explain the fall of the city, notably by the Hellenistic Jewish general and historian Josephus. He ascribed it primarily to sedition and the rise of tyrants as rulers in Jerusalem.[3] Christian writers had frequently discussed the topic but had not connected the fall with the crucifixion until early in the third century, when Tertullian developed the theme in his treatise *Adversus Marcionem*.[4] We should certainly not suppose that Eusebius got the idea from any Latin writer. Instead, he indubitably derived it from the Alexandrian–Caesarean theologian Origen, and specifically from works produced in Origen's later years at Caesarea.

Eusebius relied not only on Origen's theological point or points but also on his interpretations of first-century Christian and Jewish historical details. We intend to examine these details and then turn to conclusions.

It was helpful to correlate the Gospel accounts of the crucifixion of Jesus with statements made by non-Christian chronologists. Early

---

[1] Acts 9:24, 20:3, 19; 23:30; see also Origen, *De princ.* IV. 1. 5.
[2] Eusebius, *H. E.* VI. 3. 5; Origen, *Ioh. comm.* VI. 2, p. 108, 8–9 Preuschen.
[3] *Bell.* 1. 10; cf. II. 454–7; 539; III. 351–4; IV. 104; 137; 147–57; 318–25; etc.
[4] *Adv. Marc.* III. 23. 4–5 (*Adv. Iud.* 13. 27–8). One could mention Melito of Sardis, *Pasch. hom.* 99, but because of the author's rhetorical polemic (on which cf. K. W. Noakes, 'Melito of Sardis and the Jews', *TU* 116, 1975, 244-9) the reference is not clear. See also O. Perler, *Méliton de Sardes Sur la Pâque* (Paris, 1966), 198-9.

Christian apologists were able to find two such writers apart from the more important Hellentistic Jewish authors Philo and Josephus. These two were a Euhemerist antiquarian, of uncertain date, named Thallus,[5] and a freedman of Hadrian named Phlegon.[6] Thallus deserves little attention. Jacoby's first Testimonium, from the Armenian version of the *Chronicle* of Eusebius, states that Thallus dealt with events from the capture of Troy to the 167th Olympiad (112-109 BC). This is almost certainly wrong, not only because Thallus is said to have discussed an eclipse in the fourth year of the 202nd Olympiad 'in the third book of his *Histories*' but also because, according to Theophilus of Antioch, he held that Belos, king of the Assyrians, lived 322 years before the Trojan War.[7] Our primary concern is with the fragment on the eclipse. It comes from the Christian chronographer Julius Africanus, who wrote of the darkness at the time of the crucifixion that 'Thallus calls this darkness a solar eclipse — unreasonably, it seems to me'.[8] The unreasonableness was of course related to the time of the crucifixion, at Passover, when with a full moon a solar eclipse is impossible. It remains uncertain whether Thallus actually mentioned the 'darkness' or not. Perhaps he simply mentioned the solar eclipse of 24 November 29.[9] The references to solar eclipse, Bithynian earthquake, and the collapse of buildings in Nicaea — cited by Eusebius without reference to author[10] — may come from him.

Phlegon should be taken more seriously.[11] It looks as though he actually discussed Jesus, though not very accurately. According to Origen, in the thirteenth or fourteenth book of his *Chronicle* Phlegon 'even grants to Christ foreknowledge of certain future events, although he was muddled and said that some things which really happened to Peter happened to Jesus; and he testified that it turned out in accordance with what Jesus had said'. As for the precise reference Origen betrays his own vagueness by adding 'I think' to the book

---

[5] F. Jacoby, *FGrHist*, No. 256. The collection is not quite properly arranged because it neglects the use of one author by another.

[6] Ibid., No. 257.

[7] Theophilus (F 2-3 Jacoby) is the source of Jacoby's T 3 and F 4.

[8] *FGrHist*, 256, F 1.

[9] If so, it would be pointless to treat him as the source of Tertullian, *Apol.* 5. 1-2, and Eusebius, *H. E.* II. 2. 5; cf. C. Cecchelli, 'Un tentato riconoscimento imperiale del Cristo', *Scritti in onore di A. Calderini e R. Paribeni*, i (Milan, 1956), 351-62.

[10] *Chron. Lat.*, p. 174 Helm; Greek in Syncellus, *CSHB* I, 614, 10-11.

[11] Cf. P. de Labriolle, *La Réaction païenne* (Paris, 1934), 204-20.

numbers.[12] It is hard to tell just what he had in mind, except that in the *Commentary on Matthew* Origen relies on Phlegon for the fact that the destruction of Jerusalem and the Temple took place in about the 40th year from the 15th year of Tiberius Caesar.[13] Surely Phlegon would not have mentioned that year of Tiberius had he not been concerned with the Christian Gospel. Again in Phlegon's thirteenth or fourteenth book, 'I think', Origen knew that there were accounts of the eclipse 'in the time of Tiberius Caesar, during whose reign Jesus appears to have been crucified', and of 'the great earthquakes that happened at that time'.[14] The *Commentary on Matthew* again adds an important detail: 'Phlegon . . . wrote that this happened, but he did not indicate that it happened at full moon.'[15]

What looks like an explicit quotation is to be found in the *Chronicle* of Eusebius, where we read that in the thirteenth book Phlegon writes that:[16]

And in the fourth year of the 202nd Olympiad there was a great eclipse of the sun, surpassing all that came before it. At the sixth hour the day was turned into such complete darkness that the stars were seen in the sky; earthquakes in Bithynia overturned many buildings in the city of Nicaea.

The essence of the quotation recurs in Philoponus' treatise *De opificio mundi*.[17] There is no reason to question its authenticity. If the year was actually Ol. 202, 4, there was an eclipse of the moon on 3 April 33, and this may be what Phlegon had in mind. There is also little reason to suppose that Phlegon had the events related to Jesus in mind when he was writing such words. A passage now to be found in the remains of Africanus' *Chronicle* suggests that Phlegon actually dealt with a miraculous eclipse at the time of the crucifixion, but this is open to a good deal of suspicion. The fragment reads that 'Phlegon says that under Tiberius Caesar there was a total eclipse of the sun when the moon was full, from the sixth hour to the ninth. Clearly this is the same' as the one hinted at in the Gospels.[18] First, Africanus has already dealt with the so-called eclipse described by Thallus and has stated

---

[12] Origen, *C. Cels.* II. 14.
[13] *Matt. ser.* 40; actually 42 years later, *Jer. hom.* XIV. 13 (cited below).
[14] *C. Cels.* II. 33 (cf. 59).   [15] *Matt. ser.* 134.
[16] *Chron. Lat.*, pp. 174–5 Helm.   [17] *FGrHist*, 257, F 16 (c).
[18] Africanus, Fr. 50 Routh (*Reliquiae sacrae*, ed. 2, II. 298, 6–8), from Syncellus (*CSHB* I, 610, 12–14).

that he rejects the running together of this with the Gospels. Second, since he has dealt with Thallus there was no reason for him to deal with the analogous account in Phlegon and then accept it. The passage is to be viewed as a late interpolation by someone with more piety than intelligence.[19] It is not the normal third- or fourth-century view.

Writers about predictions and eclipses might contribute something toward confirming the Christian pictures of historical events. Obviously they did not contribute much. For greater support it was neccessary to turn to the writings of Hellenistic Jewish authors like Philo and Josephus, especially since their writings were being preserved chiefly by Christians rather than Jews, and specifically in support of apologetic theology. Since they lived and wrote in the first Christian century it could be expected that they would lend support if not credibility to the Christian accounts.

The account of Jesus now found in Josephus' *Antiquities* (XVIII. 63–4) presents many difficulties, not the least being the fact that in its present form it is essentially Christian. 'He was the Christ . . . For he appeared to them, alive again, on the third day, since the divine prophets foretold these and countless other marvels concerning him.' If Josephus said anything about Jesus, it cannot have been so complimentary, as his reference to 'the brother of the so-called Christ' (*Ant.* XX. 200) shows. In addition, Origen explicitly testifies that Josephus did not 'accept' or 'believe in' Jesus as Christ.[20] The passage, at least in its present form, cannot have stood in Origen's manuscript of Josephus, the one available in the school library at Caesarea. C. Martin has suggested that the Christian statements to which we have referred come from marginal notes in the manuscript, used by Origen or even made by him.[21] Such a suggestion has the merit of agreeing with Origen's comments and explaining how it was that Eusebius of Caesarea made use of the whole passage.[22] We may add that the passage was certainly absent from the text of Josephus which Photius carefully excerpted at Constantinople in the ninth century. Photius diligently noted the deaths of John the Precursor and James the Lord's brother, but simply said of Herod Antipas that 'in his time the salvific Passion

---

[19] Routh, op. cit., 478; Labriolle, op. cit., 210.

[20] *Matt. comm.* X. 17; *C. Cels.* I. 47.

[21] 'Le "testimonium flavianum": vers une solution definitive?', *Revue Belge de philologie et d'histoire*, 20 (1941), 416; cf. 461–2.

[22] *H. E.* I. 11. 7–8; *Dem. Ev.* III. 3, 105–6; *Theoph.* V. 44. See D. S. Wallace-Hadrill, 'Eusebius of Caesarea and the *Testimonium Flavianum*', *JEH* 25 (1974), 353–62.

took place.'[23] The question of evidence was important to Photius. In writing on the *Chronicle* of Justus of Tiberias he took pains to point out that Justus wrote nothing about Christ.[24]

The account of John the Baptist was more certainly present in the text of Josephus' *Antiquities* (XVIII. 116-19). The tetrarch Herod feared sedition or revolt because of John's preaching, even though he had urged nothing but virtue and piety, and therefore executed him. The moral Josephus draws is one which his Christian readers found attractive. 'To some of the Jews the [later] destruction of Herod's army seemed to be divine vengeance, and certainly a just vengeance, for his treatment of John.' Again, 'the destruction visited upon Herod's army was a vindication of John, since God saw fit to inflict such a blow on Herod.' Origen, and especially Eusebius, shared this kind of view.

Origen referred to the passage but interpreted it in his own special way.[25] Josephus has written that piety had to precede John's baptism. It was to be employed 'not for the pardon of various sins but for the purification of the body when the soul had already been cleansed by righteousness'. Such a description is not entirely different from what could be found in early Christian baptism, which obviously involved at least the intention of righteousness. But there are different emphases in the two cases. Origen made John's baptism thoroughly Christian, claiming that he was simply relying on Josephus. 'A man who lived not long after John and Jesus recorded that John was a baptist who baptized for the remission of sins. For Josephus in the eighteenth book of the Jewish antiquities bears witness that John was a baptist who baptized for the remission of sins.' The expression 'for the remission of sins' is thoroughly Christian and Josephus did not use it.

Eusebius cites the passage about John the Baptist as 'confirming the testimony recorded in the gospel writings about him' but more sensibly refrains from discussing the kind of baptism provided by John.[26] In the *Demonstratio* he is concerned with John as fulfilling the prophecy of 'a voice crying in the desert' (Isaiah 40) and speaks of him as proclaiming 'the cleansing of the soul'.[27] These words prove that Eusebius knew the whole passage from Josephus, though in quoting it here he brought it to a close just before the clause, 'not for the pardon of

---

[23] Cf. A. C. Bouquet, 'The References to Josephus in the Bibliotheca of Photius', *JTS* 36 (1935), 289-93. These passages in Photius occur in Cod. 238 (*PG* 103, 1188B-C and 1192B).

[24] *Cod.* 33 (*PG* 103, 66B).

[25] *C. Cels.* I. 47.

[26] I. 11. 4-6.

[27] *Dem. Ev.* IX. 5. 15.

various sins but for the purification of the body when the soul had already been cleansed by righteousness'. Eusebius obviously suppressed this as contradicting the Gospel accounts.

It is sometimes supposed that Origen made use of Josephus' description of the false prophet Theudas (*Antiquities*, XX. 97, followed by a reference to the rebel leader Judas in 102). Such a supposition is quite unnecessary. In his *Commentary on John* Origen referred to Theudas as coming before Judas but he did so not on account of any correct or incorrect reading of Josephus. He was following Acts 5:36-7 and, indeed, quoting part of verse 37.[28]

More important is what later Christian writers do with Josephus' account of James the Lord's brother (*Antiquities*, XX. 197-203). The earliest witness to the Josephan account might be supposed to be Hegesippus, as cited by Eusebius in the *Church History* (II. 23. 16-17). In this section of Hegesippus' work, as in Josephus, James is described as being stoned. But the account of Hegesippus is so confused, portraying James as thrown down from the wing of the Temple, stoned, and struck on the head with a launderer's club, that E. Schwartz thought the mention of stoning had been interpolated – though in any case from Josephus.[29] In the Nag Hammadi *Second Apocalypse* James is thrown down and then stoned in a peculiar way.[30] Probably one should conclude that neither Hegesippus nor the author of this apocalypse was acquainted with Josephus' story of the death of James. And certinly it was unknown at Alexandria. According to the *Hypotyposes* of Clement, James the Just 'was thrown down from the wing of the temple and beaten to death with a launderer's club'.[31] It is precisely the stoning mentioned by Josephus that is omitted. Clement did not know Josephus' account. Similarly Origen is ignorant of it, at least in the form in which it is known to others. He makes no reference to a 'political' narrative like the one Josephus gives. Instead, he refers twice to the theological consequences of James's death in such a way as to suggest that his interpretation has somehow replaced the original text. The first example occurs in the *Commentary on Matthew*.[32]

---

[28] *Ioh. comm.* VI. 9.
[29] 'Zu Eusebius Kirchengeschichte I. Das Martyrium Jakobus des Gerechten', *ZNW* 4 (1903), 48-61; cf. W.-P. Funk, *Die Zweite Apokalypse des Jakobus aus Nag-Hammadi-Codex V* (*TU* 119, 1976), 172-6.
[30] Cf. A. Böhlig, 'Zum Martyrium des Jakobus', *Novum Testamentum*, 5 (1962), 207-13.
[31] Eusebius, *H. E.* II. 1. 5 (cf. 23. 3).
[32] *Matt. comm.* X. 17.

Josephus . . . desirous of setting forth the reason for which the people experienced such suffering that even the temple was destroyed, stated that these things happened to them in accordance with the wrath of God because of what they ventured to do to James the brother of Jesus the so-called Christ. What is marvellous is that though Josephus did not accept our Jesus as Christ, he none the less ascribed such righteousness to James: he says that the people supposed that they suffered these things on account of James.

Origen rightly states that Josephus was concerned with the causes for the destruction of Jerusalem. The theme comes up repeatedly, especially in the *Jewish War* but also in the *Jewish Antiquities*. But there is one cause for the catastrophe which Josephus never mentions, and that is the execution of James under the high priest Ananus. Indeed, in the *Jewish War* Josephus argued that the sack of Jerusalem took its beginning from the murder of Ananus by revolutionary forces. 'The overthrow of the wall and the downfall of the Jewish state dated from the day on which the Jews beheld their high priest, the captain of their salvation, slain in the middle of the city.'[33] The oddness of this is all the greater because, as my father noted, the expression 'captain of salvation' recalls what is said of Jesus in Hebrews 2:10, while 'slain in the middle of the city' is how Melito of Sardis describes Jesus in his *Paschal Homily*.[34] What Josephus does in the *Jewish War* is ascribe cosmic significance to the death of the high priest Ananus. On the other hand, by the time he comes to describe him in the *Antiquities* and his own autobiography he is more unfavourably impressed by Ananus. acceptance of bribes to expel Josephus himself from Galilee,[35] and therefore he is glad to describe his judicial murder of James, 'brother of the so-called Christ', in an account which Origen could have used had he known it. What Origen seems to know, however, is an account in which the death of James actually led to the fall of Jerusalem, just as in Hegesippus' Christian narrative we have first the death of James and then the statement that 'and at once Vespasian began to besiege them.'[36] What he has in common with the real Josephus is no more than the name of James's brother, 'the so-called Christ', and James's death.

Origen takes up this subject again in *Contra Celsum*, I. 47, where he reiterates the thought that Josephus, though a non-believer, was seeking

[33] *Bell*. IV. 318.
[34] *Pasch. hom.* 523, 710, 712, 724–5 Perler.
[35] *Vit*. 196.
[36] Eusebius, *H. E.* II. 23. 18.

for the reason for the fall of Jerusalem and the destruction of the Temple.

He should have said that the plot against Jesus was the cause of these disasters for the people, since they killed the predicted Christ; but as if unwillingly coming not far from the truth he said that these things occurred to the Jews to avenge James the Just, who was the brother of Jesus the so-called Christ.

Origen sums up his argument a little farther on.

If then he says that the events related to the devastation of Jerusalem took place for the Jews because of James, is it not more reasonable to say that they took place because of Jesus the Christ?

It is clear that Origen has a text of Josephus that has already been altered away from Josephus' own reading of the events in the direction of a Christian theodicy rather than a Jewish one. Origen also twice states that James was famous for his righteousness or justice; this note, ascribed to Josephus, comes from the Christian tradition. But Origen does not go quite so far as to quote Josephus directly on the subject of the death of James. Similarly Eusebius, writing his early *Chronicle*, contents himself with stating that 'James the Lord's brother, whom all called the Just, was killed by stoning by the Jews.'[37] The notion of James as 'the Just' is Christian, but the death by stoning is from Josephus, as is the date in Nero's seventh year (AD 60–61 or 61–62). This must of course be approximately correct for Albinus' arrival after the death of James, for according to Josephus, *Bell.* VI. 300 and 305, Albinus was governor four years before the war, i.e. in 62.

When Eusebius wrote the *Chronicle*, we can see, he did not know or was not impressed by the account of Hegesippus, according to which James was rather more than stoned and in addition was put to death immediately before the siege of Jerusalem by Vespasian, probably in 69. He knew some Christian story on the subject but his primary source was the real Josephus.

In producing the *Church History*, however, we took Origen's comments much more seriously. Thus after quoting Hegesippus' story of the death of James and insisting (wrongly) that it agrees with Clement's, he goes on to say that 'James was so famous for his righteousness that intelligent Jews supposed that this [his death] was the cause of the siege of Jerusalem immediately after his martyrdom; it happened because of nothing else but the crime they had committed

[37] *Chron.*, pp. 182–3 Helm.

against him.'[38] Who are the intelligent Jews? None other than Josephus himself, as described by Origen in the *Commentary on Matthew*: 'He says that the people too thought that they suffered these things on account of James.' The word 'cause' (αἰτία), used in regard to Josephus' search, also comes from Origen's accounts. The word 'immediately', however, was added by Eusebius himself when he tried to connect his Origenist Josephus with the fanciful account given by Hegesippus. It was Hegesippus, not Josephus, who supposed that the siege of Jerusalem began immediately after the death of James.

Eusebius was not content with a periphrastic statement about Josephus. He wanted to appeal to Josephus himself as his authority. He therefore did so. 'As a matter of fact Josephus did not hesitate to testify to this in writing, when he speaks in the following terms: "Now these things happened to the Jews to avenge James the Just, who was a brother of Jesus the so-called Christ, since the Jews killed him though he was the most righteous of men."'[39] This is exactly what Origen had claimed Josephus said; this time the language comes from the treatise *Contra Celsum*, adjusted from indirect to direct discourse. Unlike Origen, however, Eusebius looked up the passage about James in Josephus' *Antiquities* and found it in the twentieth book. It was too valuable a passage to omit from the *Church History*, even though it did not contain the passage Origen had mentioned. Eusebius therefore proceeded to quote it.[40]

By this time he was somewhat confused, since (no matter what he says about them) his sources did not agree on crucial matters. Hegesippus called James's opponents 'scribes and Pharisees', while Josephus called the hostile high priest a Sadducee and claimed that 'strict observers of the law' (Pharisees) opposed him. Hegesippus set the siege of Jerusalem just after James's death, while according to the chronology of Josephus, it took place six or seven years later.

Apparently Eusebius at first maintained the view of Josephus, already followed in the *Chronicle*. He dates Paul's appeal to Caesar and Festus' rule in Judaea early in the reign of Nero, certainly not later than 62. For this reason he could quote a lengthy passage from the *Jewish War* in which Josephus definitely placed the rule of Albinus, procurator just after James's death, 'four years before the war'.[41] When he began

---

[38] *H. E.* II. 23. 19. For wise Jews as interpreters cf. Josephus, *Bell.* VI. 313.
[39] Ibid., 21–4.   [40] Ibid., 22. 8–23. 1.
[41] Ibid., III. 8. 7 (Josephus, *Bell.* VI. 300).

making use of Hegesippus it was necessary to do a good deal of tinkering. He made the extraordinary claim that Hegisippus belonged to the first 'succession' from the apostles and added that he gave the most accurate account of James's death.[42] Next he added the word 'immediately' to his first Origenist Josephus notice. He probably deleted the part of the story of Jesus son of Ananias in which the Roman governor was identified as Albinus.[43] And in writing Book III, still using Hegesippus, he referred to 'the martyrdom of James and the capture of Jerusalem that took place immediately afterward'.[44] All these passages illustrate the confusion resulting from contradictory sources.

In any case, by the time we reach the present state of the *Church History* the authentic text of Josephus is still present (as it was not for Origen) but it has been devalued in favour of the Origenist Josephus and Hegesippus.

Apart from episodes related to Jesus, John, and James, it was important for Christian authors to find Hellenistic Jewish support for the narratives related to the beginnings of Jewish suffering — the suffering so well deserved on account of the crucifixion. In dealing with this subject we shall vary our usual procedure and deal first with the full-blown legendary picture to be found in Eusebius' writings, then with the way in which this picture was developed. Actually we should speak of two legendary pictures, for the one in the *Chronicle* is different from the one in the *Demonstratio*. In the *Chronicle* Eusebius first discusses his pagan authorities for earthquake and eclipse, then turns to Josephus as his authority for a startling event 'around these times on the day of Pentecost'.[45] Priests experienced an earthquake and heard a voice saying, 'Let us go forth from this place.' Josephus also told how 'in the same year' at night Pilate put images of Caesar in the Temple.[46] And this was the first cause of sedition and disturbances for the Jews.' Presumably Eusebius was aware that Origen had discussed both these passages from Josephus. Like Josephus himself, Origen had given no date for the voices in the Temple.[47] This was Eusebius' contribution to this story. On the other hand, Origen

[42] Ibid., II. 23. 3.

[43] After *H. E.* III. 8. 9 the MSS ER add Josephus, *Bell.* VI. 305–9. Original or interpolation?

[44] *H. E.* III. 11.

[45] *Chron.*, p. 175; Josephus, *Bell.* VI. 299 (cf. Eusebius, *H. E.* III. 8. 6).

[46] *Bell.* II. 169 (no year mentioned, but apparently on Pilate's arrival in Judaea).

[47] *Lam. comm.*, fr. 109 Klostermann.

had stated that in the time of Pontius Pilate there was an attempt to set up a statue of Caesar in the Temple; another took place under Gaius.[48] Here Origen makes a contribution. He mixes up the episode of the military standards in Jerusalem under Pilate with that of the imperial statue in the Temple under Gaius. Unfortunately he led Eusebius astray, though the expression about the event as the first cause of sedition and disturbances seems to come from Josephus' own comment on 'very great disturbance'.

The second legendary picture is to be found in the *Demonstratio*. First Eusebius quotes the Pentecost story, noting that according to Josephus it took place after the passion of our Saviour. Then he paraphrases the account of the standards, with Josephus calling them 'images of Caesar' and claiming that they were brought by night into the Temple. Finally he comments on the 'very great disturbance' thus provoked, adding mention of trouble and sedition. Finally he claims that Philo corroborates this narrative when he says that imperial standards (Josephus' word, not Philo's) were set up in the Temple at night. Actually Philo mentions neither the Temple nor night.[49] We must be dealing with an Origenist picture of Philo or, more probably, Josephus.

One would like to imagine that Eusebius tinkered with his *Church History* after he had written passages like these. In any case, his discussion in the *History* is much more restrained. He has other axes to grind. He uses the Pentecost passage just as Josephus had used it, in the midst of a selection on omens before the fall of Jerusalem and even before the revolt.[50] The episode of the standards is still taken as punishment for crimes against the Saviour, but the standards do not go into the Temple.[51] To be sure, we are still told that according to Philo, Pilate 'attempted something contrary to Jewish law in regard to the temple then still standing in Jerusalem',[52] but we are not told what the something was. Maybe Eusebius has checked some of his references.

We have now gone through most of the quotations from earlier authors which Eusebius found meaningful as he was creating his picture of the crucifixion and the events related to it. Now we must move onward to the theological-historical inferences he drew, or claimed to have drawn, from the sequence of events in the first century. As we examine this question we shall see — it might as well be stated at once — that it was Origen, and specifically the Origen who wrote at Caesarea,

[48] *Matt. comm.* XVII. 25.   [49] *Dem. Ev.* VIII. 2. 121-3.
[50] III. 8. 6.   [51] II. 6. 4.   [52] II. 5. 7.

who influenced him in some of his wildest generalizations about the fate of the Jews in the first century. Our primary text will be the *Church History*, where his thoughts seem to be rather fully developed.

The basic points are set forth in two sections of the *History*. First comes II. 5. 6–10, 10, where we learn about the dire consequences of attacking either the Saviour or the apostles. In this section it is true that the final destruction of Jerusalem is presented as an important penalty, but most of the time the effects are immediate. The Jews like Pilate[53] suffer 'shortly afterwards' (II. 5. 6; 6. 5; 7), there is no long delay. Their penalites begin 'from the times of Pilate and the crimes against the Saviour' (II. 6. 3). To be sure, they will lead up to 'finally, the siege under Vespasian' (II. 6. 8). But after Herod Agrippa's attempt against the apostles the avenging minister of divine Justice will overtake him at once (II. 10. 1). It makes no difference that both in Acts and in Josephus the penalty is paid for deification. Second comes the more interesting passage, in which Eusebius explains the meaning of the fall of Jerusalem in relation to the crucifixion. This is to be found in III. 5. 2–8, 11. Most of the section consists of accurate quotations from Josephus, and we need not concern ourselves with them. Our purpose is to consider the historical-theological context in which Eusebius sets these materials. Basically, his setting consists of two parts: *H. E.* III. 5. 2–7, and III. 7. 7–9. We are primarily concerned with the fact that these two sections contain theological explanations of the timing of the fall of Jerusalem that are both inconsistent and not due to Eusebius himself. The first passage (III. 5. 2–7) explains that the Jews not only committed a crime against the Saviour but also plotted against his apostles — for example, Stephen, James son of Zebedee, and James of Jerusalem. The other apostles then went out on missionary journeys. Before the war, in addition, the people of the church in Jerusalem left the city in accordance with a divine oracle and migrated to Transjordanian Pella. The purpose was 'that when holy men had completely abandoned the royal metropolis of the Jews and the whole land of Judaea, the Justice of God might then visit upon them all their crimes against the Christ and his apostles, by making that generation of wicked persons completely vanish from among men'.

The flight to Pella may be interesting historically.[54] It appears that

---

[53] Celsus had asked why Pilate was not punished (Origen, *C. Cels.* II. 63. 67).

[54] Cf. S. S. Sowers, 'The Circumstances and Recollection of the Pella Flight', *Theologische Zeitschrift*, 26 (1970), 305–20; M. Simon, 'La Migration à Pella: légende ou réalité?', *RSR* 60 (1972), 37–54.

Jewish-Christian Ebionites flourished in the vicinity.[55] But as far as Eusebius' literary work is concerned, it matters only to clear Jerusalem for punishment. This generation already deserved drastic punishment, according to Josephus in a passage which Eusebius cited.[56] More than that, its vanishing is probably related to the general theme of vanishing as a fulfilment of Daniel 9:26, developed by Eusebius in III. 5. 3–4 and in the *Demonstratio* (VIII. 2. 124). But the idea that holy men protected Jerusalem until all this took place was already expressed by Origen in a rather ambiguous passage: 'As long as the word [i.e. the Logos] was with the Jews, not depriving them of the kingdom of God, so long the temple stood and the affairs of the Jews were protected.'[57] In a homily on Jeremiah written only a few years earlier, Origen clearly stated that 'the Logos of God abandoned the assembly of the Jews.'[58] In addition, though he uses the third person imperative in another homily, he is really describing past events when he says, 'Let the angels who always gave aid to Jerusalem ... abandon Jerusalem; her sins have become great, they have killed Jesus, they have laid hands upon Christ; as long as the sins were still minor, we could still make petition and exhort concerning them, we could spare Jerusalem, but who will spare after this crime?'[59] Presumably Eusebius historicizes the theological ideas of Origen by referring to the departure of the holy men. This is his primary concern: to summarize from Josephus 'how many' penalties of one sort or another came upon the Jews, to point out that (nearly) three million Jews must have attended Passover at Jerusalem, and to follow him in noting the coincidental date of the destruction of the Temple. Where Josephus compared the date with that of the first destruction of the Temple,[60] Eusebius compares it with that of the passion of Christ. He then goes on to give excerpts from Josephus about the punishment given by God for the crime against the Christ of God.[61]

A historian tends to historicize, especially if he has theological guidance. Origen had taught him that the 'seventy weeks until the coming of Christ the governor' predicted in Daniel 9:24 had already

---

[55] Cf. Epiphanius, *Haer.* XXX. 2. 7–8 (Ebion to Kokabe); Julius Africanus in Eusebius, *H. E.* I. 7. 14; Eusebius, *Onom.*, p. 172, 2–3 Klostermann.
[56] Josephus, *Bell.* V. 566 (*H. E.* III. 6. 16); cf. V. 442–5; VI. 408.
[57] *Matt. comm. ser.* 29.   [58] *Jer. hom.* XIV. 15.
[59] *Jer. hom.* XIII. 1.   [60] *Bell.* VI. 250; 268.
[61] III. 5. 7 (cf. 5. 6; 7. 1). The term is Lucan (9:20; cf. 23:35) and Jewish (Origen, *C. Cels.* I. 49).

taken place. They were no longer in the future.[62] Eusebius shared this view and denounced a writer of Origen's time who thought they were still future.[63] Thus it is not surprising that underneath his comments on the fall of Jerusalem is an emphasis on the fulfilment of Daniel's predictions (Dan. 9:25–7). We hear of the mysterious 'disappearance' or 'vanishing' of 'that generation' and of the Temple itself (Dan. 9:26). And we learn that 'the abomination of desolation announced by the prophets was set up in that famous temple formerly God's' (Dan. 9:27). Comparison with the *Eclogae propheticae* and the *Demonstratio* shows how important Eusebius found the theme. His eschatology is historicized, not futuristic.[64]

The second passage again owes much to Origen, as well as to Josephus. It speaks of 'the philanthropy of the all-good providence' which respected the protection given by apostles living in Jerusalem, especially James, and exhibited patience in case the Jews repented. Oddly enough, Josephus says something like this in regard to the Emperor Titus. 'Throughout the war he had compassion on the populace, walled in by the insurrectionists, and many times he put off the capture of the city and by means of the siege gave the guilty ones time for repentance.'[65] Of course 'philanthropy' and 'providence' are characteristic of God and emperors alike. Origen, on the other hand, insisted that God's longsuffering had come to an end after the crucifixion.[66]

If you examine the date of the passion, that of the fall of Jerusalem and of the destruction of the city, and in what way God abandoned this people because they had killed Christ, you will see that God did not use longsuffering with this people! Or if you prefer, listen: from the 15th year of Tiberius Caesar to the destruction of the temple there were only 42 years. A little time for repentance had to be allowed, especially because of those who were to be converted from the people by the signs and wonders to be achieved by the apostles.

These forty-two years, presumably from Phlegon as suggested earlier, turn into 'forty whole years' when Eusebius paraphrases the passage. He too is concerned with God's longsuffering but he wants to insist upon

---

[62] Origen, *De princ.* IV. 1. 5.   [63] VI. 7.

[64] R. Wilken points out that in writing against the Christians Porphyry too had treated Daniel's predictions as fulfilled — but under Antiochus Epiphanes. Eusebius finds a different time for fulfilment but agrees that it lies in the past.

[65] Josephus, *Bell.* I. 10.

[66] Origen, *Jer. hom.* XIV. 13. In the next section he refers to 'the plot of the people against our Saviour'.

how long it lasted. And his signs and wonders come from Josephus,
not from memories of the book of Acts.[67]

Finally, of course, we should speak of the ambiguous oracle found
in the sacred writings, that 'at that time one from their country would
rule the earth.' Josephus says that many Jews in spite of wisdom went
astray in interpreting it. He himself was able to explain that it referred
to Vespasian.[68] Origen does not refer to this passage in his extant
writings,[69] and therefore we cannot be sure how he would have taken
it. Probably, however, he would have argued with Eusebius that
Vespasian ruled only the Roman Empire, while Christ, as stated in
Old Testament predictions, ruled over the ends of the earth.[70] As
usual, Eusebius gives us a reinterpreted version of Josephus, in this
instance not certainly, but possibly, relying on Origen.

It is thus clear that whenever Eusebius is making statements about
the theological-historical importance of the Jewish people in the first
century, he relies on ideas already set forth first by Josephus and
then by Origen. Of the two, Josephus was the more reliable. It is a
pity that so many of Origen's influential comments had little
foundation or none at all.[71]

For dealing with events in Jewish history after 70 Eusebius suffers
from several kinds of disabilities. The moralizing of Josephus has
come to an end; so has the moralizing of Origen; and for the later
events Eusebius' sources are inadequate, distasteful, or both.

The first of them was Hegesippus, who told something about Jewish
and Christian history at least up to the reign of Trajan. Eusebius clearly
indicates Hegesippus as his source for the notion that 'after the capture
of Jerusalem Vespasian ordered a search made for all who were of
the family of David, so that no one from the royal tribe might be left
among the Jews; for this reason a very great persecution was again
inflicted on the Jews.'[72] Perhaps Hegesippus relied on Josephus for
this notion. It is clear that mopping-up operations continued well after

[67] Even Eusebius' idea that the people could have obtained 'salvation'
(σωτηρία, III. 7. 9) is anticipated in Josephus' words (*Bell.* VI. 310).
[68] *Bell.* VI. 312-13.
[69] Cf. H. Schreckenberg, *Die Flavius-Josephus-Tradition in Antike und
Mittelalter* (Leiden, 1972), 73-6.   [70] III. 8. 10-11; Ps. 2:8; 18:5.
[71] Note that R. Helm ('De Eusebii in Chronicorum libro auctoribus', *Eranos*,
22 (1924), 34) suggested after Schürer that Eusebius may have used Josephus
via Africanus. Origen seems a more likely candidate. See also E. Fascher,
'Jerusalems Untergang in der urchristlichen und altkirchlichen Überlieferung',
Theologische Literaturzeitung, 89 (1964), 81-98.   [72] III. 12.

the fall of Jerusalem, and not just at Masada. Vespasian suspected that new revolts might arise. In addition, he investigated 'the most reputable Jews both in Alexandria and in Rome', acquitting them only 'on the intercession of Titus', and having their accuser burned alive.[73] A writer dealing with Jewish Christianity might well regard these event as a persecution of the Jews. According to Eusebius, Domitian, unlike Vespasian, persecuted Christians, but the passage he cites from Hegesippus does not prove the point. 'Domitian ordered the execution of those who were of the family of David', and for this reason the grandsons of Jude were arrested, then released by the emperor.[74] Exactly the same situation recurred under Trajan. Explicit quotations from Hegesippus show that the grandsons of Jude were accused again 'on the same charge' (III. 32. 6 – wrongly described as faith in Christ in a summary, 32. 5) or in a parallel but more worked-over quotation, 'of being descended from David and a Christian' (III. 32. 3, wrongly summarized as 'for being a Christian', 32. 2). Eusebius' judicious combination of quotations and summaries has made it hard to see that according to Hegesippus Christians suffered as Jews under Domitian and Trajan.

On the other hand, in dealing with the revolts under Trajan and Hadrian, both in the *Chronicle* and in the *Church History*, Eusebius clearly has rather reliable sources.[75] The Trajanic campaigns make some sense, and the end of the revolt under Hadrian is correctly described. But since Eusebius has no theological guide like Origen he has to do his own interpreting, as we should expect, relying on Josephus once more. 'The calamities of the Jews were at their height, and disaster followed upon disaster.' A revolutionary 'movement' arose. There was 'an evil spirit of sedition'. Words related to *stasis* appear four times in this brief section about events under Trajan (IV. 2). For affairs under Hadrian Eusebius uses terms like 'rebellion' (ἀποστασία), revolution, and 'folly' (ἀπόνοια). The Jewish leader Bar Cochba was an assassin and a robber (IV. 6. 1–3). But Eusebius treats separately his demand that Christians should deny that Jesus was the Christ. This point, taken from Justin Martyr, is not integrated theologically with

---

[73] Josephus, *Bell.* VII. 421; 447–50; *Vit.* 424–5.

[74] III. 19–20.

[75] Cf. A. Fuks, 'The Jewish Revolt in Egypt (A. D. 115–117) in the light of the papyri', *Aegyptus*, 33 (1953), 131–58; H. Mantel, 'The Causes of the Bar Kokba Revolt', *Jewish Quarterly Review*, 58 (1967/8), 224–42, 274–96 (esp. 277–9). R. L. Wilken suggests that perhaps Eusebius got his information from Jews at Caesarea.

his other materials (IV. 8. 4). And while Eusebius notes that finally 'the city was emptied of the nation of the Jews and its old inhabitants utterly destroyed, and colonized by an alien race', he is content to add that it was called Aelia in honour of Hadrian (IV. 6. 4). Evidently Eusebius' source at this point, Aristo of Pella, did not engage in reflection on the end of Jerusalem. And without the guidance provided by a Josephus or an Origen, Eusebius himself was unable to do so. This may be why his narratives concerning the revolts under Trajan and Hadrian are both more factual and less rhetorical–theological than what he had to offer in regard to the first revolt. He will not reach his earlier level of rhetoric again until he comes to deal with Constantine's opponents Galerius, Maximin, and Licinius. Then he will pull out all the stops and offer a grand crescendo on the theme of the fate of the enemies of God.

X

THE FIFTH THEME: PERSECUTION AND MARTYRDOM

In regard to persecution and martyrdom we possess five important documents written by Eusebius. These are the *Chronicle*, the *Collection of Ancient Martyrdoms*, two versions of the *Martyrs of Palestine*, and the *Church History* in its final form. To see what changes his mind may have experienced we begin with the *Chronicle*.

Early Martyrs in the *Chronicle*

The *Chronicle* does not mention the martyrdoms of either Stephen or James son of Zebedee, for presumably Eusebius regarded these persons as part of the sacred history related in Acts. He gave dates for events in Acts only when they could be confirmed from Josephus or on the basis of comparison with other New Testament books (II. 22). Neither Stephen nor the son of Zebedee could be given a date for a chronicle. On the other hand, the death of James the Lord's brother, by beheading could be set in the year 62 because of the evidence of Josephus.[1] At this point Eusebius obviously did not know how Hegesippus correlated the death of James with the siege of Jerusalem under Vespasian (II. 23. 18-19). Paul and Peter were put to death at Rome late in the reign of Nero (II. 22. 7-8; 25. 5). In the *Chronicle* Eusebius cites an otherwise unknown Bruttius as the authority for unnamed Christian martyrs under Domitian, but he is absent from the *Church History*.

Eusebius places another group of martyrs and persecutors around the middle of the reign of Trajan, dating the death of Symeon of Jerusalem in 106/7, that of Ignatius of Antioch in 107/8, and the Pliny-Trajan letters about Christians in 108/9. All three items fall within the 221st Olympiad, and it may be that Eusebius' source or sources possessed no date more precise than that. We have seen that it is not likely that he could date either Symeon or Ignatius from local bishop lists (Chapter IV). Could he have assigned a date to the Pliny-Trajan letters? It is significant that A. N. Sherwin-White, relying on internal evidence, reaches the date 110, but we must recall that

---

[1] Josephus, *Bell.* II. 166; *Ant.* XX. 197-203.

Eusebius could not have used this method. He had read not the letters but a summary of two of them in a Greek version of the *Apology* of Tertullian. While some of the language in Jerome's version of the *Chronicle* comes from Pliny himself, not from Tertullian, disagreements with Eusebius' version of Tertullian (III. 33. 3) prove that it was only Jerome who had read Pliny. Perhaps the most probable conclusion is that the date was chosen simply because it was toward the middle of Trajan's reign, although it is also conceivable that a learned critic at Caesarea had indicated a date for Ignatius in the manuscript Eusebius used.

The next martyr to be discussed was the Roman apologist Justin, whose death, dated in 156/7, was ascribed to the plotting of a Cynic named Crescens. Justin had convicted him as a glutton and an impostor. The language comes from the remarks of Justin's disciple Tatian, explicitly quoted in the *Church History* (IV. 16. 9) but obviously known during the composition of the *Chronicle*. In preparing both works Eusebius was aware that he had no reliable account of Justin's martyrdom and had to rely on Tatian. Why the date? Eusebius knew that Justin addressed his *Apology* to Antoninus Pius (IV. 11. 11). When he wrote the *Chronicle* he obviously did not suppose that he addressed another to Marcus Aurelius ('Antoninus Verus', IV. 18. 2). But there is a good deal of confusion in the *Chronicle*'s dating just at that point. Eusebius seems to have exchanged the true date of Justin's martrydom for the true date of Polycarp's. In other words, Polycarp should have been set in 156/7, Justin a decade later.

The *Chronicle* for 166/7 says that 'when persecution broke out in Asia, Polycarp and Pionius achieved martrydom; written accounts of their sufferings are extant.' Furthermore, 'very many in Gaul perished gloriously for the name of Christ; their struggles are preserved in books to the present day.'

Pionius lived in the third century and his martyr-acts may come from the fourth. Eusebius set him in connection with Polycarp because he came from Smyrna and commemorated Polycarp's martyrdom. But why was Polycarp himself set in 166/7? He visited Rome under Anicetus, as Eusebius pointed out in the *History* (IV. 14. 5); but the date of this visit did not need to be set later than 156/7 (IV. 10; 11. 6-7). Conceivably the date was chosen because Eusebius understood Melito of Sardis to imply that Lucius Verus may have persecuted but that Marcus Aurelius did not do so (IV. 26. 6, 11). Therefore the persecution at Smyrna, as in Gaul (V. 5. 1), had to be set under Lucius

Verus, or at some point between 161 and 169.

It may also be the case that the martyr-acts of Pionius had already been transmitted along with the *Martyrdom of Polycarp* and that, along with the letter of Polycarp to the Philippians, a collection of materials related to Polycarp was coming into existence. Given Eusebius' dating for the martyrdom of Polycarp himself, it was almost inevitable that Pionius should have been set at the same time. And it is possible, but most uncertain, that Eusebius or some predecessor was sufficiently impressed by parallels between the *Martyrdom of Polycarp* and the *Acts of the Gallican Martyrs* to set the events around the same year.[2]

In the *Chronicle* Eusebius does not refer to the martyrdoms of Carpus, Papylus, and Agathonice (IV. 15. 48) or that of Apollonius (V. 21). The Gallicans are the last second-century martyrs in the *Chronicle*. After them we hear only of Leonides, the father of Origen, three bishops under Decius, and Peter of Alexandria.

The *Collection of Ancient Martyrdoms*

Eusebius' *Collection of (Ancient) Martyrdoms* (or *Martyrs*) is mentioned at four points in the *Church History*. He refers 'interested readers' to it three times (IV. 15. 47, V. 4. 3; 21. 5), and once explains that it contains the whole account of the deeds of the Gallican martyrs (V, pr. 2). It certainly included the martyr-acts of Pionius and, because of the connection with Polycarp, probably those of the bishop as well. It is a question whether it contained the *Acts of Carpus, Papylus, and Agathonice*. Did Eusebius want to include the story of a woman who was a volunteer martyr, virtually a suicide? On the other hand, he obviously did include the *Acts of Pionius* which tell of three Christians who wore chains around their necks even before they were arrested; he admired the would-be voluntary martyrdom of Origen (VI. 2. 3–5) and the actual voluntary martyrdoms of Basilides (VI. 5. 5–6) and three men at Caesarea (VII. 12). Though in discussing the martyrs Eusebius was able to condemn voluntary martyrdom, rigorism in confession, and sectarian conduct, he does not seem to have included or excluded early martyrdoms on any basis other than doctrinal orthodoxy. Naturally Montanist and Marcionite martyrs were not acceptable

---

[2] *Mart. Pol.* 2. 2 // V. 1. 51 (neither murmuring nor groaning because conversing with the Lord/God); *Mart. Pol.* 2. 3 // V. 1. 26 (brief punishment versus eternal torment). But Eusebius omits the *Mart. Pol.* expressions in his paraphrase (IV. 15. 4).

(IV. 15. 46; V. 16. 20–2; VII. 12; *Mart. Pal.* 10. 3). The last martyr-act to be included was that of Apollonius at Rome under Commodus.[3] Apollonius was worth mentioning because of the learned apology for Christianity which he presented before the Roman senate (V. 21).

We may suggest that as part of Eusebius' preface to the *Eclogae propheticae* passed into the preface to the *Church History*, so the preface to the *Collection of Martyrdoms* may have passed into the preface to Book V.

Other writers of historical narratives would have transmitted in writing, to the exclusion of all else, victories won in war and conquests over enemies, the prowess of generals and the brave deeds of warriors — defiled with the blood of myriads whom they slew for the sake of children and fatherland and other possessions. But our narrative of God's commonwealth will inscribe on everlasting monuments the record of most peaceful wars fought for the very peace of the soul, and of those who therein contended valiantly for truth rather than fatherland, for religion rather than their dearest ones; it will proclaim for everlasting remembrance the steadfastness of the champions of religion, their deeds of bravery and much endurance, the conquests, too, over devils, and victories won over invisible foes, and the crowns gained when all was done.

This artfully constructed passage (with chiasmus) does not introduce the reader just to the *Gallican Martyrs*. Presumably it once led him into the *Ancient Martyrdoms* as a whole. The point of it is that true heroism is not military and heroic history is not military history. What Eusebius has to say looks rather like the criticisms of Thucydides' military history current among rhetoricians and historians, but diverted for Christian use. (See also III. 4. 4, p. 26 above.)

If there was a special occasion for such a preface it may have been during the last persecution, which according to Eusebius began in the army (*Chron. Lat.*, p. 227; VIII. App. 1; 4. 2–3).

The Use of the *Martyrdoms* in the *Church History*

When used in the *Church History*, the martyr-acts obviously contained narratives that were 'not just historical but instructive as well' (V, pr. 2)[4] the most obvious example of such instruction is given in Eusebius' paraphrase of the account of Pionius. He provided 'welcomes to those who had fallen before the trial in the persecution' (IV. 15. 47).

---

[3] The others listed by H. Musurillo (*The Acts of the Christian Martyrs*, Oxford, 1972, lv) are not what Eusebius called 'ancient'.

[4] Similarly a story about the apostle John is historical and useful (III. 23. 19).

The same point is made at greater length with exact quotations from the letter of the Gallican martyrs (V. 2), and their attitude is contrasted with the 'inhuman and merciless'[5] attitude of rigorists like the Novatianists, Melitians, and Donatists (V. 2. 8). Another story about them shows the error of living on bread and water when in prison (V. 3. 1–3). The martyrs could serve as models for the later Church. Thus the account of Polycarp shows that the Phrygian Quintus 'turned cowardly when he saw the wild beasts'. Even though he 'had given himself up and had forced some others to give themselves up voluntarily', later on he took an oath by the gods and offered sacrifice. In the *Acts* (ch. 4) the point is made in these words: 'This is why, brethren, we do not approve of those who come forward voluntarily; the gospel does not teach thus.' In the *History* Eusebius wanted to make it more explicit. 'The narrative of the aforementioned document showed that this man rushed before the court with others rashly but not with discretion; when he was convicted he offered to all a clear proof that such men should not make rash and indiscreet ventures' (IV. 15. 8).

Conceivably Eusebius' venture into paraphrasing much of the *Martyrdom of Polycarp* was responsible for his close attention to phrasing and his reproduction of some of it in his own *Martyrs of Palestine*. Thus he quoted words about Polycarp as 'the twelfth martyr in Smyrna' (IV. 15. 45), as 'an apostolic and prophetic teacher' (15. 39), and as 'putting an end to the persecution by his martyrdom as though adding the seal' (15. 3). So the martyrs with Eusebius' teacher Pamphilus 'were in total twelve and had been judged worthy of a prophetic or apostolic gift and number' (*Mart. Pal.* 11. 1). Not long after their death a certain Eubulus, 'last of the martyrs of Caesarea, set the seal upon the contests' (11. 30), and still later Silvanus of Gaza 'became the final seal for the whole struggle in Palestine' (13. 5). Probably it was from the *Martyrdom* (as cited IV. 15. 40) that Eusebius developed his language about the jealousy and envy of the Devil, though the account of the Gallican martyrs also contains many references to diabolical activity.[6]

Eusebius devotes more than a sixth of Book IV to the *Martyrdom of Polycarp,* nearly a third of Book V to the Gallicans. Why so much attention to the latter? The *Commentary on I Peter* by Oecumenius

    [5] The phrase is used of Pamphilus' judge (*Mart. Pal.* 11. 18).
    [6] V. 1. 5. 14. 16. 25. 27. 42. 57; 2. 6.

tells us that Irenaeus was the author of the *Gallican Martyrs*.[7] Pierre Nautin and others have substantiated this view with parallels to which more might be added.[8] What are we to suppose Eusebius knew about the question? Certainly in the *Church History* he lost his way chronologically because he realized that he had to move the Gallicans from about 167 to about 177. The reason for doing so was the accession of Eleutherus of Rome, 'in the seventeenth year of the emperor Antoninus Verus' (V, pr. 1), as related to a (second) letter from the martyrs in Gaul addressed to Eleutherus and commending Irenaeus to him (V. 4. 2). The martyr-acts could not have been written before the episcopate of Eleutherus. Does Eusebius believe that martyr-acts should be anonymous or, at least, written in the name of a church? Certainly this is what he says about the *Martrydom of Polycarp*. It was written 'in the name (ἐκ προσώπου)' of the church of Smyrna (IV. 15. 2), just as I Clement was written 'in the name' of the church of Rome (III. 38. 1). The only clue Eusebius offers to suggest that he knew who the author was is his description of 'the brethren in Gaul' as 'ambassadors for the sake of the peace of the churches' (V. 3. 4). The letter includes a passage containing a panegyric on peace (V. 2. 7)[9] just as a letter from Irenaeus to Victor of Rome offers praises of peace (V. 24. 13. 16-17). On the letter to Victor Eusebius says that Irenaeus 'deserved his name, making peace in this way and thus serving as a promoter and ambassador on behalf of the peace of the churches' (V. 24. 18). If Eusebius did not conclude that Irenaeus wrote *Gallicans* his work was more desultory than usual.

The last document which Eusebius had included in his *Ancient Martyrdoms* was the account of the trial and execution of a certain Apollonius, 'famous for his culture and philosphy', at Rome under Commodus (V. 21). Eusebius has to provide an introduction to the account in the *Church History*, for the martyrdom came under Commodus and according to the anti-Montanist author he ha~ just cited (V. 16. 19) there was universal peace in his reign, even for Christians. Under these circumstances rich and noble Romans (like Apollonius) turned to Christianity. It was the Devil who brought the martyr into court, using one of his own servants (cf. IV. 7. 2) as an informer. Eusebius ends his introduction by stating that the judge

---

[7] *PG* 119, 536-D; Irenaeus, Fr. gr. XIII Harvey.

[8] *Lettres et écrivains des iie et iiie siècles* (Paris, 1961), 54-9.

[9] The section also includes a rather unusual allusion to Ps. 20:5; cf. Irenaeus, *Adv. haer.* II. 34. 2.

has the informer put to death by breaking his legs (cf. John 19:31-7; Cicero, *Phil.* XIII. 27). He inflicted this penalty because of 'imperial decree' dealing with 'informers on such matters'. The matters in question were obviously the profession of Christianity. What of the 'imperial decree'? From the Greek mistranslation of Tertullian's *Apology* which he used, Eusebius concluded that Tiberius had threatened to punish accusers of Christians by death (II. 2. 6), and from Melito's *Apology* he could suppose that imperial policy had remained basically consistent from the beginning. Only bad emperors like Nero and Domitian had modified it (IV. 26. 5. 8-9). In addition, a decree which Eusebius did not recognize as a forgery ascribed the same idea to either Antoninus Pius or Marcus Aurelius: 'the accuser shall be liable to penalty' (IV. 13. 7). It thus appears that everything in the introduction to Eusebius' account of Apollonius comes from the Church historian's own creativity — except for the name of the martyr and that of his judge 'Perennius', presumably the praetorian prefect Tigidius Perennis.

What of the trial itself? Evidently it was a conspicuous feature of the martyr acts, for Eusebius lays emphasis on Apollonius' preliminary discussion with Perennis, the judge's request to him to provide a defence before the Roman senate, and the 'very learned' defence he then set forth. In the Armenian and Greek apologies now extant the arguments are close to the more leisurely discussions provided by Clement of Alexandria[10] and Theophilus of Antioch. Eusebius refers the interested reader to the *Collection of Ancient Martyrs*.

At the end we learn that Apollonius was 'perfected' (a word frequent in the *Church History*) by 'capital punishment' (a term also used in *Mart. Pal.* 9. 5). His execution was carried out 'as by decree of the senate', presumably the decree 'that Christians shall not exist' mentioned in the Greek *Acts* (13. 14. 23. 45). It should be noted, however, that Eusebius appends another explanation for Apollonius' death. There was 'an ancient law' that punishment had to be inflicted once Christians came into court. And in describing it, Eusebius turns once more to the language of Tertullian in the Greek translation. Several key phrases come directly from his earlier Tertullianistic passages (II. 2. 2; III. 33. 2-3).

We conclude that the description of the *Acts of Apollonius* in

---

[10] Cf. H. Paulsen, 'Erwägungen zu Acta Apollonii 14-22', *ZNW* 66 (1975), 117-26.

V. 21 owes almost everything to Eusebius' own ideas as to what such *Acts* should have contained. For the purposes of the *Church History* he was not concerned with the apologetic sections which constitute much of the Armenian and Greek *Acts*. As far as authentic *Acts* are concerned, we should infer that the Armenian version is relatively close to what Eusebius included in his *Ancient Martyrdoms*, while the later Greek *Acts* have strayed far away, often with use — or rather misuse — of Eusebius' own ideas.

Contemporary Martyrdoms

Martyrs and martyrdom were highly important to Eusebius in his own time, and we shall presently see what he wrote about them and why. First, however, we should recall that among the main emphases of his *Apology for Origen* (and therefore of Book VI of the *History*) was the problem of Origen's attitude toward martyrdom, discussed in relation to his youth as well as his old age. Similarly Dionysius of Alexandria felt it necessary to defend himself against charges that he had taken flight during persecution 'on his own and apart from God' (VI. 40. 1). The whole Novatianist controversy, which vexed the Church at the middle of the third century, had to do with the controversies between confessors and non-confessors. The Egyptian bishop Germanus, a confessor, tried to 'defame' Dionysius (VII. 11. 1; cf. 11. 18-19). Eusebius cites only documents that express the 'official' episcopal view.

Like other Christians of varying viewpoints he found accounts of martyrs inspiring. He repeated Dionysius' account of his miraculous escape (VI. 40) and also his tales of Egyptian martyrs (VI. 41-2), especially those who like the Gallicans in the second century (V. 2) showed mercy toward those who had fallen away (VI. 42. 5-6).

From Caesarean local tradition he described the martyrdom of the soldier Marinus, presumably during the persecution under Valerian and Gallienus (VII. 15; sacrifice to emperors, plural, involved). Certainly it was in this persecution that three other men were martyred there as voluntary confessors. Eusebius tells about them without commenting on the voluntary aspect; he notes that there was also an anonymous woman martyr who belonged to the sect of Marcion (VII. 12).

After a brief period of persecution 'beginning with the brethren in the army' (VIII. 1. 7; 4, 2-4) outright war against the churches began in the nineteenth year of Diocletian, and it lasted, off and on, for ten years. Eusebius carefully observed what went on. The volunteer martyr

Apphianus stopped the governor Urbanus from sacrificing and was put to death; he had come from the house where Eusebius was (*Mart. Pal.* 4. 8). Eusebius himself witnessed the earthquake which washed Apphianus' body up from the sea 'before the city gates' (4. 15). Apparently this martyr was put to death on 2 April 306. Eusebius also witnessed martyrdoms at Tyre, in Egypt, and in the Thebais (VIII. 7-9). He also witnessed, under unexplained circumstances, something of what went on near the copper mines at Phaeno, where confessors were sent for hard labour (*Mart. Pal.* 13. 6-10). Evidently he was in contact with Phaeno, for the *Apology for Origen* was destined for the confessors there. And Eusebius worked on it with Pamphilus while the latter was in prison at Caesarea before being put to death.

Beginning with the *Gallican Martyrs*, Eusebius reports cruel and seemingly unusual tortures and punishments seemingly unparalleled until modern times. He lays emphasis on the torments suffered by the martyrs whether he found them in his sources or not. Such descriptions heighten the effect of his praise of the martyrs, even though, as G. E. M. de Ste. Croix has pointed out, there seem to have been ninety-one of them in Palestine during eight years of persecution.[11]

On the other hand, his remarks about bishops are extremely cutting and he devotes a special chapter to indicating that during the persecution in the East eleven bishops were martyrs (VIII. 13). He does not bother to say that three of the eleven seem to have been Meletians. Elsewhere, however, he refers to the pre-persecution situation in which 'rulers attacked rulers and laity formed factions against laity', while 'those supposed to be our shepherds, casting aside the sanctions of the fear of God, were enflamed by contentions with one another and did nothing but add to the struggles and threats, the jealousy, enmity and hatred that they used toward one another, claiming primacies as if they were tyrants' spoils' (VIII. 1. 7-8). When the persecution came on, Eusebius himself saw these shepherds 'some shamefully hiding themselves here and there while others were ignominiously captured and mocked by the enemies' (2. 1). He has decided not to discuss either the pre-persecution squabbles or the persecution-time disasters. He does say, however, in VIII. 3 (*Mart. Pal.* 1. 3-4) that while many rulers of churches kept the faith, there were many others who 'proved weak at the first assault'. Such cowardice was exemplified in the case of Stephen of Laodicea (near Antioch), mentioned because Eusebius

[11] 'Some Aspects of the "Great" Persecution', *HTR* 47 (1954), 75-113.

wants to contrast him with his own friend, Stephen's successor (VII. 32. 23), the Bishop Theodotus, to whom he dedicated the *Praeparatio* and *Demonstratio Evangelica.*

Eusebius' criticisms of such persons could be modified. Thus he vigorously praises Meletius, a bishop of the churches in Pontus, for his asceticism, erudition, and rhetorical ability — adding that 'we knew him during the time of the persecution when he was in flight in the Palestine area for seven whole years' (VII. 32. 28). He praises Pierius too, even though according to Clodius Culcianus, Prefect of Egypt, he offered sacrifice to the gods (P. Bodmer XX). His ideal bishop, however, was Peter of Alexandria. Peter was an ascetic who 'cared in no hidden manner for the general good of the churches' and became a martyr (VII. 323. 31). His care for the churches involved denouncing rigorists and excommunicating the rigorist Meletius. He was joined by three presbyters and four bishops in Egypt, soon to be martyrs themselves. Eusebius names them all in VIII. 13. 7.

The situation was hard to write about. Eusebius admired heroism but not suicidal heroism. He favoured the state but not at the expense of the Church. He was opposed to the rigorist Novatianists (VI. 42–6), Meletians (presumably envisaged in *Mart. Pal.* 12), and Donatists (subject of Constantine's letters cited in X. 5. 18–6. 5), but not to the martyrs among them. He therefore did not precisely identify those who were carried away by 'the lust for power' and therefore took part in 'the rash and unlawful ordinations and the schisms among the confessors themselves', though he does describe the process as involving

all that the young agitators eagerly devised against the remnants of the church, heaping fresh innovations on what were still novelties, adding with an unsparing hand to the misfortunes of the persecution and building evil upon evil (*Mart. Pal.* 12).

Like Eusebius' attitude, his own activities during the persecution may have seemed somewhat equivocal. The point was made by one of Athanasius' supporters, the Confessor-Bishop Potammon, at the Council of Tyre in 335. 'Tell me', he cried out to Eusebius,

were you not in prison with me during the persecution? I lost an eye on behalf of the truth, while you seem not to have any part of your body maimed. You were not a confessor but simply stood there, alive and without mutilation. How did you get out of prison unless because you promised the persecutors that you would do what is unlawful, or because you did it?[12]

[12] Epiphanius, *Haer.* LXVIII. 8. 4.

We have no means of answering Potammon's question; Eusebius himself replied with abuse. But it could well be that the Egyptian was among those sent to Palestine on their way to Phaeno. He could have met Eusebius during the imprisonment of Pamphilus, when Eusebius seems to have been free to come and go, just as long before, Origen had been with the holy martyrs in prison at Alexandria but escaped martyrdom thanks to 'divine and heavenly grace' (VI. 3. 4–5). Though as it happened Eusebius was neither a confessor nor a martyr, he ran the risk of death and did so willingly. His praise of martyrs and rejection of volunteering was consistent with what came to be the view of the Church as a whole.

This moderation apparently had apologetic value. At any rate, by the autumn of 309 the pagans of Palestine, according to Eusebius (*Mart. Pal.* 9. 3) viewed the imperial policy without enthusiasm. They considered it wretched, excessive, disgusting, palling, and burdensome. Such an attitude seems to have gained some support in government circles (VIII. 12. 8–9). Athanasius casts some light on the situation when he describes hearing about the persecution under Galerius when 'Greeks concealed our Christian brethren from search and in many instances lost money and underwent imprisonment in order not to become betrayers of those in flight; for they guarded those who had taken refuge with them and were desirous of running risks on their behalf.'[13] Such non-Christian sympathizers would have been alienated by Christians who either denied their faith or volunteered for martyrdom. They must have been among the readers whom Eusebius had in mind.

In spite of what Eusebius hints about the severity of the persecution in 311 to 312, he knows the names of only three martyrs (and mentions two others without naming them). These are Peter of Alexandria, a martyr on 26 November 311,[14] Lucian of Antioch, put to death on 7 January 312,[15] and Silvanus, Bishop of the churches about Emesa in Phoenicia. The basic account is to be found in Book IX (6. 1–3). Peter 'was arrested for no reason at all and quite unexpectedly' and then 'unaccountably beheaded, as if by order of Maximin'. In view of the date, less than six months after the death of Galerius, it is possible that Peter had been forbidden to assemble

---

[13] *Historia Arianorum*, 64. 2 (218. 20–5 Opitz).

[14] F. H. Kettler, 'Petrus I (1) Bischof von Alexandria', *RE* XIX (1938), 1281–8.

[15] G. Bardy, *Recherches sur saint Lucien d'Antioche et son école* (Paris, 1936), 71.

Christians in a cemetery at Alexandria (IX. 2; cf. VII. 13). As for Lucian, since he was 'brought to the city of Nicomedia, where the emperor was then staying' and then presented arguments on behalf of Christianity — denouncing Roman ancestral traditions and the forged *Acts of Pilate*, according to Rufinus[16] — it is quite possible that his imprisonment and execution were related to the attempts of both Antiochenes and Nicomedians to be freed from Christians. All three martyrs are mentioned again in the late addition to Book VIII (13. 1-7), where Eusebius is listing 'rulers of the church martyred in famous cities'. And Peter's name appears in VII. 32. 31, with the statement that he was beheaded in the ninth year of the persecution, because though Book VII ends before the persecution it also completes Eusebius' discussion of the episcopal successions up to 'the destruction of the places of prayer'.

---

[16] Rufinus, *H. E.* IX. 6. 3; cf. Eusebius, *H. E.* IX. 5. 1.

XI

A RECURRENT THEME: THE CANON OF SCRIPTURE

The present introduction to the *Church History* contains no reference
to the canon of scripture, but in V. 8. 1 Eusebius wrote that 'when
beginning this work we made a promise to set forth from time to time
quotations from the ancient ecclesiastical presbyters and authors in
which they committed to writing the traditions that came down to
them about the canonical scriptures.' A promise of this sort does
occur in III. 3. 3: 'As the history goes forward, I shall endeavour to
indicate along with the successions which of the ecclesiastical authors
from time to time used what sort of disputed books, and what was said
by them about the canonical and acknowledged writings and about
those that are not such.'[1] This presumably means that when Eusebius
first wrote his introduction he promised to discuss the canon. Later
the promise was deleted there and transferred to the beginning of
the third book.

The removal of the promise from the very beginning was
accompanied by a changed, and very negative, view of the Apocalypse
of John. Originally Eusebius treated the book as a work of 'the apostle
and evangelist'.[2] He recognized that questions had been raised about
it, but his response to them was to collect testimonies to its use and
high valuation by Justin (IV. 18. 8), Theophilus (IV. 24), Melito
(IV. 26. 2), Irenaeus (V. 8. 5-6), Apollonius (V. 18. 4), Clement of
Alexandria (III. 23. 6),[3] and Origen (VI. 25. 9-10). Later Eusebius'
thought passed through two stages of negative thinking. Presumably
in his second edition he treated the Apocalypse as beyond the pale,
forged by Cerinthus to advance the cause of millenarianism (III. 28.
1-5). Such a book was not even 'disputed' but as a heretical forgery
was completely wicked and impious (III. 25. 7). Eusebius quoted a
tale ultimately from Polycarp about how the apostle John denounced
Cerinthus (III. 28. 6). This supposedly proved that the apostle cannot
have written the Apocalypse. Eusebius then goes on to quote a defence

---

[1] Augmentations of III. 3. 3 appear in III. 3. 5; 24. 16. 18; 25. 2.

[2] This was also his view when he wrote the *Chronicle* (pp. 192-3 Helm).

[3] Eusebius did not treat the Apocalypse as 'disputed' when discussing
Clement's usage (VI. 13. 6; 14. 1-4).

of Nicolaus, presumed founder of the Nicolaitans denounced in the Apocalypse, and to supply evidence on the apostles as married men (III. 29-30). This seems directed against the extreme asceticism welcomed in the Apocalypse. Otherwise it is hard to see what Eusebius means when he calls the quotations 'related to the present subject'. Finally, when he read all he needed from Dionysius of Alexandria (VII. 24-5) rather than just a misinterpreted excerpt (III. 28. 4-5), his mind changed again and he must have viewed the Apocalypse as canonical but by an author different from the evangelist.

In regard to the most important or most widely accepted books of the New Testament few questions created widespread controversy, and Eusebius deals with matters related to the Synoptic Gospels only occasionally and to the major Pauline epistles not at all. The simplest way to view his opinions on these matters is to go through the *Church History* book by book, noting what he has said in regard to the canonical and non-canonical books.

The matter first came to Eusebius' attention when he wrote Book I. He was aware that many people thought Matthew disagreed with Luke in regard to the genealogy of Jesus and that Christians ignorant of the truth made guesses about the passages in question; but he was convinced that Julius Africanus had solved the problem by genealogical analysis (I. 7). In the first two books he frequently points out how Matthew or Luke or Acts is in agreement with the testimony of Josephus, 'the most famous historian among the Hebrews' (I. 5. 3).

In Book II we find three passages in which New Testament books are discussed, but all three discussions are merely incidental to Eusebius' main interests. Thus in II. 15 he has been discussing Simon Magus and Peter's triumph over him when it occurs to him to set forth something about Mark's relation to Peter and thus to provide a transition to his subsequent treatment of Christianity at Alexandria (II. 16-17). The hearers of Peter, says Eusebius, urged Mark, Peter's follower, to leave them (presumably as he left for Alexandria) an account of the doctrine they had received. In addition, Eusebius says that 'the apostle, knowing by the revelation of the Spirit what had been done, was pleased at their zeal and ratified the document for reading in the churches.' This information, he claims, comes from the *Outlines* of Clement of Alexandria and is confirmed by Papias, Bishop of Hierapolis. Proof of the desultory nature of Eusebius' interest comes from examining the different account by Papias as cited in III. 39. 15 and the partly different account of Clement paraphrased in VI. 14. 6-7.

The idea that the apostle was moved by the Spirit could be based on what Clement said about either Peter or John, but Clement explicitly said that Peter gave neither disapproval nor commendation to Mark's Gospel.

In a second instance Eusebius treats Philo's account of the Therapeutae, a first-century Jewish sect, as referring to early Christians. He is aware that the sacred scriptures they studied must have been the Old Testament books, but he is also aware that they had 'writings of ancient men who were founders of their sect and left many memorials of the ideas expressed allegorically' (II. 17. 11; Philo, *Vit. cont.* 28). Eusebius identifies these books as probably 'the gospels and the writings of the apostles and some exegetical treatises after the fashion of the ancient prophets, such as are contained in the Epistle to the Hebrews and many other epistles of Paul' (II. 17. 10). This is an explanation of what the Therapeutae were reading, not a comment on the canon. But they read Hebrews — written by Paul.

Third, after discussing the martyrdom of James the Lord's brother, Eusebius says,

Such is the story of James; the first of the so-called catholic epistles is said to be his; but it must be observed that it is not genuine, since not many of the ancients mentioned it, any more than the so-called epistle of Jude, itself one of the seven called catholic; but we know that these letters, along with the others, have been publicly read in most churches. (II. 23. 24–5.)

Undeniably this is a notice about the canon, important here to Eusebius, who never cited either James or Jude. The subject came up because he was closely following the text of Origen's *Commentary on Matthew* (X. 17), where the author claimed that Josephus ascribed the fall of Jerusalem to the death of James and then mentioned Jude as author of a letter that was 'short but full of powerful words of heavenly grace'. Origen did not mention the epistle of James. This is the note that Eusebius added here. Though his primary concern was with James, not the New Testament, he has modified Origen's words about James in order to create a notice about the canon.

Toward the end of Book II (II. 25. 5) Eusebius spoke of the martyrdoms of Paul and Peter. At the beginning of Book III he spoke of them again and referred to Linus as first Bishop of Rome (III. 1–2). The apostolic age is evidently nearing its end, even though the remarkable longevity of the apostle John will keep it from terminating until early in the reign of Trajan (III. 31. 6). The repeated mentions of the deaths of Peter and Paul make it appropriate to list their writings.

The third chapter of Book III therefore contains, as the chapter heading states, a discussion 'concerning the letters of the apostles'. In regard to Peter, Eusebius accepts the First Epistle on the ground that 'the former presbyters' did not question its authenticity, but he does not regard 2 Peter as 'canonical' (though it has seemed 'useful'). No ecclesiastical writer has ever accepted the Acts, Gospel, Preaching, or Apocalypse ascribed to him. This statement is more emphatic than accurate. Later on Eusebius himself will note that Clement of Alexandria used the *Apocalypse of Peter* (VI. 14. 1); it is a fact that Clement also used the Preaching. Perhaps Eusebius actually felt the lack of adequate information on this kind of subject. In any event, just here (III. 3. 3) he promised that hereafter he would note, along with the 'successions', which of the books in dispute were used by which ecclesiastical writers, and what the authors had to say. Much later, after neglecting the promise in regard to many of the authors treated, he came back to it (V. 8. 1). Now he claimed that he had made it 'at the beginning of this work' — thus it was obviously very important — and he was going to quote from Irenaeus, for he was one of 'the ancient ecclesiastical presbyters and authors'. In actual fact, Eusebius has studied the work of Irenaeus more carefully than those of any other second-century authors.

But before coming up to Irenaeus' time we must consider what else Eusebius wrote on the letters of the apostles. He says that the fourteen letters of Paul are 'obvious and clear', but then he immediately corrects himself: there are those who raise questions about Hebrews and say that the church of Rome rejects it as not Paul's; he will give further evidence later. *The Acts of Paul* have also been questioned. People say that the Hermas of Romans 16:14 wrote the *Shepherd*; there are varying opinions on this book too. In the subsequent chapter (III. 4) we hear about Paul's lieutenants as described in Acts and the Pastoral Epistles, and we also learn, therefore, about Luke and Acts.

The next time we hear of a canon is after Eusebius' account of the Jewish war of 66 to 70, begun in II. 26 and completed in III. 5-8, with lavish use of Josephus' *War*. Since Josephus is one of his most important sources, Eusebius discusses his life and works and quotes a passage to show that among the Hebrews there are twenty-two 'undisputed' books: five with the Law and the early tradition, thirteen by prophets on contemporary events, and four with hymns and precepts. Such books as 1 and 2 Maccabees are on a lower level (III. 10).

In Eusebius' view, Josephus himself wrote 4 Maccabees. Since he does not say that the number of New Testament books should equal that of the Old, we are not justified in assuming that he wanted to make an exact correlation. Because of his interest in numerology, more notable in later works than in the *Church History*, we should suppose that he noticed the resemblance. The five books of law and early tradition might be equivalent to the Gospels and Acts; the prophets' thirteen books would be analogous to the thirteen unquestioned Pauline epistles; and the four books remaining would be constituted by 1 Peter and 1 John, and probably — since we are considering Eusebius' earlier opinions — Hebrews and the Apocalypse of John.

As he wrote this section of the *Church History*, however, Eusebius' principles concerning the canon were not very rigid. His principal authorities, Irenaeus and the early Alexandrians, had accepted and used 1 Clement. Eusebius describes it as 'great and wonderful' and says that it is 'acknowledged' and has been publicly read in many churches both long ago and recently (III. 16). Only a later discussion will show that Clement belonged to the post-apostolic age and that his letter should not, therefore, be regarded as scripture (III. 38).

We now come to Eusebius' first discussion of John 'the apostle and evangelist', who was 'condemned to live on the island of Patmos' and therefore was the author of the Apocalypse (III. 18. 1). For his date Eusebius relies on Irenaeus, who said that the revelation was seen 'toward the end of the reign of Domitian'. Like Irenaeus, Eusebius obviously upheld the common authorship of Gospel and Apocalypse. In another passage he insisted upon the longevity of this author, appealing to two witnesses (an echo of John 8:17 — and even of Rev. 11:3?) who advocated ecclesiastical orthodoxy, Irenaeus and Clement of Alexandria. Irenaeus insisted that after returning from Patmos, John the Lord's disciple remained at Ephesus until the reign of Trajan (III. 23. 3-4). Clement spoke of John's return 'after the death of the tyrant' when he was 'an old man' (23. 6. 17-18). In III. 18. 20 and 23 there is no question whatever concerning the identity of the author of the Apocalypse (on Patmos) with the 'apostle and evangelist'.

Eusebius had earlier made the same point in his *Chronicle*. There he had stated that under Domitian 'the apostle John, banished to the island of Patmos, saw the apocalypse which Irenaeus expounds.' He had added that it was said that the apostle John came back from exile to Ephesus. And he had said that 'Irenaeus writes that the apostle John remained until the times of Trajan' (he was relying on the passages later used in the *Church History*). 'After him', Eusebius wrote, 'came his distinguished hearers, Papias the Hieropolitan bishop and Polycarp the Smyrnaean and Igantius the Antiochene' (*Chron. Lat.*, pp. 192–3 Helm). Here Eusebius obviously treats the author of the Apocalypse as an apostle and also as the teacher of Papias, Polycarp, and Ignatius – in that order.

In the *Church History* we still read that Polycarp, Papias, and Ignatius – in *that* order – were alive in the time of Trajan but only Polycarp is closely linked to the apostles, and not specifically to John (III. 36. 1). Eusebius is employing the language of Irenaeus, however (cited V. 14. 3), and we cannot suppose that at this point he questioned the relations of these three with John the apostle.

Beyond this, we must note that according to Irenaeus, cited in III. 39. 1, Papias was definitely a hearer of John and a companion of Polycarp and an 'ancient man'. This, as we have just seen, was the view of Papias which Eusebius accepted when he wrote his *Chronicle*. The link between Papias and John, author the Apocalypse, was important for all who valued the literal interpretation of apocalyptic eschatology. Irenaeus was one of such enthusiasts. At one time Eusebius was another. As he wrote his first version of Book III of the *Church History* he continued to hold the view of the Apocalypse he had held at the time he wrote the *Chronicle*. Indeed, it was the view set forth by four of his highly revered mentors: Justin, Irenaeus, Clement, and Origen. He makes it plain that Theophilus, Melito, and Apollonius knew the book but does not say what they thought about authorship.[4]

In spite of all these positive notes about the Apocalypse, Eusebius changed his mind about the work and traces of the change are present in Book III of the *Church History*. The shift in attitude becomes evident at the point where he mentions John's banishment to Patmos. There he says that Irenaeus wrote about 'the so-called Apocalypse of John' (III. 18. 1). Actually Irenaeus raised no question about the authorship of the book. Eusebius tells us nothing about its contents at this point or, for that matter, any other. What we have in its place seems significant. Instead of describing the descent to earth of the heavenly Jerusalem or the thousand-year kingdom on earth, he tells how the grandnephews of the Lord, when asked about the kingdom

---

[4] Melito's title, *On the Devil and the Apocalypse of John*, suggests that he viewed the book as scripture; if as scripture, presumably apostolic. Theophilus (*Ad Autol.* II. 22) speaks of the evangelist as 'spirit-inspired'. This must be an allusion to Rev. 1:10, 'I was in the Spirit.'

of Christ, explained that it would be 'neither worldly nor on earth but heavenly and angelic'. Upon hearing it described thus, the Emperor Domitian freed them and terminated a persecution of the Church (III. 20. 4-5). Two points are made in this tale, paraphrased from Hegesippus. First, Christ's kingdom was definitely not as described in the Apocalypse of John. Second, when the true doctrine of the kingdom is understood by a Roman emperor he stops persecuting Christians. Both points are important for the development of Eusebius' thought on apocalyptic and politics.

The materials that follow this discussion of the kingdom reflect Eusebius' old synthesis about John. It is notably expressed in III. 23. 1, where John is called 'the one whom Jesus loved' (John 13:23, etc.), 'at the same time apostle and evangelist', and the one who 'returned from banishment on the island after the death of Domitian'. The island is Patmos (Rev. 1:9) and the Domitianic date comes from Irenaeus.

Chapter 24 is quite different from what goes before it. It follows a long quotation from Clement of Alexandria, supposedly included 'an account of the history and also the edification of future readers' (23. 19; 'edification' may explain why the quotation was so long). Then Eusebius offers a rather awkward transitional sentence. 'Come now, let us indicate the undisputed writings of this apostle', (i.e. John). We are to learn why his Gospel, universally accepted, is listed fourth, after the other three. But the point of the explanation becomes clear toward the end of the discussion. If the interrelations of the Gospels are properly understood, they 'no longer appear to disagree' (24. 13). This implies that someone thought they did disagree; and we happen to know that this was the view of Gaius of Rome, answered by Hippolytus with comments not unlike those of Eusebius.[5] Why does Eusebius not mention Gaius? It seems that he is already working toward a discussion of the Apocalypse, which Gaius also rejected. He is planning to appeal to the authority of Gaius on the Apocalypse while rejecting his view on the Gospel. For this reason he certainly prefers to leave out Gaius' name at this point. The discussion of John's works ends, oddly enough, with a comment on Luke and the promise to give citations from 'the ancients' on the Gospels (24. 16); then we learn that neither the Gospel nor the First Epistle of John has been

---

[5] *Dionysius Bar Salibi in Apocalypsim, Actus et Epistulas catholicas*, trans. I. Sedlacek (*CSCO Scriptores Syri*, series 2a, Tomus CI, versio), 1-2; Epiphanius, *Haer.* LI, *passim*.

questioned (not quite correct, as we have seen), while the Apocalypse has been both questioned and accepted. The 'testimony of the ancients' will be provided (24. 17-18).

Before coming to any such testimonies Eusebius now recapitulates the already mentioned writings of the New Testament. In III. 3 he had made use of two categories: acknowledged (unquestioned, undisputed, canonical) and disputed. In III. 25 the categories are different. There are acknowledged books and disputed books, but the disputed books are of two kinds: those known to many and those that are not genuine but spurious. Beyond these categories lie the forged books used only by heretics. Naturally such an account, based almost entirely on the writings of Origen, is welcome. What Eusebius is doing with it, however, is reiterating his downgrading of the works ascribed to John, apart from the Gospel and First Epistle, both of which are 'acknowledged'. In his view the Apocalypse is either Acknowledged or Disputed (Spurious), while 2-3 John are Disputed (Known to Many).[6]

At the end of this discussion Eusebius denounces the heretical forgers because the character of their style differs from that of the apostles and their doctrine is different from true orthodoxy (25. 7). The phraseology is Origen's (cf. VI. 25. 11) but the intent is Eusebius' own. He is going to describe apostolic orthodoxy as the reverse of heresy and by implication dispose of the Apocalypse. We therefore leave the canon and 'turn to the subsequent history' by discussing the heretic Menander (III. 26). Menander promised his disciples that they would gain 'eternal immortality in this life itself, no longer dying but remaining here without ageing and destined to be immortal'. Eusebius is sure that this doctrine was inspired by the Devil. It is intended to demolish the ecclesiastical doctrines on 'the immortality of the soul and the resurrection of the dead' (26. 4). In other words, he is presenting Menander's view as the expression of a this-worldly apocalyptic eschatology like the doctrine he finds in the Apocalypse of John. Another heresy supposedly worth discussing here is that of the Ebionites. Their diabolical doctrines include the notion that Christ was the son of Mary and her husband, and they venture to attack the apostle Paul. Bar Salibi, whose testimony we noted above, stated that these were doctrines of Cerinthus, and his information came from

---

[6] Perhaps written by someone not an apostle but named John (III. 25. 3; cf. Dionysius of Alexandria in VII. 25. 14; a different view, VII. 25. 11). Note that Origen proposed three categories when discussing the *Preaching of Peter*: genuine, spurious, mixed (*Ioh. comm.* XIII. 17, p. 241, 15 Preuschen).

Hippolytus' attack on Gaius. We infer that at this point Eusebius is again leading up to the Apocalypse.

The most important passage is the explicit discussion of Cerinthus (III. 28). We find Gaius cited as an authority on the heresy.

Moreover Cerinthus, who through revelations (apocalypses) written down as if by a great apostle, falsely introduces wonders to us as if shown to him by angels, saying that after the resurrection the kingdom of Christ will be on earth and that mankind, living in Jerusalem, will again be enslaved to lusts and pleasures. And as the enemy of the scriptures of God, he says in his desire to deceive that there will be a period of a thousand years spent in a wedding feast.[7]

Gaius' target is obviously the Apocalypse of John, with its emphasis on revelation to John by an angel (1:1, 9, 10; 22:8), on the kingdom at Jerusalem (20:3, 6; 21:2, 10), and on the wedding feast (19:7, 9). In order to support Gaius' authority Eusebius also quotes from Dionysius of Alexandria and his comments made 'as from prior tradition' (III. 28. 3). What Eusebius thus quotes is obviously based upon Gaius. What he does not quote at this point is Dionysius' statement, cited more fully in VII. 25, that the Apocalypse was being assigned to Cerinthus and that he himself disagreed with Gaius' view. Only when he reached Book VII, after observing that his hero Origen accepted the Apocalypse (VI. 25. 10), could he accept the notion that while the apostle John had not written the Apocalypse, nevertheless it was not to be rejected. At this point in Book III he was using every available weapon to discredit the book.

His concluding remarks in III. 28. 6 make use of Irenaeus' testimony, based on Polycarp, to denigrate the Apocalypse further. If one looked at Irenaeus' account of the heresy of Cerinthus one would not find any trace of Jewish or Christian apocalyptic ideas. Therefore Eusebius eagerly passes over his account, stating that he set forth some of Cerinthus' 'more secret' doctrines. What really counts is an excerpt from a passage later to be quoted more fully (IV. 14. 3–8). In it we learn that 'the apostle John' (actually called 'John the Lord's disciple' by Irenaeus, but Eusebius makes no distinction between the terms) once fled from a bath-house when he knew that 'Cerinthus, the enemy of the truth', was inside. This story usefully differentiates John 'the apostle' and teacher of Polycarp from Cerinthus, the heretic and author of the Apocalypse.

---

[7] The Greek of both sentences is corrupt but this must be the sense.

So much for Cerinthus. It seems likely that two more chapters, rather oddly appended at this point, have to do with the same point about the Apocalypse. Chapter 29 begins by speaking of 'the so-called heresy of the Nicolaitans of which the Apocalypse of John makes mention'. Like Irenaeus (I. 26. 3), Eusebius correlates them with the Nicolaus mentioned in Acts 6:5. What follows, however, is a strange story about Nicolaus, taken from Clement of Alexandria and intended to free him from the legendary suspicion of immorality. The point must be that the Apocalyptist's hatred of the Nicolaitans (Rev. 2:6, 15) was not fully justified.[8] In Chapter 30 Eusebius cites Clement's list of married apostles 'on account of those who reject marriage' and then goes on to quote Clement's story about Peter and his wife. He claims that these quotations are 'related to the subject under discussion'. But what is the subject under discussion? The story about Nicolaus indicated that it was permissible for him to have a beautiful wife. It was clear from the New Testament, even apart from Clement's list, that some of the apostles were married. One would suppose, given the context in Eusebius' work, that the subject under discussion might be the Apocalypse of John. In this case, it is significant that the only passage in the New Testament where sexual abstinence is set forth as an absolute goal is Rev. 14:3-5, where certain men are described as 'redeemed from the earth' and 'blameless' because they 'did not defile themselves with women'.[9] In an effort to oppose the teaching of the Apocalypse, Eusebius was willing to cite Clement on married apostles even though at other times his own view was that the apostles rejected marriage (or their wives) because of their exalted chastity and purity of body and soul alike (see Chapter XIII).

This whole section of Book III comes to an end in Chapter 31 after some citations on the burial of John and a daughter of Philip at Ephesus and Philip and his (other?) daughters at Hierapolis. A quotation from Gaius actually disagrees with one from Polycrates of Ephesus, but Eusebius says that there is complete harmony (III. 31. 4). A summary touches upon 'the apostles and apostolic times' and the writings left by them or disputed and used by many or, finally, the ones that are completely spurious and 'alien to apostolic orthodoxy' (31. 6;

---

[8] Clement, *Str.* III. 25. 5-26. 2; contrast Epiphanius, *Haer.* XXV. 1. 4-5; cf. P. Prigent, 'L'hérésie asiate et l'église confessante', *VC*, 31 (1977), 12-16.

[9] The passage from the Apocalypse was cited with enthusiasm by Eusebius' adversary (see below) Methodius (*Sympos.* I. 5, VI. 5; cf. VII. 3). Note also Methodius' praise of the asceticism of John, Peter, and Paul (*De res.* I. 59. 6).

for the expression cf. 38. 5).

In Book III, then, we find two views of the Apocalypse. According to Eusebius' original opinion, earlier expressed in the *Chronicle*, it was written by John the apostle, who also wrote the Gospel ascribed to him. Later on, under the influence of Gaius of Rome, whose work Eusebius may have encountered in the library at Jerusalem as he was working on Book VI, he changed his mind and ascribed the book to the heretic Cerinthus. Only when he finally reproduced the bulk of Dionysius' comments on the Apocalypse did he attain to a more moderate view on the subject (VII. 24-5).

The alterations in his view of the Apocalypse were accompanied by alterations in his view of Papias of Hierapolis, an ardent exponent of apocalyptic realism. We have already cited some of Eusebius' early statements about Papias. To them we should add a comment preserved in *Church History*, III. 36. 2 by four manuscripts (ERBD). Papias was a man 'in every respect most learned, and knowledgeable in scripture'. The words may come from a Byzantine monk, as Schwartz suspected, but the opinion is in harmony with what Eusebius at first thought of Papias.

The full account of Papias in III. 39 seems to fall, or at least can be divided, into two parts. First we have Irenaeus' favourable statement about him, along with Papias' own discussion of his use of oral tradition (3-4), examples of traditions derived from the daughters of Philip, perhaps a comment on a New Testament 'Justus' (9-10), information about the evangelists Mark and Matthew (14-16), and some comments on various books he used (17). These materials are in harmony with Eusebius' early appreciative attitude toward Papias. In addition, and rather easily separable, are his comments reflecting criticisms of Papias and the claim that he was not a disciple of apostles. Papias was not a hearer or eyewitness of the sacred apostles (2; not like Polycarp, III. 36. 1), for the John he heard was not the apostle; there were two of them, both buried at Ephesus (5-8). Papias recorded inauthentic parables and used mythical materials. He was a stupid millenarian enthusiast. He led Irenaeus and others astray (11-13).

The latter attitude of Eusebius is related to the change in his view of the Apocalypse. It is also related to the discussions of apostolic tombs by Gaius of Rome (II. 25. 7) and Dionysius of Alexandria (VII. 25. 16). As heir to the traditions of the anti-chiliastic and anti-Montanistic Christians, Eusebius works out their ideas in historical terms, then applies them to the canon of the New Testament.

Another book with which he was especially concerned was the

Epistle to the Hebrews. There was no real question about it in the East. Clement of Rome used it, as Eusebius noted (III. 38. 1). Irenaeus mentioned, and cited passages from, both it and 'the so-called Wisdom of Solomon' (V. 26). Clement of Alexandria (VI. 13. 5; 14. 3–4) and Origen (VI. 25. 11-14) were concerned with its relation to Luke and Clement of Rome. Dionysius of Alexandria ascribed it to Paul (VI. 41. 6). So did Eusebius himself. As early as the time when he wrote III. 3 he was aware, however, that 'some persons' rejected Hebrews and said it was disputed on the part of the Roman church as not being Paul's. This statement is apparently based on Eusebius' knowledge, such as it was, of the contemporary church of Rome. In VI. 20. 3 he says that 'to this day' some at Rome do not consider it Paul's. His reference to Gaius as holding the same view does not point to the source of his current information. It is not clear whether or not he knows other Roman witnesses against Pauline authorship. According to Photius, Hippolytus held that Paul did not write the epistle (*PG* 103, 404A), but Eusebius does not seem to have known that Hippolytus was Roman. Stephanus Gobarus says that neither Hippolytus nor Irenaeus thought Paul wrote it (Photius, *PG* 103, 1104D); this may explain Eusebius' rather enigmatic remarks about Irenaeus (V. 26).

What especially interests Eusebius about Hebrews, as finally about the Apocalypse, is the question of how to reconcile style (φράσις) and content (νοήματα) with such aspects of the universally accepted letters of Paul. To judge from his quotations from Clement and Origen on the subject, he took from the former the notion that the letter was written by Paul in Hebrew and from the latter the idea that it was translated by either Luke or Clement (III. 38, 1–3).

As for the 'heretical' gospels and apocalypses, it is unfortunate that Eusebius did not say more. His principle is clear enough. 'No man belonging to the successions of the ecclesiastics has judged it right to mention any of them in any way in his writings' (III. 25. 6). Why should Eusebius quote from them or discuss their authors? Only in II. 13. 7 do we find even an allusion to the content of such books. There Eusebius speaks of the greater secrets of the Simonians and says that he who first hears of them will be astonished and 'according to a written oracle of theirs will marvel'. The oracle is apparently the Gospel of Thomas,[10] though a similar saying is found in the Gospel

---

[10] Cf. R. M. Grant, 'Eusebius and Gnostic Origins', *Paganisme, Judaïsme, Christianisme: Mélanges offerts à Marcel Simon* (Paris, 1978); P. Oxy. IV. 654, 7–8; Nag-Hammadi II. 32. 17–18; cf. Clement, *Str.* V. 96. 2.

according to the Hebrews. If it comes from Thomas, Eusebius may have found a reference in the library at Caesarea. In works written there Origen used a saying from this Gospel, using the expression, 'I have read somewhere . . .'[11] If it comes from Hebrews, Eusebius may have taken it from Hegesippus, who discussed Simonians (IV. 22. 5) and quoted from that Gospel (22. 8).[12]

Historical and theological considerations were not all that Eusebius took into account when he discussed the canon. His enemy Methodius, mentioned in the *Apology for Origen* (see Chapter IV), was a chiliast[13] and according to Photius, claimed that Origen had misunderstood the divine plan by assigning 6,000 years to the period from the beginning of creation to Adam, 1,000 years to the divine rest, and another 6,000 from the rest to us — a total of 13,000 years![14] Methodius himself relied strongly on the 'Christ-possessed' author of the Apocalypse of John.[15] This was enough to raise Eusebius' suspicions about the book. In addition, Methodius made use of the *Apocalypse of Peter* and included it among 'the divinely inspired scriptures'.[16] Eusebius was aware that Clement of Alexandria had commented on the *Apocalypse of Peter* in his *Hypotyposes* (*H. E.* VI. 14. 1), but he took more pleasure in the rejection of the Gospel of Peter by Serapion of Antioch (VI. 12. 2). He was aware that many books used by Clement were not genuine, such as the *Acts of Paul,* the *Shepherd*, the *Apocalypse of Peter*, the *Epistle of Barnabas*, and 'the so-called Didachai of the Apostles' (III. 25. 4; cf. VI. 13. 6; 14. 1). But in III. 3. 2 he went out of his way to state that none of the pseudo-Petrine literature was handed down among the writings generally received. 'No ecclesiastical author among ancients or moderns has used testimonies taken from them.' This is not a randomly aimed shot at apocryphal literature. Eusebius' target is his contemporary Methodius.

More than that, while Eusebius basically agreed with Methodius in regard to the theological authority of the Wisdom of Solomon, placing it rather high, he was not going to accept Methodius' simple-minded attribution of it to Solomon himself. He was aware that his favourite Jewish author, Josephus, had not accepted it at all, and he knew that

[11] Origen, *Jos. hom.* IV. 3; *Jer. hom. lat.* I (III). 3, p. 324 Nautin.
[12] Note, however, that Eusebius thinks that Hebrews may be disputed but Thomas is heretical (III. 25. 5–6).
[13] *Sympos.* IX. 1, p. 114 Bonwetsch.
[14] *De creatis* 12, p. 499.
[15] *Sympos.* I. 5, p. 13; cf. V. 7, VI. 5, VIII. 4. 7, IX. 3; *De res.* II. 28. 5.
[16] *Sympos.* II. 6, p. 23; cf. VIII. 2, p. 83.

its place in second–century Christianity had been ambiguous at best. His statements on this subject deserve to be disentangled. First, he tells us that not only Hegesippus but also Irenaeus and 'the whole chorus of the ancients' called Proverbs 'all-virtuous Wisdom' (IV. 22. 9). The remark is wrong as to 'all-virtuous Wisdom', for the term, apparently invented by Clement of Rome (I Clem. 57. 3), does not occur in Irenaeus' extant writings. Irenaeus does refer, however, to Wisdom as speaking through Solomon in the book of Proverbs,[17] and Melito of Sardis, as quoted by Eusebius himself, identifies Proverbs with Wisdom.[18] Second, Eusebius seems unwilling to tell us what Irenaeus actually said about both the Epistle to the Hebrews and the Wisdom of Solomon. He does state that Irenaeus composed 'a book of various discourses, in which he mentions the Epistle to the Hebrews and the Wisdom called Solomon's, citing certain expressions from them' (V. 26). We venture to guess that Irenaeus was comparing the two just as Eusebius compared I Clement with Hebrews (III. 38. 1). His point was presumably the one mentioned by Stephanus Gobarus, who says that he rejected the Pauline authorship of Hebrews.[19] It is surely significant that in Irenaeus' treatise against heresies there are explicit references to all the Pauline epistles except Philemon, but none to Hebrews, and only one possible allusion to that letter (three words).[20] In addition, there is no mention of the Wisdom of Solomon, though there is the one allusion (six words) noted by Eusebius.[21]

Eusebius was of course aware that Clement of Alexandria frequently made use of the Wisdom called Solomon's and the Wisdom of Jesus son of Sirach (VI. 13. 6). More important, he knew that his hero Origen used both books, even though neither can have appeared in the list of Old Testament books which Eusebius cites (VI. 25. 2). The list is said to contain twenty-two books and actually contains twenty-one, but the missing item must be the book of the Twelve Prophets. This means that even though a significant text from Origen's *De principiis* is extant only in Latin, it may well express Origen's attitude. It refers to 'Wisdom, a book which is said to be Solomon's but is certainly not regarded as authoritative by all'.[22]

Methodius raised no such questions. In his *Symposium* he referred to

---

[17] *Adv. haer.* IV. 20. 3.   [18] *H. E.* IV. 26. 14.
[19] *PG* 103, 1104D.   [20] *Adv. haer.* II. 30. 9 (Heb. 1:3).
[21] *H. E.* V. 8. 8; *Adv. haer.* IV. 38. 3 (Wisd. 6:20).
[22] *De princ.* IV. 4. 6; cf. *After the New Testament* (Philadelphia, 1967), 70–82.

'all-virtuous Wisdom' twice, and he meant the Wisdom of Solomon. In his anti-Origenist treatise *On the Resurrection* he explicitly ascribed the work to Solomon (six times).[23]

Since Eusebius wanted to use the ideas of Wisdom but also wanted to differentiate himself from Methodius he pointed toward second-century evidence (Methodius greatly admired Irenaeus) concerning the book. In his own later writings, notably the *Praeparatio*, he would clearly indicate that there were questions about Solomonic authorship.[24] But like Methodius he would use the expression 'all-virtuous Wisdom' in regard to this book, not Proverbs![25] His confusion confuses us when we read in the *Chronicle* (p. 133, 18) that 'Jesus son of Sirach composed a book of Wisdom which is called all-virtuous.'

Conclusion

Various changes, within the *Church History* as well as outside it, show that Eusebius' thought about the New Testament canon developed as he was writing the book. The most significant changes took place in regard to the Apocalypse of John, politically and theologically unattractive during the years just after the Diocletianic persecution. On the other hand, Eusebius was willing to defend eastern views against Rome on the Pauline authorship of Hebrews, especially because he found this letter theologically so congenial.[26] (Ideas related to Hebrews are worked out in his sermon for the church at Tyre.) He attacked the apocryphal Petrine literature as used by his enemy Methodius and went far out of his way to insist that while the Wisdom of Solomon could be used, Solomon did not write it.

In Eusebius' view no question arose about the canonicity of the four Gospels, the Acts, the fourteen Pauline epistles (including Hebrews), 1 Peter, and 1 John (III. 3. 25). Among the 'disputed books' he included James, Jude, 2 Peter, and 2–3 John (III. 25. 3), for Origen had raised questions about all of them.[27] In fact, Eusebius disagreed with Origen only in regard to the Apocalypse of John. He rejected it, as did many eastern writers of the fourth century beginning with Cyril

---

[23] *Sympos.* I. 3; II. 7; *De res.* I. 36. 2; 52. 1; 56. 2; 62. 5; II. 9. 12; 19. 13.

[24] *Praep. ev.* VII. 12. 6; XI. 7. 5; 14. 8; cf. *Dem. Ev.* V. 1. 24.

[25] Methodius, *Sympos.* I. 3; II. 7; Eusebius, *Praep. Ev.* XI. 7. 5.

[26] Cf. I. 2–4; G. Bardy, 'La Théologie d'Eusèbe de Césarée d'après l'Histoire Ecclésiastique', *RHE* 50 (1955), 5–20.

[27] James and Jude; II. 23. 24–5, based on Origen; 2 Peter: VI. 25. 8, from Origen; 2–3 John: VI. 25. 10, from Origen.

of Jerusalem.[28]

Even at this point it appears that he was following a lead given by Origen. Nautin has pointed out that in the newly published papyrus *On the Pascha* Origen apparently refers to 'the Apocalypse attributed to John', while in his late *Homily VII on Joshua* he cites only the Gospel and the Epistles as works of John.[29] Eusebius may not have known these works, however. Perhaps he simply recapitulated Origen's changing attitude.

---

[28] R. Pfeiffer (*History of Classical Scholarship from the Beginnings to the End of the Hellenistic Age*, Oxford, 1968, 207 n.4) suggests that Eusebius (VI. 25. 3) may supply 'the earliest evidence of the word [κανών] for the canon of scripture', but in that passage Eusebius is simply referring to the Church's rule of accepting only four gospels.

[29] O. Guéraud–P. Nautin, *Origène Sur la Pâque* (Paris, 1979), 119 n. 23.

XII

THE FINAL THEME: THE MERCIFUL AND GRACIOUS HELP OF OUR SAVIOUR

After the theme of persecution and martyrdom in his own time, Eusebius proposed to discuss 'the final merciful and gracious help of our Saviour'. Laqueur thought that this promise was added to the others only when Eusebius was expanding his seven-book edition to eight,[1] but since in our view the whole preface and perhaps the whole προκατασκευή (I. 1–4) was one of the last elements in the *Church History* we need not separate this promise from the others.

When was the promise fulfilled? For Eusebius the most important event of this kind was evidently the deathbed decree of Galerius providing toleration for Christians. 'When the divine and heavenly grace showed that it watched over us with gracious and merciful regard, then indeed our rulers also . . . changed their mind in a most marvellous fashion and gave utterance to a recantation' (VIII. 16. 1 = *Mart. Pal.* 13. 14). As political events continued to unfold, he could use the same language to speak of God as showing himself to be merciful and gracious when he brought Constantine forward (IX. 8. 15).[2] God is by nature 'gracious and merciful' (*Ecl. proph.* I. 3), but he is not 'gracious and merciful' toward a disobedient Church (VIII. 1. 8), in need of corrective punishment.

Obviously the existence of propitious and favouring help is most fully evident when unusual events suggest the presence of divine activity. Before turning to examine the place of such events throughout the *Church History* we should take a look at the language Eusebius uses when he discusses such events. Next we shall consider the probable sources of his ideas, as well as the miraculous events he reports. Finally we shall turn to the political evidence.

Eusebian Language

What we find especially characteristic of Eusebius' theological rhetoric is his tendency to use two adjectives wherever one would do. Ramsay

---

[1] R. Laqueur, *Eusebius als Historiker seiner Zeit* (Berlin–Leipzig, 1929), 3–4.
[2] Cf. also *Vit. Const.* IV. 13.

MacMullen has discussed this habit among civil servants, ancient and modern, in a vigorous treatment of 'Roman Bureaucratese'.[3] In Eusebius we see it carried over into the Church bureaucracy as well. We should expect this from a Christian author who could speak of 'ecclesiastical grace' (*C. Marcell.* I. 6).

Thus it might be expected that in the introductory chapters (I. 2–4) he would refer to the Logos of God as 'divine' and 'heavenly'. What is especially Eusebian is saying 'divine and firstborn' and 'divine and heavenly'. At the beginning of Book VI Eusebius tells us that Origen was not a martyr at an early age because his mother hid his clothes and the modest youth stayed home. The result was due to 'divine and heavenly providence, acting for the general good through his mother' (VI. 2. 4). When he later risked martyrdom he miraculously escaped because 'the divine right hand' was helping him. 'The same divine and heavenly grace' saved him 'again and again . . . when plots were laid against him' (VI. 3, 4–5). The ideas come from Origen himself. Nautin draws attention to a reference to the days of his youth, when people 'saw miraculous and wonderful signs' (*Jer. hom.* IV. 3).[4] Again, in his *Commentary on John* (VI. 2) he speaks of later plots against himself and the aid he received from 'the heavenly Logos'. The apostles too were saved from plots 'by some divine power' (*De princ.* IV. 1. 5). But Eusebius himself adds emphasis on the 'divine and heavenly', just as when he tells how Fabian was chosen as Bishop of Rome because of 'the divine and heavenly grace'. A dove lighted on his head to show that the Spirit had chosen him (VI. 29. 2–3).

Such terms proliferate when Eusebius tells about the victory of the apostle Peter over Simon Magus and his patron the Devil, 'the evil power who hates the good'.[5] He mentions 'the divine and super-heavenly grace', 'the divine Logos', 'divine and marvellous effulgence', 'the all-good and most philanthropic providence', and even 'the divine armour' metaphorically worn by the apostle (II. 14).

Galerius' recantation was due to 'divine and heavenly grace', as we have already seen. Eusebius could use the same expression when he referred to the happy state of the Constantinian Church (X. 8. 1–2). He could also speak of 'divine and heavenly judgement' (VII. 30. 2), 'the divine and heavenly hand' (VIII. 1. 6), 'divine and ineffable power' (VIII. 7. 4; 12. 11; *Adv. Hierocl.* 4), and 'the divine and ineffable

---

[3] *Traditio*, 18 (1962), 364–78.
[4] P. Nautin, *Origène: Homélies sur Jérémie*, i (Paris, 1976), 264–5.
[5] Cf. G. J. M. Bartelink, 'Μισόκαλος, epithète du diable', *VC* 12 (1958), 37–44.

wisdom' (*Adv. Hierocl.* 2).

It is possible that Eusebius liked to use 'divine and heavenly' (etc.) because in the third and fourth centuries the term 'divine' was so often used to mean 'imperial'.[6] Indeed, the imperial orders of various kinds, either called 'royal' by Eusebius or left without adjectives, are all called 'divine' in the papyri.[7]

E. Seidl, writing on 'the oath in Roman-Egyptian provincial law', found the earliest oath by 'the divine and heavenly fortune' dated in 342, in the reign of the Emperors Constans and Constantius II.[8] He supposed that 'heavenly' could be traced back to the Lord's Prayer — in which the word does not appear — and suggested that the Roman government was using expressions that 'could find points of contact in the Christian religious life'.[9] Actually such oaths go back to the reign of Constantine,[10] and a clear 'chancery' hand of the early third century refers to what must be restored as 'divine and heavenly' (τῆς [θεί]ας καὶ οὐρα[νίου]) and may be 'fortune'.[11] In the variously dated, but obviously tetrarchic, P. Oxy. XVII. 2106 we find what the editors restored as ἡ θεία καὶ [σεβασμία τύχητ] ὧν δεσποτῶν ἡμῶν αὐτοκρατόρων κα [ὶ καισάρων]. Obviously one could as well read [οὐράνιος τύχη τ].

All aspects of Eusebius' language thus find official precedent.

Eusebian Ideas

Here we are concerned primarily with what Eusebius has to say about 'divine providence' (as early as Euripides)[12] and 'divine grace'. The term 'divine providence' was of course Christian and it had been used by Alexander of Jerusalem in a letter quoted by Eusebius himself (VI. 11.

---

[6] e.g., P. Oxy. XII. 1464. 6 (Decian decree ordering sacrifice). But Constantine too speaks of 'divine providence' (X. 5. 18) and 'the holy and superheavenly Power' (X. 5. 21).

[7] Διατάγματα (VIII. 17. 2; cf. 16. 1; IX. 9a. 9; 10. 10. 12; *Mart. Pal.* 9. 2; 13. 14): P. Cair. Isid. 1. 8. 15. Γράμματα (VIII. 2. 4; cf. 2. 5; IX. 1. 1. 6; 9. 13; 9a. 7; 10. 8): P. Oxy. XVII. 2106. 3; Wilcken, *Chrest.* 158. 19. Διατάξεις (IX. 7. 1; 10. 6. 12; X. 4. 14; 5. 1; 8. 11; 9. 8): Wilcken, *Chrest.* 41. III. 20 (AD 232). Πρόσταγμα (VIII. 17. 8; IX. 10. 9; X. 5. 14. 17): P. Cair. Isid. 2. 6; 3. 5; 4. 5; 5. 4 (all AD 299), etc. Πρόσταξις (*Mart. Pal.* 8. 13): P. Merton I. 31. 3. 9. 16 (AD 307); P. Thead. 33. 5 (probably 308).

[8] P. Flor. 34.

[9] *Münchener Beiträge zur Papyrusforschung und Antiken Rechtsgeschichte*, XXIV (1935), 22.

[10] P. Strassb. II. 129 = SB 7685.   [11] P. Hibeh, 274. 14.

[12] *Phoeniss.* 637.

5). Both Clement and Origen employed it, as reference given in the *Patristic Greek Lexicon* show. Beyond these theologians, reference to divine providence was common in two historians Eusebius knew, Diodorus Siculus and Dionysius of Halicarnassus, as well as in one he knew well, Josephus.[13] The idea was shared with emperors and their subordinates. Thus Maximin Daia insisted upon the providential care provided by the gods and by himself (IX. 7. 3; 10. 7). A proclamation abolishing some compulsory services between 245 and 248 speaks of 'the divine providence of our lords the Augusti',[14] while between 302 and 306 the anti-Christian prefect Culcianus refers to 'the divine providence of the all-victorious emperors and the most renowned Caesars'.[15]

Just as providential care is an important feature of ancient thought (for Origen it involved the care of the universe, peoples, institutions — notably the Christian Church — and individuals)[16] so also the idea of grace was important, and not among Christians alone. When one uses the word he is referring to the beneficence of God or an emperor extended to a person or persons who cannot claim it as a right. Thus in the second century a petitioner speaks of taking refuge with 'the grace of the most renowned emperor'.[17] And according to Cornelius of Rome, writing in the year 251, all the persons receiving aid in his church were supported by 'the grace and philanthropy of the Master'. He added that the number was increasing 'through the providence of God' (VI. 43. 10). This is rather like the way in which others spoke of the grain-doles provided by emperors, for example at Hermopolis, Egypt, in 261: 'I am enrolled for the . . . coming distribution . . . of the grain-dole allotted us by the munificence of our lords the Caesars Augusti Macrianus and Quietus.'[18] A large group of papyri from Oxyrhynchus includes applications for the years 268 to 272 in which the dole is called 'distribution', 'gift', 'donation', and even 'philanthropy'.[19] We can find 'grace' at an earlier date. In Philo's *Legatio* there is a description of the monthly distribution of money or grain at Rome in the time of Augustus. Philo refers to what was

---

[13] Cf. H. W. Attridge, *The Interpretation of Biblical History in the Antiquitates Judaicae of Flavius Josephus* (Missoula, Mont., 1976), 160–5.

[14] P. Oxy. XXXIII. 2664.

[15] P. Oxy. XXXI. 2558.

[16] Cf. B. Drewery, *Origen and the Doctrine of Grace* (London, 1960), 75–86.

[17] *BGU* I. 19, col. I, 21 (AD 135).

[18] P. Lond. 955 (III, pp. 127–8) = Wilcken, *Chrest.* 425.

[19] J. Rea, P. Oxy. XL (1972). 'Philanthropy': Nos. 2918, 2919, 2921.

distributed as 'the grace' (i.e. bounty) and 'the common philanthropy'.[20] The language is religious only in the sense that it is imperial. And one can trace it farther back. Toward the end of the second century BC the priests of Isis at Philae requested royal permission to erect a stele 'on which we shall write down the philanthropy given us by you in these matters, so that your grace-bounty may remain ever-memorable with her forever'.[21] Priestly and royal language are blended.

Our purpose in this section is not so much to insist upon the common language and ideas as to suggest that when Eusebius used them he was readily understood by his readers both pagan and Christian. Constantine had no difficulty in saying that he had received 'perfect grace from the divine providence'.[22] He could inform various churches that 'the heavenly and divine grace', as expressed at Nicaea, was meant to be obeyed.[23]

Eusebius looked for the expression of divine providence and divine grace in miraculous events, and notably in Books VIII and IX he found the miraculous in the political history of the Roman Empire. The persecution came to an end 'by the grace of God'. First 'the divine and heavenly grace' showed that it watched over Christians; then the rulers recanted. This was not because of anything human or pity or philanthropy. Instead, the care given by divine providence exhibited itself, and divinely sent punishment came upon Galerius (VIII. 16). Drought, famine, and plague struck Maximin's empire when God showed forth his 'heavenly alliance' with Christians (IX. 7. 16-8. 1). God's providential care was miraculously expressed when Constantine came on the scene (IX. 8. 15-9. 1). When he defeated Maxentius men stopped viewing the Exodus as a myth (IX. 9. 4). Finally God struck down Maximin and his grace restored the churches (IX. 9. 12; 10. 13; 11. 1).

Eusebius thus understood the events of his own time as controlled by God's providence and grace (two ideas sometimes correlated by his mentor Origen)[24] and he expressed his understanding of the events through language perhaps more imperial than Christian, as might be

[20] Philo, *Leg.* 198.

[21] *OGI* 139, 20–1 (reference from H. Conzelmann, *Theologisches Wörterbuch zum Neuen Testament*, IX (Stuttgart, 1973), 365).

[22] H.-G. Opitz, *Athanasius Werke*, III, 1: *Urkunden zur Geschichte des arianischen Streites* (Berlin, 1935), Urk. 25 (p. 52, 2).

[23] Ibid., Urk. 26, 12 (p. 57, 10).

[24] Drewery, op. cit., 96.

expected. Miracles were by no means limited to his own time, however. As a Bible reader he was aware of miraculous occurrences in both Testaments, and his picture of Church history involved the miraculous help of God along the way.

Eusebian Miracles

Before speaking directly about miracles we should add a few words concerning Eusebius' idea of the divine justice or judgement as expressed in historical events. The divine justice punished both Herod the Great (I. 8. 3) and Herod Antipas (II. 10. 1; both examples from Josephus). It also punished the Jews for their 'crimes against Christ' (II. 6. 8; III. 5. 3. 6; the view of Origen) or against James the Just (II. 23. 20; supposedly from Josephus actually from Origen). Naturally it also punished persecutors, especially emperors (VII. 30. 21; VIII. 16. 2-3; IX. 7. 2; 9a. 12; cf. X. 9. 1) but also their subordinates (II. 7; IX. 11. 5; X. 4. 29; *Mart. Pal.* 7. 7). It punished bad bishops (VIII. 1. 7-2. 3; *Mart. Pal.* 12) and the opponents of good ones (VI. 9. 7-8). When Herod was punished for his 'crime against the Christ and the other children', his sufferings were only 'a prelude to what he would receive after his departure hence' (I. 8. 3). Fourth-century disasters, however, provided preludes to a this-worldly disaster, the overthrow of Maximin (IX. 8. 3; *Mart. Pal.* 7. 7-8).

When one thinks of divine judgement in an ancient context one is likely to remember tragedy, especially in regard to literary precedents. Josephus had already pointed in this direction. As Thackeray put it, he described Herod the Great and his family in the first book of the *War* with 'all the pathos and the technical terminology of a Greek drama'.[25] Just so, Eusebius notes that this account 'overshadows every tragic drama' (I. 8. 4). Similarly the fall of Jerusalem as described by Josephus could be called a 'tragedy' (III. 6. 1), perhaps especially because of the mother who killed and ate her infant son. Similar terms appear in relation to the martyrs of Palestine. In the shorter version Eusebius speaks of unburied corpses as offering 'a spectacle worse than any account or tragic report' (9. 11). In the longer version he refers to 'the drama concerning the marvellous Apphianus' (4. 15). And in both versions he calls the torture of a Christian 'drama' (11. 13).

Eusebius' miracle stories or references are not usually 'tragic',

---

[25] H. St. J. Thackeray, *Josephus the Man and the Historian* (New York, 1929), 65.

however. They are ordinarily to be found either in theological or apologetic summaries or in an atmosphere close to folklore. We shall give examples having to do with the miracles of Christ and his apostles and their immediate successors, with their predictions, and with the magic ascribed to heretical teachers. Then we shall discuss the signs preceding the fall of Jerusalem (from Josephus), the question of the renewal or continuation of miraculous powers raised by the Montanists, the continuing presence of miracles especially in relation to bishops and other prominent persons, and finally the problem of credibility as raised by Eusebius himself.

Eusebius speaks of the incarnate Logos as 'doer of wonderful works' (I. 2. 23). Oddly enough, the expression comes from the forged or at least altered account of Jesus in Josephus' *Antiquities*, cited in I. 11. 7, and Eusebius uses it again in *Demonstratio* III. 4. 21.[26] He works miracles and teaches, just as his disciples do (II. 3. 2). In the introductory section Eusebius goes on to speak, without further definition, of 'the marvel of his birth'. If a reader possessed only the *Church History* he would not know what was meant, even with the aid of I. 5. 2 ('in accordance with the prophecies concerning him'), until he reached II. 1. 2 ('the virgin . . . was discovered to have conceived by the Holy Spirit', Matt. 1:18).[27] There are further references to Jesus' miracles, his resurrection from the dead, and his 'divine restoration to the heavens' (cf. Acts 3:21). The importance of the miracles is stressed again at the end of Book 1, where they attract the attention of King Abgar of Edessa, who corresponds with Jesus to get his aid. Indeed, 'the divinity of our Lord and Saviour Jesus Christ became famous among all men because of his wonder-working power, and led myriads to him . . .' (I. 13. 1). After Jesus' resurrection and return to heaven, Thomas, one of the twelve, sent Thaddaeus, one of the seventy, who 'by the power of God' performed 'great and marvellous deeds' (I. 13. 12). In Book II Eusebius tells another story about rulers who after 'the miraculous resurrection and ascension into heaven' were convinced of Jesus' divine nature. Pontius Pilate informed Tiberius not only about these events but also of 'his other wonders'. Tiberius thereupon asked the Roman senate to approve the deification of Jesus, but the senate rejected his proposal. According to Tertullian, Eusebius' source, Tiberius 'threatened death to the accusers of the Christians' (II. 2).

[26] J. Stevenson, *Studies in Eusebius* (Cambridge, 1929), 21 n. 1.
[27] Irenaeus' discussion of Isaiah 7:14 is noted in V. 8. 10 (cf. VI. 17).

Both Abgar and Tiberius are obviously mentioned because of their importance as witnesses to Jesus' miraculous powers.

Miracle was by no means confined to the period when Jesus was on earth. His resurrection and ascension showed that it would continue, and Eusebius lays some emphasis on the wonder-working achieved by the apostles 'by divine power' or 'by the power of Christ' (II. 1. 11; 3. 2). The apostle Peter was rescued from prison 'by a divine epiphany' (II. 9. 4). Herod Agrippa died after being acclaimed as a god. According to Acts an angel smote him, and Eusebius therefore modifies the parallel passage in Josephus[28] so that Agrippa would see not an owl as a messenger of God but simply a messenger (= angel) of God (II. 10. 6).[29]

The fall of Jerusalem was important for the miracles related to it. First, even before the war an oracle warned Jerusalem Christians to abandon the city and emigrate to Pella (III. 5. 3; see Chapter VI). Second, the fall of the city had been noted by 'the inerrant prediction of our Saviour' (III. 7. 1). Events took place in accordance with his 'prognostic predictions', for he foresaw them 'by divine power as if already present' (7. 3). 'If anyone compares the expressions of our Saviour with the narratives of the historian about the whole war, how could he not marvel and acknowledge that both the foreknowledge and the prediction of our Saviour is truly divine and supernaturally wonderful?' (7. 6).

More than that, the existence of divine and miraculous signs before the war is confirmed by Josephus, who explicitly sets them forth in the sixth book of his *Jewish War* (III. 7. 9–8. 9). But there was something even more wonderful. Josephus tells about an oracle, found 'in the sacred writings', to predict that at that time one from their land would rule the world. Josephus thought this was Vespasian. Vespasian did not rule the world, however, and the oracle really referred to Christ (III. 8. 10–11).

The continuation of miraculous powers among the apostles and their successors is made clear in generalizing passages in Book III. Eusebius says that 'the inspired and truly godly men' were 'bold in the divine and wonder-working power given them by the Saviour', 'the thaumaturgic power of Christ' (24. 3). They were 'serving a greater

---

[28] *Ant.* XIX. 346.
[29] Similarly in IV. 15. 39 when Polycarp has finally been killed by a *confector*, Eusebius has 'much blood' come out, rather than 'a dove and much blood' as in *Mart. Polyc.* 16. 1. A different text? Incredulity?

and superhuman ministry' (24. 4). Their successors too ministered 'with the grace and co-operation of God, since many wonderful miracles of the divine Spirit were still being effected by them at that time' (37. 3). Apparently Eusebius is generalizing from the 'traditions' he gives from Papias: the daughters of 'the apostle Philip' told him about the resurrection of a dead man and about the way in which Justus Barsabbas, years earlier, drank poison without harmful effect (III. 39. 9). A little later, Quadratus spoke of some persons cured or raised from the dead by Jesus who had 'reached our times', perhaps at the end of the first century (IV. 3. 2).

The miracles performed by heretics, however, were all to be ascribed to magic,[30] since Justin and Irenaeus had already so ascribed them. In addition, it could be noted that Menander was empowered by 'diabolic energy' (III. 26). Two Montanist leaders were inspired to commit suicide, while another was said to have fallen to earth while in a trance. Eusebius' authority refuses to accept responsibility for these stories, but Eusebius gladly quotes them (IV. 16. 13-15). He was sure that there were anti-heretical miracles. The Monarchian bishop Natalius was often warned by the Lord through visions but did not repent until angels scourged him all one night (V. 28. 11-12).

The Montanists were especially important because they made acute the question about spiritual gifts and their continuance or revival in the Church. Naturally the Montanists claimed to be prophesying, whether they or their opponents called their effort 'new'. Others rejected their claim but held that prophecy and spiritual gifts still existed in various more conventional churches.

The anonymous anti-Montanist cited by Eusebius claims that Montanus 'with measureless desire of soul for first rank' proceeded to prophesy 'contrary to the church's custom handed down by tradition and in succession'. His claims were encouraged by some (within the Church) 'exalted as if by the Holy Spirit and the prophetic gift' (V. 16. 7-8). Upon reflection, Montanists and anti-Montanists alike seem to have appealed to the precedent of the daughters of Philip.[31] The Montanists seem to have traced a succession from them to a certain Quadratus and 'Ammia in Philadelphia',[32] then to the women disciples of Montanus (V. 17. 4).

---

[30] II. 1. 11; 13. 1; IV. 7. 9; II. 4.   [31] III. 30-1; V. 17.

[32] Is Ammia the daughter of Philip whose name seems to have disappeared from Polycrates' list (III. 31. 3 = V. 24. 2)?

In answer to the Montanist claim, Christians insisted that according to the apostle Paul 'the prophetic gift must exist in every church until the final coming of Christ' (V. 17. 4; 1 Cor. 1:7). Eusebius, like his predecessors, looked for witnesses to the continuation of the gifts and found them reported by Justin (IV. 18. 8) and Irenaeus (V. 7. 6). Indeed, he hinted that the gift was given Origen (VI. 2. 11), more ambiguously to Fabian of Rome (VI. 29. 3). Indeed, the continuation of miraculous powers in various churches allowed Montanism to seem credible (V. 3. 4; cf. 7. 1).

Cities of Miracle

Jerusalem, we have already seen, was a city of miracle for Christian and non-Christian Jews. So it had been in New Testament times, notably according to Luke-Acts. There, after the resurrection, the Lord had transmitted *gnosis* to some of the apostles (II. 1. 4). There the throne of James the Lord's brother, first bishop of the church in the city, was still preserved in Eusebius' time (VII.19).

Eusebius is not himself a witness to the long-time preservation of a little of the water miraculously transformed into oil by Narcissus of Jerusalem. He contents himself with mentioning it in connection with a story told on the basis of oral tradition. At the all-night paschal vigil the deacons ran out of oil. Narcissus had water drawn and after prayer had it poured into the lamps. 'Contrary to all reason, by miraculous and divine power its nature was changed from water to the quality of oil.' This was only one of Narcissus' miracles. It obviously resembles both the changing of water into wine (John 2:1-11) and the inexhaustible 'widow's cruse' (2 Kings 4:1-7).[33] Fully folkloristic, the story is important only because it depicts a miracle in the service of ecclesiastical authority and ritual, while at the same time it introduces a note of unexpected spirituality into the cult (VI. 9. 1-3).

Another story about Narcissus is equally miraculous. Three wretches for a reason unnamed plotted against him and spread slander not detailed. They guaranteed their slander by oaths. One said, 'May I be destroyed by fire', another, 'May my body be consumed by a dreadful disease', the third, 'May my eyes be blinded'. The great eye of justice[34]

---

[33] Cf. T. H. Gaster, *Myth, Legend, and Custom in the Old Testament* (New York, 1969), 518-19.

[34] Proverbial according to Polybius, XXIII. 10. 3 (cf. (Menander), *Monost.* 225 Jäkel; Diphilus in *Praep. Ev.* XIII. 13. 47); Josephus, *Bell.* I. 84. 378; *Laus Constantini*, 17. 6.

punished all three. A small spark fell on the house of the first and burned him up with his whole family. The second was covered by disease from head to feet. The third, impressed by the fate of the others, made public confession and wept so hard that both eyes were destroyed (VI. 9. 4-8). Here too we are in the folklore world.

This is not all, however. When Narcissus had reached the age of 115 or so, and had resumed office after retirement to the desert, he received a coadjutor in a manner entirely miraculous. Alexander, Bishop in Cappadocia and formerly a pupil of Pantaenus at Alexandria, received a revelation in a vision at night. He thereupon journeyed to Jerusalem in order to pray there and visit the holy places. Meanwhile some of the Christians of Jerusalem had received a similar revelation. Those who were 'especially zealous' were to 'go forth outside the gates and welcome as their bishop the one foreordained by God'. Neighbouring bishops consented to his translation (VI. 11. 1-2). What choice had they?

Eusebius tells us nothing more about miracles in Jerusalem. In regard to Alexandria, we have already seen divine and heavenly providence and grace protecting Origen. We need only add that at a later date it also miraculously protected Dionysius, as he himself stated (VI. 40. 3-5). At the beginning of the third century the Church gained many converts when the martyr Potamiaena appeared and called them in their dreams (VI. 5. 6-7).

At Rome, as we have indicated, miracle played a part in the selection of at least one bishop. The nondescript rustic Fabian was selected when a dove suddenly flew down from above and lighted on his head, 'in clear imitation of the descent of the Holy Spirit "in the form of a dove" [Luke 3:22] upon the Saviour'. The people responded 'as if moved by one divine spirit' (VI. 29. 2-4).

When he reaches the persecution under Valerian, Eusebius turns aside from his accounts of the major sees (especially Alexandria) to give some local traditions, first about martyrs (VII. 12. 15) then about their senatorial admirer Astyrius and his friends (16-17). Astyrius' friends 'who have survived to our day' tell how at Caesarea Philippi a sacrificial victim thrown into the source of the Jordan, perhaps in honour of Pan, would disappear rather than float. This circumstance was regraded as a great marvel. Astyrius once attended the event and asked God to convict the demon and end the deception. The sacrifice at once came to the surface, and 'no further marvel ever took place about that place.'

Like the folklore cited before, this seems to be a Christian version of someone else's story. According to Zosimus, the Aphrodite of Aphaka at the source of the river Adonis predicted the destruction of Palmyra in 273. Offerings cast into a lake near her temple ordinarily sank if they were acceptable, floated if they were not. Shortly before Palmyra was destroyed the gold and silver previously accepted came to the surface.[35] At the very least the stories about Astyrius and Aphrodite reflect cultic rivalry. According to *Laus Constantini*, 8.6, Constantine took pains to destroy the temple at Aphaka.[36]

Credibility

Questions of credibility are expressed in two citations from Josephus' *War* concerning events in the fall of Jerusalem. When the historian introduced his account of a woman who killed and ate her baby he said that such an event had been narrated 'neither by Greeks nor by barbarians — horrible to tell, incredible to hear'. He would have left it out had there not been countless witnesses (III. 6. 20; *Bell.* VI. 199). Again, an apparition 'of incredible size' would have seemed merely fabulous had it not been described by those who saw it (III. 8. 5; *Bell.* VI. 297). Eusebius takes these over without comment and obviously accepts Josephus' point.

At another point, however, he seems to express a 'non-committal attitude on the miraculous'. This is to be found in V. 5, where he is summarizing the story of the Christian legion whose prayers brought rain to Romans, lightning to barbarians on the Danube in the time of Marcus Aurelius. Eusebius has grave chronological difficulties with the story, as we have seen (pp. 18, 118–19). It seems impossible that he can have doubted its authenticity, for he uses it apologetically.

The story is told by authors who are far from our doctrine . . . and has also been explained by our own. The outside historians, unfamiliar with the faith, have set forth the miracle but have not acknowledged that it took place by the prayers of our people; but our authors, as friends of truth, have handed down in simple and harmless fashion what actually happened' (V. 5. 3).

At the end of his discussion, however, he says, 'But let these things be as anyone will.'[37] This kind of expression, related by Thackeray chiefly

[35] Zosimus, *Hist.* I. 58. 1–3; cf. F. Paschoud, *Zosime: Histoire nouvelle*, i (Paris, 1971), 168.

[36] Cf. *Vit. Const.* III. 55. 2.

[37] H. St. J. Thackeray, op. cit., 57–8. Cf. G. MacRae, 'Miracle in the *Antiquities* of Josephus', *Miracle* (ed. C. F. D. Moule, London, 1965), 127–47; H. R. Moehring, 'Rationalization of Miracles in the Writings of Flavius Josephus', *TU* 112 (1973), 376–83.

to Josephus and Dionysius of Halicarnassus, was actually widespread among historians.[38] In fact, almost any historian was expected to use it, no matter what he thought of startling events and their occurrence. Its presence in V. 5. 7 proves nothing about Eusebius' attitude.

Indeed, three passages in his writings in which he deals with contemporary events prove that he was a believer, not a sceptical historian. 'Who that saw them' — martyrs at Tyre — 'was not struck with amazement' at their sufferings and their 'marvellous endurance'? Eusebius himself was present and 'beheld the present, divine power of our Saviour'. The wild beasts were driven back 'by a divine and mysterious power I cannot explain', or rather 'by divine providence' (VIII. 7. 2-6). This is the account of an eyewitness. Second, Eusebius tells of the martyr Apphianus, tortured and then drowned in the sea. The subsequent miracle was seen by all the residents of Caesarea. An earthquake brought Apphianus' corpse up out of the deep and cast it ashore by the gates of the city (*Mart. Pal.* 4. 14-15). Several years later, when burial was denied to martyrs, 'contrary to the laws of nature' and 'by a beastly and barbarous counsel', a miracle took place and the very stones wept 'by an ineffable reason'. Eusebius 'knows well that this account will seem a delusion or a myth to those after us, but not to those for whom the event made the truth credible' (9. 8-9, 12-13).

Around this time Rabbi Abbahu died at Caesarea too, and his disciples also spoke of weeping stones.[39] Did Christians borrow from Jews, or vice versa? Or did both interpret phenomena in the light of their different faiths?

For the Christian author, telling about divine aid in the midst of suffering, such miracles pointed ahead to the event in which he saw God as finally vindicating his people. Miracles in the past were important, but they paled when compared with the political miracle of the early fourth century, when the Roman Empire turned toward Christ and his epiphany (cf. X. 8. 1).

Imperial Documentation

The most conspicuous feature of Books VIII-X is the presence of collections of imperial documents issued by Galerius, Maximin, and Constantine with Licinius. We have already discussed the framework

---

[38] G. Avenarius, *Lukians Schrift zur Geschichtsschreibung* (Meisenheim/Glan, 1956), 163-4.

[39] S. Lieberman, 'The Martyrs of Caesarea', *Annuaire de l'institut de philologie et d'histoire orientales et slaves*, 7 (1944), 400.

of miracle within which Eusebius sets the death of Galerius, the triumph of Constantine, and the defeat of Maximin. Now we turn to the tangible consequences of these events, to be found in imperial letters and decrees.

In the course of the *Church History* Eusebius is always concerned with imperial documentation, finding it wherever he can. Thus a rescript of Hadrian comes from the *Apology* of Justin (IV. 9), a letter of Gallienus perhaps from the correspondence of Dionysius of Alexandria (VII. 13). His selection of a rescript from either Antoninus Pius or Marcus Aurelius is less fortunate, since the document seems to be a forgery (IV. 13). It is hard to imagine how he would acquire copies of such venerable documents, in any event. Josephus had access to the imperial archives at Rome,[40] but while writing the *History* Eusebius seems to have gone no farther than Egypt.

An important inscription from Ephesus in the early fourth century shows how one could look things up.[41] A governor writes to the city of Ephesus and gives instructions for defending traditional precedence in the province of Asia. Full documentation is to be sent him for forwarding to 'the deity of our masters'.[42] It is to be derived from 'the ancient laws' as cited in Ulpian's treatise *De officiis* (presumably *De officiis proconsulis*), from the 'divine constitutions' (i.e. imperial), and from the *senatus consulta*. Eusebius would not have consulted Ulpian, but Lactantius tells us that in his seventh book he collected anti-Christian rescripts.[43] This book also contained rescripts on 'assassins and poisoners' and 'astrologers and seers'.[44] The only anti-Christian document Eusebius cites, however, is a rescript of Maximin which he claims to have seen on a bronze tablet at Tyre (IX. 7. 3–14).

Eusebius was therefore concerned with the edict of toleration issued by Galerius on his deathbed, with the series of documents which showed how Maximin grudgingly accepted toleration, and finally with documents favouring the Church issued by Constantine and Licinius in 313 to 314. (Lactantius used Latin versions of the edict of Galerius and the joint letter of Constantine and Licinius, but they are not exactly the same as Eusebius' documents.) The mention of Constantine

---

[40] H. St. J. Thackerary, op. cit., 70–2.
[41] J. Keil–G. Maresch, 'Epigraphische Nachlese zu Miltners Ausgrabungsberichten aus Ephesos', *JAOI* 45 (1960), Beiblatt 83–4; L. Robert, 'Sur les inscriptions d'Ephèse', *Revue de Philologie*, 41 (1967), 46.
[42] Cf. IX. 1. 3. 5.   [43] *Div. inst.* V. 11. 9.
[44] *Coll. leg. Mos. et Rom.* I. 3. 6; XV. 2.

and Licinius probably points toward Eusebius' sources for his documentation. When Constantine took Rome in 312 he discovered, and undoubtedly circulated at least to a restricted group, the letters Maximin had exchanged with Maxentius. Along with statues and images of Maximin, these documents constituted part of Constantine's successful propaganda campaign against the memory of Maxentius and the waning power of Maximin.[45] The success of the campaign is evident from Eusebius' portraits of both emperors. In addition, Eusebius' use of the documents from Maximin is intended to prove how inconsistent and grudging his policy toward the Christians was. Laqueur[46] pointed out that Maximin's praetorian prefect must have favoured the Christians, but he added that the documents probably passed through the hand of officials of Constantine and/or Licinius.

Of course Eusebius indicates something of the content of the anti-Christian legislation of the first three centuries. But he never quotes it exactly. He reserves quotation for the pro-Christian enactments of the emperors. Thus there are no quotations from the edicts of Diocletian and his fellow tetrarchs. Indeed, even an attempt by Maximin to moderate the severity of the persecution appears only in paraphrase (VIII. 12. 7-9).

It is necessary for you, noble and law-abiding judges, to exercise merciful and humane conduct in your dealings with the Christians. It is not fitting to defile your cities with the blood of your own citizens, or to involve the supreme authority of the emperors in an accusation of cruelty, since this government is well-disposed and mild toward all men. Therefore the benefit of our humane imperial authority is to be extended to all, and the death penalty is not to be imposed upon the Christians.

Unfortunately this expression of 'humanity' was accompanied by the announcement of a new penalty (VIII. 12. 10).

The penalty now to be imposed upon those Christians who refuse to recant is the gouging out of an eye and the maiming of a leg. This lighter punishment will be characteristic of our humane imperial authority.

Thus Lactantius says that Maximin claimed to exercise clemency by forbidding the killing of Christians, but he ordered them 'debilitated'

---

[45] Lactantius, *Div. inst.* 44. 10; cf. 43. 3.
[46] R. Laqueur, *Eusebius als Historiker seiner Zeit* Berlin–Leipzig, 1929), 175, 179.

in this way.[47] The date was probably 308.[48] Constantine stopped the practice, but only in 316.[49] In a letter which Eusebius cites (IX. 9a. 2-3) Maximin claims that when he first came to the Orient 'under happy auspices' (probably as Augustus) he stopped banishment, harsh treatment, and insults in the case of Christians. Obviously he has in mind the problems of upper-class Christians, not their inferiors. In the same letter he refers to extortion 'at the hands of the *beneficiarii*' and other officials (9a. 7). Problems of extortion by so-called *Caesariani* were conspicuous from 305 onward.[50] Persecution usually leads to fraud. Eusebius passes over the problems of upper-class Christians to lay emphasis on the sufferings of those not exempted from torture and extreme forms of the death penalty.

The edict of Galerius, issued before his death in mid-311, is either quoted in the form in which Maximin re-issued it or in a version from which his name has dropped out (VIII. 17. 3-5). Certainly it underwent revision. Galerius (or Maximin) is given the ironical titles 'Aegyptiacus Maximus' and 'Thebaicus Maximus' for victories over his own people in Egypt and the Thebaid. And in the late version represented by bDM the name and titles of Licinius have been deleted. Presumably the name and titles of Maximin vanished earlier, perhaps by accident. Galerius' name was Galerius Valerius Maximianus, while Maximin's was Galerius Valerius Maximinus.[51] After the lengthy preamble, with its historical justification of imperial policy, the point of the edict is reached in VIII. 17. 9-10.

Christians may exist again and build the houses in which they assembled, providing that they do nothing contrary to order.

They are also required to pray to their god for the security of emperor, people, and themselves. Presumably Diocletian had ordered *ne Christiani sint*.

Historically analysed, the five imperial documents preserved in Books VIII and IX shed a bright light on Maximin's problems from 311 onwards. The edict of Galerius stated why the emperors had persecuted – in order to restore the ancient laws and public order – and why they had failed – because of the self-will and folly of the Christians, most of

---

[47] *De mort. persec.* 36. 6-7.   [48] *Mart. Pal.* 8. 1.
[49] *Cod. Theod.* IX. 40. 2.
[50] *CIL* III, 12134; cf. V, 2781, lines 31-4, O. Seeck, 'Caesariani', *RE* III (1897), 1295-6; *AE* 1935, 168.
[51] I formerly held that because of imperial titulature the edict in its present form should be ascribed to Maximin. T. D. Barnes has persuaded me otherwise.

whom abandoned Christianity but did not return to paganism. Now they were to be pardoned and allowed to exist, even to build churches. A later instruction would tell the 'judges', i.e. provincial governors, about procedure.

Galerius died before such a letter went out, at least in the diocese of Oriens, but Eusebius possessed the letter sent by Sabinus, praetorian prefect of the Emperor Maximin (IX. 1. 3-6). This letter contains the themes of the edict of Galerius, repeating its emphasis on restoration and on the obstinacy of Christians. Because of the danger to which they had exposed themselves, the emperors were willing to liberate them and not to continue bringing charges of not worshipping the gods. Now the governors were to transmit Sabinus' orders downward to urban and rural officials.

Similarly when we look at the two documents in IX. 9a and 10 we see that the first is from Maximin to the praetorian prefect instructing him to issue a decree in his own name, while the second is such a decree though from the emperor, not from Sabinus. The parallels suggest that the second is what Maximin had asked Sabinus to send out. Perhaps he refused to do so on his own responsibility.

Both documents begin with semi-historical sketches of the goals of Diocletian and Maximian, authors of the persecution, and of Maximin's own attempts to mitigate the severity of the penalties. In the first document there is an unconvincing account of his efforts not to banish Christians from Nicomedia and other cities (IX. 9a. 4-6). This narrative disappears from the parallel document, presumably because it was so palpably misleading. The first document ends with an order to Sabinus to use only persuasion when calling provincials to the worship of the gods, and to allow freedom of worship. The second goes much farther. Emphasis is laid on the extortion and robbery characteristic of officials, who are reminded that freedom of worship has been allowed. Now it is being emphasized again. Christians are finally allowed to build churches and recover confiscated property.

Eusebius points out that these concessions were made 'less than a whole year after the ordinances against the Christians set up by him [Maximin] on tablets' (IX. 10. 2). Naturally he took pains to obtain a copy of these ordinances, for he knew they were inconsistent with Maximin's claim to have been tolerant. He found the emperor's rescript on a bronze tablet at Tyre. In it (IX. 7. 3-14) Maximin answered a petition to banish Christians by lengthily describing the providential care of the immortal gods, hampered by Christian godlessness but favourably affected by Maximin's own sacred rites (the priesthoods he restored). He went on to agree that intransigent Christians should be 'separated and driven far from your city and countryside' in order to free the city from pollution.

In Eusebius' view all such petitions were inspired by the emperor himself or by the Curator of Antioch (IX. 2). This official dealt with finances and presumably was active in the 'extortion' of Christians' funds (cf. IX. 9a. 7; 10. 8. 11). From a petition found at Arykanda in Lycia and preserved at Istanbul we can see how similar the petitions and their answers must have been.[52] In IX. 9a. 6 Maximin admits that he confirmed the request they made. He says he insisted on toleration, but only verbally. It was this fatal wavering that had to be glossed over in IX. 9a and forgotten in IX. 10. The Christians did not forget, and Eusebius' collection of documents helped them remember.

Laqueur noted that in the *Church History* Maximin died three times. Indeed, the figure could be raised to four. He 'perished by a most disgraceful death at the hand of Licinius' (IX.9. 1.), was 'struck down by the divine justice' (9. 12), 'ended his life by a miserable death' (10. 6), and finally 'gave up the ghost' (10. 15). Laqueur thought these repetitions pointed toward various sources and editions of Book IX, but it seems likely that much is due to rhetorical emphasis. We should not exclude the possibility that in IX. 10. 13-15 Eusebius was making use of Lactantius, *De mortibus persecutorum* or, more probably, of common sources, written or oral. It is worth noting that where Lactantius hinted at a trace of human sympathy with Maximin's family, Eusebius saw only the work of divine justice in Licinius' killings.

Originally, as we have said after Schwartz, Laqueur, and others, there was no Book X. The documents from Constantine and Licinius later included in X. 5-7 came at the end of Book IX. Probably in 315, however, Book X was elaborately justified (X. 2) and enlarged by including the panegyric Eusebius had preached at Tyre for the dedication of the new church there, one of the 'temples rising once more from their foundations to a boundless height' (X. 2. 1; cf. VIII. 1. 5). Peace and concord (X. 3. 1) made the new era quite different

---

[52] *CIL* III, 12132 = *OGI* 569. By now Eusebius had stopped reading Josephus, in whose *War* he could have found out how the people of Antioch once asked Titus to expel the Jews from their city and to destroy the bronze tablets listing their privileges. Titus noted that since their native city had been destroyed no other place would receive them (*Bell.* VII. 108-10). But Eusebius would not have regarded this as a parallel (see Ch. IX).

from the period before the persecution (VIII. 1. 7). Eusebius quotes his long and ornate panegyric in full, for the 'temple' at Tyre was a counterpart to the spiritual temple of God in heaven and its whole symbolical meaning had to be explained (X. 4).

In Eusebius' view it was important that the fall — even death and burial — of the Church in the persecution was due, as in VIII. 1. 7-2. 3, to her own envious sinfulness (X. 4. 12, 57-8). This is not to say that evil and tyrannical persecutors did not deserve their punishment (X. 4. 14, 29).

In X. 2. 2 Eusebius describes the imperial documents provided in ATERM at X. 5-7 but deleted from BD and the Syriac version. There were 'successive imperial constitutions' which extended 'the bounty from God toward us'. There were personal letters to the bishops with honours and gifts of money. This description exactly corresponds with the documents. The first (X. 5. 2-14) is almost identical with a Latin decree which Lactantius says Licinius had published in Nicomedia on 13 June 313.[53] In Eusebius' version there is a preamble to explain that previously the emperors had provided religious liberty but that various conditions, which 'seemed clearly to have been added in that rescript', kept Christians from taking advantage of the opportunity (X. 5. 2-3). The Constantinian-Licinian document thus resembles the letter and the edict of Maximin (IX. 9a. 6; 10. 9),[54] in which the emperor's desire for religious liberty is contrasted with the repressive attitudes of citizens or provincial governors. On the other hand, in X. 5. 6 we read that the 'conditions . . . were contained in our former letters' and that they were related to matters 'wholly unfortunate and foreign to our clemency'. Constantine and Licinius, now victors over Maximin, must be explaining away how it was that the persecutor associated them with himself in his legislation hostile to Christians. The Arykanda inscription shows that the provincials sent their anti-Christian petition to Maximin and Licinius, though not to Constantine. Presumably, then, the rescript banishing them was, or should have been, issued in the name of both.

The Constantinian-Licinian document is even more repetitious than the enactments of Maximin. Batiffol tried to differentiate the original from 'glosses' dealing with details.[55] Nesselhauf thought that the

---

[53] *De mort. persec.* 48.

[54] Also *cum feliciter ego* (Lactantius, *De mort. persec.* 48. 1); cf. X. 5. 10; IX. 9a. 2. 4.

[55] 'Les Étapes de la conversion de Constantin. II. L'édit de Milan', *Bulletin d'ancienne littérature et d'archéologie chrétiennes*, 3 (1913), 244-7.

equivalent of X. 5. 5-6 (Lact. 48. 3-4) comes from Constantine and is framed by Licinius' statements in X. 5. 4, 7 (Lact. 48. 2. 5).[56] Castritius argued that these ascriptions should be reversed.[57] Moreau claimed that as a whole the document came from Licinius. In the realms of Constantine the edict of Galerius had remained in force; indeed, it was in force as late as 15 February 314.[58] Laqueur, anticipating the general position of MacMullen, pointed out that a Hellenistic king could produce legislation equally turgid. A fourth-century imperial chancery could do no less.[59]

This, then, was the first of the documents to which Eusebius referred as 'successive imperial constitutions'. Two others follow, the first immediately. This is called an imperial command but is actually a letter addressed to the Proconsul of Africa and instructing him to restore the property of the Church at once. It is thus a pendant to the more general constitution already discussed (X. 5. 15-17). Eusebius or an earlier collector of documents supposed that it showed that property was to be restored only to the Catholic Church in Africa, not the Donatists. The letter indicates that this question had not yet come to the attention of the emperors. Quite soon, however, the question did come up, and another letter addressed to the proconsul, providing exemption from compulsory civic duties for clerics, refers to 'the Catholic Church over which Caecilian [Bishop of Carthage] presides' (X. 7. 1-2).

Between the two letters addressed to the Proconsul of Africa Eusebius has placed three letters from Constantine to the Bishops of Rome, Syracuse, and Carthage. Eusebius describes the first as related to 'the union and concord of the churches', the second to 'removing all division among the bishops', and the third to gifts of money to the churches. His descriptions are not quite ingenuous. After the peace of the Church the divisions already present in the African church resulted in outright schism. The consequent squabbles lasted for more than a century, and even in 321 Constantine had to abandon his hope of settling them by state authority. Actually, the first of Eusebius' three letters instructs the Bishop of Rome to preside over a synod

---

[56] H. Nesselhauf, 'Das Toleranzgesetz des Licinius', *Historisches Jahrbuch*, 74 (1955), 46-9.

[57] H. Castritius, *Studien zu Maximinus Daia* (Kallmünz, 1969), 80-1.

[58] J. Moreau, *Scripta minora* (Heidelberg, 1964), 99-105; cf. *CSEL* 26, 203.

[59] R. Laqueur, 'Die beiden Fassungen des sog. Toleranzedikts von Mailand', ΕΠΙΤΥΜΒΙΟΝ *Heinrich Swoboda* (Reichenberg, 1927), 139 n. 5; cf. *OGI* 5.

dealing with the affairs of Caecilian of Carthage along with ten plaint-
iffs and ten allies. The emperor asks him to 'leave no schism or division
in any place'. The second looks back to the first and orders the Bishop
of Syracuse to attend another synod, to meet at Arles on the first
of August (in 314). The third is placed last although it was written
before the others. Constantine discusses the distribution of funds in
Africa by Caecilian 'in accordance with the schedule sent you by
Ossius' (of Cordova, Constantine's adviser). Caecilian can obtain the aid
of the proconsul in dealing with schismatics (X. 5. 18–6. 2).

The Constantinian–Licinian constitution rightly comes at the end
of the persecution. The other documents are related to the church in
Africa, about which Eusebius has previously said virtually nothing
(VI. 43. 3; VII. 3; VIII. 6. 10). He must have possessed them because
they presented the imperial position in regard to the question of
African schism in 313 and 314. Presumably the dossier, such as it was,
came into existence before the Synod of Arles. When the final edition
of Book X appeared it was clear that the emperor had not solved the
problem and Eusebius therefore deleted the documents.

Eusebius' account of the fall of Licinius and the victory of
Constantine betrays hasty analysis and composition (X. 8–9). 'The
envy that hates good and the demon that loves evil' (an odd expression!)
could not put up with the sight of the peace of the Church and the
Empire. Thus inspired and neglecting the fate of the tyrants, Licinius
plotted against his benefactor, brother-in-law, and co-emperor, then
openly warred against him and persecuted Christians. Indeed, he went
mad and warred against God. He drove Christians away from his palace
(cf. VII. 1) and forced soldiers to offer sacrifices (cf. VIII. 4. 3–4).
His laws were abominable. He forbade the sending of aid to prisoners,
under penalty of imprisonment. He altered the laws of marriage and
inheritance and raised taxes, tax valuations, and fines. He banished
the innocent and arrested 'noble and highly esteemed men', offering
their wives to his own household slaves and satisfying his lust with
many women (X. 8. 1–13). The language is virtually the same as that
used of Maxentius and Maximin in late sections of Book VIII
(14. 2. 11–12).

Licinius' moves against the Church, however, were far more
significant. He put bishops unnamed to death, demolished some
churches in Pontus (cf. VIII. 12. 6), and deposited the bodies of some
Christians in the sea after cutting them to pieces (cf. VIII. 13. 4). He
planned a universal persecution, but God intervened through

Constantine (X. 8. 14-19).

The last chapter of the *Church History* is a panegryic on the victorious Constantine and his son Crispus, whom Eusebius compares with God the universal king and his son, the Saviour of all (X. 9. 4). *Damnatio memoriae* followed the defeat of Licinius, and he suffered the fate of the older tyrants — i.e. death. The Empire was restored by Constantine, 'resplendent with every virtue that godliness bestows', and Crispus, 'in all respects like his father'. All tyranny was purged away, and the Empire was preserved 'for Constantine and his sons alone'.

The discussion of the laws in chapter 8 is obviously related to the repeal of Licinius' acts in December 324. The panegyric in chapter 9 must have something to do with the fact that Eusebius, excommunicated by a synod at Antioch toward the end of 324, had been given the right to appeal to an ecumenical synod which Constantine was convoking in the spring of 325. This means that in the winter of 324 to 325 Eusebius completed the *Church History*. He deleted many of his earlier references to Licinius and made the whole work, especially the last three books, worthy of the emperor whom he expected to deliver him from his enemies at Ancyra or Nicaea.

Conclusion

The theme announced last by Eusebius combines theological and political terminology and ideas. We began by discussing the theological aspects of his thought. We end with politics, and another suggestion. Codifications of imperial laws were provided by bureaucrats fairly early during the reign of Diocletian in the Codex Gregorianus (up to May 291, though including also the rescript against the Manichees of 297 or 302) and the Codex Hermogenianus (up to 294). Obviously in the changed conditions after Galerius' edict of toleration the previous anti-Christian legislation was out of date. It is conceivable that in the new setting Eusebius was concerned with copying down the tangible evidence for 'the merciful and gracious help of our Saviour' and its continuing effects (VIII. 16. 1; also IX. 8. 15). Such documents would be useful to Christians and pagans alike as they dealt with the legal situation of Christians and churches after the downfall of Galerius and Maximin. The anti-Christian legislation of Maximin, attested by an extant inscription, was included simply in order to show how inconsistent Maximin was.

XIII

EUSEBIUS AS CHURCH HISTORIAN

We have reached the end of what may seem rather a long journey. Its purpose, variously defined at various points during the last ten years, now seems fairly clear. It is to cast some light on Eusebius and his times by tracing, or trying to trace, modifications in his views as expressed in the *Church History*. Everyone agrees that such modifications can be found in Books VIII–X. Our purpose has been to find them in the first seven books as well. It does not make much difference whether we are illuminating the first quarter of the fourth century or, in addition, the last years of the third century. In either case our sources for the history of Christianity are so meagre that closer analysis can only prove helpful. And whether or not one agrees with every detail of the portrait of Eusebius that begins to emerge, it is at least a picture of a human being, neither a saint nor intentionally a scoundrel. Eusebius' work is important not just because of the documents he used but because of the ways in which he used them. These ways illuminate the history of the Christian Church in one of its most important transitions, a transition in which Eusebius himself played a prominent part.

His life bridged the forty years of peace at the end of the third century, the decade of persecution, and the quarter-century of peace under Constantine. We do not know much about his biography. To judge from the volume of his writings, he was essentially an exegete and scholar, not a man of action. He tells us that Dionysius of Alexandria, who died in 265, lived into his own era (III. 28. 3), but we know nothing directly about what he was doing before he saw the young Constantine and the older Diocletian on their way from Palestine to Egypt in 296 (*Vit. Const.* I. 19. 1). Apparently he stood close to the Bishop Agapius (VII. 32. 24), closer to the philanthropist and presbyter Pamphilus, a fervent admirer of Origen (VII. 32. 25). Certainly by the time the persecution began, in 303, Eusebius had made much use of the library founded by Origen and continued by Pamphilus at Caesarea. He witnessed the destruction of churches as the persecution began (VIII. 2. 1), and was living in a house with other Christians of Caesarea when Apphianus left them to become a voluntary martyr (*Mart. Pal.* 4. 8). At other times during the persecution he was at Tyre

(VIII. 7) or in the Thebaid in Egypt (VIII. 9. 4–5). During 308 to 310, when Pamphilus was in prison at Caesarea, Eusebius worked with him on their joint *Apology for Origen* (VI. 33. 4).[1] Since the *Apology* was addressed to the confessors in the copper mines at Phaeno, Eusebius' visit there may have been undertaken so that he could deliver it to them.[2] After Agapius' death Eusebius himself became Bishop of Caesarea and preached the sermon for the rededication of the Christian basilica at Tyre probably in 314 (X. 4). Deposed by a synod at Antioch late in 324, he was vindicated by the Council of Nicaea and became a trusted friend of the Emperor Constantine. It may be that Constantine knew something about the *Church History*, for in a letter he referred to Eusebius' erudition and modesty (*Vit. Const.* III. 60. 3). Eusebius' modesty had been expressed in his description of his own preaching at Tyre (X. 4. 1).

Eusebius was vulnerable especially at two points. First was his failure to be a martyr, or even a confessor, during the persecution. A vehement Egyptian bishop and confessor, devoted to Athanasius and hostile to Eusebius, attacked him at the Council of Tyre. We have already discussed (Chapter X) the accusation brought against Eusebius by Potammon (and later noted by Athanasius).[3] Eusebius did not really reply but counter-attacked. The time was not ripe for an analysis of Roman policy in various provinces or for pointing out that Eusebius himself had not even been arrested; he was visiting Pamphilus to work with him in the defence of Origen — against similar charges. It is clear, however, that there was no simple answer to be given to those who had actually suffered during the persecution, especially since Constantine had shown special favour to one of them, Paphnutius, at the Council of Nicaea (Socrates, *H. E.* I. 11). Eusebius could only claim that he admired martyrs and had shown his admiration by collecting ancient martyrdoms and by what he had written in Books VIII and IX of the *Church History*.

The second point was more difficult to deal with and has less to do with Eusebius' historical work. This was the problem of his old-fashioned theology, partly based on New Testament passages, partly on a simplified version of Origen's views. Whether or not Eusebius intended to become involved in theological controversies, Arius was able to bring him into Christological debates by claiming that he and

---

[1] Cf. Photius, *Bibl. cod.* 118 (*PG* 103, 396C).
[2] Ibid., 397C; cf. M. J. Routh, *Reliquiae sacrae*, iv (ed. 2, Oxford, 1846), 341.
[3] Athanasius, *Apol. sec.* 8. 3 (p. 94, 8 Opitz).

practically all his fellowbishops in the East taught that God existed
without a beginning while the Son did not.[4] Eusebius blithely informed
the Syrian Bishop Euphration that this was indeed his view; he
explained that the Father was first and the Son second, that the Son
had said, 'The Father who sent me is greater than I', and that he had
prayed to 'the only true God'. The apostle Paul set forth 'ineffable
and mystical theology' when he called Christ 'the one mediator
between God and man, the man Christ Jesus'.[5] Half a century later
Athanasius still recalled his statements with distaste.[6]

These are the controversies in which we know Eusebius was involved
as he wrote and rewrote his *Church History*. In addition, two questions
discussed at the Council of Nicaea seem to find echoes. First, under
Ossius of Cordoba the Synod of Elvira in Spain had forbidden sexual
relations between clerics and their wives. Perhaps under his auspices,
some bishops at Nicaea tried to make the prohibition mandatory in
the East, but the aged ascetic and confessor Paphnutius was able to
stop them. In Eusebius' *Demonstratio* (III. 5. 75) he had argued that
the disciples of Jesus 'rejected even the wives permitted by law, not
under compulsion from physical pleasure or enslaved by the desire
for children and descendants'. In the *Church History* on the other
hand, he provided testimony from Clement of Alexandria about
married apostles, their wives, and their children, and claimed that the
remarks were 'relevant to the present matter' (III. 30). It seems likely
that this passage was written just before, or even during, the Council
of Nicaea. It therefore comes from the edition of 325. Second, the
Council of Nicaea, supported by imperial letters, made it mandatory
that the Easter usage of Rome was to be followed.[7] Eusebius soon
wrote a treatise *On the Paschal Celebration* in order to explain that
local traditions, even in the East, had to yield when unity was desired.
The narrative in the *Church History* about an earlier controversy
looks as if it had been altered in order to suit the new situation. It is
hard not to agree with the conclusion of B. Lohse that Eusebius'
account in V. 23-5 is completely tendentious.[8] But why? Eusebius
lays much emphasis both on Irenaeus' apparently successful appeal

[4] H. G. Opitz, *Athanasius Werke*, III: *Urkunde* (Berlin, 1936), Urk. 1, 3
(p. 2, 4).

[5] Ibid., Urk. 3 (pp. 4-6).

[6] Athanasius, *De synodis*, 17. 3 (p. 244, 27 Opitz).

[7] Opitz, Urk. 26 (p. 56, 23).

[8] *Das Passafest der Quartadecimaner* (Gütersloh, 1953), 134-6.

for diversity and on the absolute unanimity with which the churches outside Asia agreed. In the light of actual practice before Nicaea we must infer that the emphasis on diversity is ante-Nicene, that on absolute unanimity under Roman leadership post-Nicene. At the end of Eusebius' little dossier on the Quartodeciman question he cites a letter from the Palestinians perhaps to the Roman church, just as possibly to the Asians with Polycrates.[9] Eusebius implies and, indeed states that the Palestinians agreed with Rome and that the Alexandrians agreed too, celebrating the same day, i.e. Easter Sunday. Perhaps they did not agree. Irenaeus had to write a letter to an Alexandrian explaining that the feast of the Resurrection should be celebrated on the first day of the week.[10] It is at least possible that in the late second century the Alexandrians shared Quartodeciman ideas with the Palestinians (and Asians), even though by 325 Egypt and Asia were following the Roman lead.[11] If so, this passage would provide one more example of Eusebius' desire to tinker with his history.

Finally we turn to the question of Eusebius' audience. For whom did he write and rewrite? Momigliano has recently raised this question about ancient historians generally.[12] Presumably for Eusebius his readers would be those for whom his history would be 'useful', a term not very sharply defined (see Chapter IV). Given his subject matter, his readers were likely to be Christians or even pagans concerned with Church affairs. Certainly the continuous changes at the end of the *History* reflect political considerations appropriate for readers within or on the edge of the imperial administration (cf. VIII. 1. 1–6). As a whole the *History* looks forward to something like the situation of collaboration between Church and State reflected in X. 5–7.

Perhaps we can best approach the question by looking at two kinds of 'history' he did not want to write. First, Aulus Gellius tells a story about how he found and bought bundles of old Greek books at Brindisi. They were 'full of marvellous tales, things unheard of, incredible'.[13] Certainly Eusebius did not wish to compete with 'paradoxographers' like these authors. He had little use for the crudely

---

[9] P. Nautin, *Lettres et écrivains chrétiens des iie et iiie siecles* (Paris, 1961), 85–9, prefers Roman recipients.

[10] Irenaeus, Fr. syr. 27 (II. 456 Harvey).

[11] Letter of Constantine in Eusebius, *Vit. Const.* III. 19. 1.

[12] A. Momigliano, 'The Historians of the Classical World and their Audiences: Some Suggestions', *Annali della Scuola normale superiore di Pisa, Classe di Lettere e Filosofia*, s. III, VIII, 1 (1978), 59–75 (see Bibliography).

[13] A. Gellius IX. 9. 3. 12.

miraculous, in spite of his lack of concern with social, economic, or psychological factors.[14] Like Gellius, he would have been 'seized with disgust for such worthless writings, which contribute nothing to the enrichment or profit of life'.

Second, Eusebius would not have written a Church History like one Jerome proposed to write, telling the whole story

from the apostles to the excrement of our own time, how and through whom the church of Christ was born and, when adult, flourished under persecution and was crowned with martyrdoms; and after it came to Christian rulers, became greater in power and riches but inferior in virtues.

Syme, to whom we owe this quotation, put it sardonically: 'The narration of that declension would have been congenial to his idiosyncrasy.'[15] It would not have been congenial to Eusebius'. He was both less mordant and less experienced. He actually believed that the biblical injunction, 'Put not your trust in princes' (Ps. 146: 3), applied only to the followers of the pagan Emperor Maximin Daia (IX. 11. 8).

The best parallel, as in other cases, is expressed in a passage from Polybius. He is discussing the poverty of a Roman general.

If this seems incredible to anyone, I beg him to consider that the present writer is perfectly aware that this work will be perused by Romans above all people, containing as it does an account of their most splendid achievements, and that it is impossible either that they should be ignorant of the facts or disposed to pardon any departure from truth.[16]

Of course we must add two qualifications: for 'Romans' read 'Romans who know Greek', and add 'Greeks concerned with politics'. But for either group we may substitute 'orthodox Christians' or 'those concerned with Christians' and we approximate the viewpoint of Eusebius. The 'splendid achievements' are related to the rise of Rome or the rise of Christianity. Eusebius uses more florid rhetoric than Polybius does, but many of the motifs are the same. Like Polybius and other Greeks who admired Rome, he tells of a deadly struggle, but one against the Devil and heretics and persecutors. 'Like some noble general of God, clad in divine armour', Peter 'brought the

---

[14] G. F. Chesnut, *The First Christian Histories* (Paris, 1977), 61–131.

[15] Jerome, *Vita Malchi* 1 (*PL* 23, 53); R. Syme, *Ammianus and the Historia Augusta* (Oxford, 1968), 210. For Jerome's picture of the Church and the clergy cf. D. S. Wiesen, *St. Jerome as a Satirist* (Ithaca, 1964), Ch. III. There is no satire in Eusebius.

[16] Polybius XXXI. 22. 8–9.

priceless merchandise of the spiritual light from east to west' and overcame Simon Magus (II. 14. 6). The Christian struggle is not, however, a literal military campaign but a war waged for the peace of the soul, with everlasting monuments and everlasting remembrance as the reward (V, pr. 4). So too Eusebius' account of the conflict is no static compilation but like the work of other historians, even including Thucydides, the result of a long process including much revision. In relation to the history of the Christian Church it can even be called 'not a prize essay to be heard for the moment but a possession for all time'.[17]

---

[17] Thucydides applies these words to his own work (I. 22. 4); Eusebius does not.

BIBLIOGRAPHY

Abramowski, L., 'Irenaeus, *Adv. haer.* III. 3. 2 . . . and . . . 3. 3', *JTS* 28 (1977), 101–4.

Arnold, G., 'Mk 1 1 und Eröffnungswendungen in griechischen und lateinischen' Schriften', *ZNW* 68 (1977), 123–7.

Attridge, H. W., *The Interpretation of Biblical History in the Antiquitates Judaicae of Flavious Josephus.* Missoula, Mont., 1976.

Audet, T.-A., 'Orientations théologiques chez saint Irénée', *Traditio*, 1 (1943), 15–54.

Augar, F., *Die Frau im römischen Christenprocess. TU* 38, 4, Leipzig, 1905.

Avenarius, G., *Lukians Schrift zur Geschichtsschreibung.* Meisenheim/ Glan, 1956.

Bacher, W., *Die Agada der bablyonischen Amoräer.* Ed. 2, Frankfurt a.M., 1913; repr. Hildesheim, 1967.

Balanos, D. S., 'Zum Charakterbild des Kirchenhistorikers Eusebius', *Theologische Quartalschrift*, 116 (1933), 309–22.

Bardy, G., 'Aux origines de l'école d'Alexandrie', *RSR* 27 (1937), 65–90.

— — *Eusèbe de Césarée: Histoire Ecclésiastique.* Paris, 1952–60.

— — 'Pour l'histoire de l'école d'Alexandrie', *Vivre et Penser*, 2 (= *RB* 51, 1942), 80–109.

— — *Recherches sur saint Lucien d'Antioche et son école.* Paris, 1936.

— — 'Sur Paulin de Tyr', *Revue des sciences religieuses*, 2 (1922), 34–45.

— — 'La théologie d'Eusèbe de Césarée d'après l'Histoire Ecclésiastique', *Revue d'histoire ecclésiastique*, 50 (1955), 5–20.

Barnes, T. D., 'The Chronology of Montanism', *JTS* 22 (1971), 403–8.

— — 'Legislation Against the Christians', *JRS* 58 (1968), 32–50.

— — 'A Note on Polycarp', *JTS* 18 (1967), 433–7.

— — 'Origen, Aquila, and Eusebius', *Harvard Studies in Classical Philology*, 74 (1970), 313–16.

— — 'Porphyry Against the Christians: Date and the Attribution of Fragments', *JTS* 24 (1973), 424–42.

— — *Tertullian.* Oxford, 1971.

— — 'The Composition of Eusebius' *Onomasticon*', *JTS* 26 (1975) 412–15.

Bartelink, G. J. M., 'Μισόκαλος, epithète du diable', *VC* 12 (1958), 37–44.

Batiffol, P., 'Les Étapes de la conversion de Constantine. II. L'édit de Milan', *Bulletin d'ancienne littérature et d'archéologie chrétiennes*, 3 (1913), 241–64.

— — *La Paix constantinienne et le catholicisme.* Ed. 2, Paris, 1914.

Bauer, W., *Orthodoxy and Heresy in Earliest Christianity*. Philadelphia, 1971.

Baynes, N. H., 'The Chronology of Eusebius'. See Lawlor, H. J.
—— 'Eusebius and the Christian Empire', *Byzantine Studies and Other Essays* (London, 1960), 168–72.

Birt, T., *Das antike Buchwesen*. Berlin, 1882.

Böhlig, A., 'Zum Martyrium des Jakobus', *Novum Testamentum*, 5 (1962), 207–13.

Boehmer, H., 'Zur altrömischen Bischofsliste', *ZNW* 7 (1906), 333–9.

Boer, W. den, 'Some Remarks on the Beginnings of Christian Historiography', *TU* 79 (1961), 348–62.

Boor, C. de, 'Neue Fragmente des Papias, Hegesippus und Pierius in bisher unbekannten Excerpten aus der Kirchengeschichte des Philippus Sidetes', *TU* 5, 2 (1888), 165–84.

Bouquet, A. C., 'The References to Josephus in the Bibliotheca of Photius', *JTS* 36 (1935), 289–93.

Bureth, P., *Les Titulatures impériales dans les papyrus, les ostraca et les inscriptions d'Egypte (30 a. C.-284 p. C.). Papyrologica Bruxellensis*, 2. Brussels, 1964.

Byatt, A., 'Josephus and Population Numbers in First Century Palestine', *Palestine Exploration Quarterly*, 105 (1973), 51–60.

Cadbury, H. J. *The Making of Luke-Acts*. New York, 1927.

Campenhausen, H. von, *Bearbeitungen und Interpolationen des Polykarpmartyriums. Sitzungsberichte der Heidelberger Akademie der Wissenschaften, Philosophisch-historische Klasse*, 1957, No. 3.

Caspar, E., *Die älteste römische Bischofsliste*. Berlin, 1926.
—— *Geschichte des Papsttums*, i. *Römische Kirche und Imperium Romanum*. Tübingen, 1930.

Castritius, H., 'Der Armenienkrieg des Maximinus Daia', *Jahrbuch für Antike und Christentum*, 11/12 (1968/1969), 94–103.
—— *Studien zu Maximinus Daia. Frankfurter Althistorische Studien*, 2. Kallmünz, 1969.

Cataudella, M. R., 'Per la cronologia dei rapporti fra cristianesimo e impero agli inizi del IV sec.', *Siculorum Gymnasium*, 20 (1967), 83–110.

Cecchelli, C., 'Un tentato risconcimento imperiale del Cristo', *Scritti in onore di A. Calderini e R. Paribeni*, i (Milan, 1956), 351–62.

Chadwick, H., 'Ossius of Cordova and the Presidency of the Council of Antioch, 325', *JTS* 9 (1958), 292–304.
—— 'The Relativity of Moral Codes: Rome and Persia in Late Antiquity', *Early Christian Literature and the Classical Intellectual Tradition*, ed. W. R. Schoedel–R. L. Wilken (Paris, 1979), 135–53.

Chesnut, G. F., *The First Christian Histories: Eusebius, Socrates, Sozomen, Theodoret and Evagrius*. Paris, 1977.

Conybeare, F. C., *Philo About the Contemplative Life*. Oxford, 1895.

Cranz, F. E., 'Kingdom and Polity in Eusebius of Caesarea', *HTR* 49 (1952), 47–66.

Cross, F. L., 'The Council of Antioch in 325 A. D.', *Church Quarterly Review*, 128 (1939), 49–76.

Diels, H., *Doxographi Graeci*. Berlin, 1879.

—— *Parmenides Lehrgedicht*. Berlin, 1897.

Dillon, J., *The Middle Platonists*. London, 1977.

Drewery, B., *Origen and the Doctrine of Grace*. London, 1960.

Drijvers, H. J. W., *Bardaisan of Edessa*. Assen, 1966.

Ehrhardt, A. A. T., *The Apostolic Succession*. London, 1953.

Emonds, H., *Zweite Auflage in Altertum. Klassisch-Philologische Studien*, 14. Leipzig, 1941.

Farina, R., *L'impero e l'imperatore cristiano in Eusebio di Cesarea (La prima teologia politica del Cristanesimo)*. Bibliotheca Theologica Salesiana, Ser. I, No. 2. Zurich, 1966.

Fascher, E., 'Jerusalems Untergang in der urchristlichen und altkirchliche Überlieferung', *Theologische Literaturzeitung*, 89 (1964), 81–98.

Fitzmyer, J. A., 'The Bar Cochba Period'. *The Bible in Current Catholic Thought*, ed. J. L. McKenzie (New York, 1962), 133–68.

Fotheringham, J. K., *The Bodleian Manuscript of Jerome's Version of the Chronicle of Eusebius*. Oxford, 1905.

Freudenberger, R., 'Ein angeblicher Christenbrief Mark Aurels', *Historia*, 17 (1968), 251–6.

—— 'Christenreskript. Ein umstrittenes Reskript des Antoninus Pius', *ZKG* 88 (1967), 1–14.

—— 'De Überlieferung vom Martyrium des römischen Christen Apollonius', *ZNW* 60 (1969), 111–30.

—— *Das Verhalten der römischen Behörden gegen die Christen im 2. Jahrhundert* (dargestellt am Brief des Plinius an Trajan und den Reskripten Trajans und Hadrians). *Münchener Beiträge zur Papyrusforschung und antiken Rechtsgeschichte*, 52. Munich, 1967.

Fuks, A., 'The Jewish Revolt in Egypt (A.D. 115–117) in the light of the papyri', *Aegyptus*, 33 (1953), 131–58.

Funk, F. X., *Didascalia et Constitutiones Apostolorum*, I. Paderborn, 1905.

Funk, W.-P., 'Die Zweite Apokalypse des Jakobus an Nag-Hammadi-Codex V'. *TU* 119, 1976.

Gaster, T. H., *Myth, Legend, and Custom in the Old Testament*. New York, 1969.

Geffcken, J., 'Augustins Tolle-lege-Erlebnis', *Archiv für Religionswissenschaft*, 31 (1934), 1–13.

Gelzer, H., *Sextus Julius Africanus und die byzantinische Chronographie*, i–ii. Leipzig, 1885–98.

Gelzer, M., *Die Achaica im Geschichtswerk des Polybius. Abhandlungen der Preussischen Akademie der Wissenschaften*, 1940, *Philosophisch-historische Klasse*, 2.

—— *Ueber die Arbeitsweise des Polybius. Sitzungsberichte der Heidelberger Akademie der Wissenschaften*, 1956, 3.

—— 'Die hellenische *prokataskeuē* im 2. Buch des Polybius', *Hermes*, 75 (1940), 27–37.

Geppert, F., *Die Quellen des Kirchenhistorikers Socrates Scholasticus.* Leipzig, 1898.

Gifford, E. H., *Eusebii Pamphili Evangelicae Praeparationis Libri* XV. Oxford, 1903.

Grant, R. M., *After the New Testament.* Philadelphia, 1967.

— — 'Eusebius, H. E. VIII: Another Suggestion', *VC* 22 (1968), 16–18.

— — 'Early Alexandrian Christianity', *Church History*, 40 (1971), 133–44.

— — 'Eusebius and his Church History', *Understanding the Sacred Text: Studies in Honor of Morton S. Enslin,* ed. J. Reumann (Valley Forge, 1972), 235–47.

— — 'Manichees and Christians in the Third and Early Fourth Centuries', *Ex Orbe Religionum: Studia Geo Widengren,* i (Leiden, 1972), 430–9.

— — 'Papias in Eusebius' Church History', *Mélanges d'histoire des religions offerts à Henri-Charles Puech* (Paris, 1974), 209–13.

— — 'Eusebius and his Lives of Origen', *Forma Futuri: Studi in onore del cardinale Michele Pellegrino* (Torino, 1975), 635–49.

— — 'Eusebius and Gnostic Origins', *Paganisme, Judaïsme, Christianisme: Mélanges offerts à Marcel Simon* (Paris, 1978), 195–205.

— — 'Eusebius and the Martyrs of Gaul', *Colloques Internationaux du Centre Nationale de la Recherche Scientifique,* 575: *Les Martyrs de Lyon* (177) (Paris, 1978), 129–36.

Gustafsson, B., 'Eusebius' Principles in handling his Sources as found in his Church History', *TU* 79 (1961), 429–41.

Habicht, C., 'Zur Geschichte des Kaisers Konstantin', *Hermes,* 86 (1958), 360–78.

Harl, M., 'L'histoire de l'humanité racontée par un écrivain chrétein au debut du IVe siècle', *Revue des études grecques,* 75 (1962), 522–31.

Harnack, A., *Die Zeit des Ignatius und die Chronologie der antiochenischen Bischöfe bis Tyrannus.* Leipzig, 1878.

— — *Die griechische Überlieferung des Apologeticus Tertullians. TU* 8, 4. Leipzig, 1892.

— — *Geschichte der altchristlichen Litteratur bis Eusebius.* Leipzig, 1893–1904. (*Die Chronologie der altchristlichen Litteratur,* i. 1897).

— — *Porphyrius 'Gegen die Christen'. Abhandlungen der Preussischen Akademie der Wissenschaften zu Berlin,* 1916, *Philosophisch-historische Klasse,* No. 1.

Hartmann, P., 'Origène et la théologie du martyre d'après le Protreptikos de 235', *ETL* 34 (1958), 773–824.

Heinrici, G., *Das Urchristentum in der Kirchengeschichte des Eusebius. Beiträge zur Geschichte und Erklärung des Neuen Testaments,* i. Leipzig, 1894.

Helm, R. 'Eusebius' Chronik und ihre Tabellenform', *Abhandlungen der Berliner Akademie* 1923, *Philologisch-historische Klasse,* 4, 3–56.

— — 'De Eusebii in Chronicorum libro auctoribus', *Eranos,* 22 (1924), 1–40.

Helm, R., 'Hieronymus und Eutrop', *Rheinisches Museum*, 76 (1927), 138–70; 254–306.

Holl, K., *Epiphanius (Ancoratus and Panarion)* I–III. Leipzig, 1915–33.

Hornschuh, M., 'Das Leben des Origenes und die Entstehung der alexandrinischen Schule', *ZKG* 71 (1960), 1–25; 193–214.

Hyldahl, N., 'Hegesipps Hypomnemata', *Studia Theologica*, 14 (1960), 70–113.

Jacoby, F., *Apollodors Chronik. Philologische Untersuchungen*, 16, 1902.

—— —— *Die Fragmente der griechischen Historiker.* Berlin, 1923–; new edn., Leiden, 1957–.

Janne, H., 'L'histoire ecclésiastique d'Eusèbe et le système de M. Laqueur', *Byzantion*, 8 (1933), 741–9.

Javierre, A.-M., 'Le Thème de la succession des apôtres dans la littérature chrétienne primitive', *Unam Sanctam*, 39 (1962), 171–221.

Jones, A. H. M., with Skeat, T. C., 'Notes on the Genuineness of the Constantinian Documents in Eusebius' Life of Constantine', *JEH* 5 (1954), 196–200.

Keil, J.–Maresch, G., 'Epigraphische Nachlese zu Miltners Ausgrabungs-berichten aus Ephesos', *JAOI* 45 (1960), Beiblatt, 75–100.

Keller, E., *Eusèbe historien des persécutions.* Geneva–Paris, 1912.

Kemler, H., 'Hegesipps römische Bischofsliste', *VC* 25 (1971), 182–96.

Kettler, F. H., 'Petrus I (1) Bischof von Alexandrien', *RE* XIX (1938), 1281–8.

Klein, R. 'Der νόμος τελεώτατος Konstantins für die Christen im Jahre 312', *Römische Quartalschrift*, 67 (1972), 1–28.

Klotz, A., 'Die Arbeitsweise der älteren Plinius und die Indices Auctorum', *Hermes*, 42 (1907), 323–9.

Knauber, A., 'Das Anliegen der Schule des Origenes zu Cäsarea', *Müncheners Theologische Zeitschrift*, 19 (1968), 182–203.

Kretschmar, G., 'Origenes und die Araber', *Zeitschrift für Theologie und Kirche* 50 (1953), 258–79.

Kroll, W., 'Plinius der älterer', *RE* XXI (1951), 271–439.

Kühnert, N., 'Der antimontanistische Anonymus des Eusebius', *Theologische Zeitschrift*, 5 (1949), 436–46.

Labriolle, P. de, *La Réaction païenne.* Paris, 1934.

Lake, K., *Eusebius: The Ecclesiastical History*, I. London, 1926.

Lampe, G. W. H., *A Patristic Greek Lexicon.* Oxford, 1968.

—— —— 'Some Notes on the Significance of ΒΑΣΙΛΕΙΑ ΤΟΥ ΘΕΟΥ, ΒΑΣΙΛΕΙΑ ΧΡΙΣΤΟΥ, in the Greek Fathers', *JTS* 49 (1948), 58–73.

Laqueur, R., 'Die beiden Fassungen des sog. Toleranzedikts von Mailand', ΕΠΙΤΥΜΒΙΟΝ *Heinrich Swoboda* (Reichenberg, 1927), 132–41.

—— —— 'Ephoros', *Hermes*, 46 (1911), 161–206; 321–54.

—— —— *Eusebius als Historiker seiner Zeit.* Berlin–Leipzig, 1929. See also Emonds, H., Janne, H.

Lawlor, H. J., *Eusebiana*. Oxford, 1912.

—— with N. H. Baynes and G. W. Richardson, 'The Chronology of Eusebius', *Classical Quarterly*, 19 (1925), 94–100.

—— with J. E. L. Oulton, *Eusebius: The Ecclesiastical History and the Martyrs of Palestine*. London, 1928.

Lazzati, G., 'Nota su Eusebio epitomatore di Atti dei Martiri', *Scritti in onore di A. Calderini e R. Paribeni*, i (Milan, 1956), 377–84.

Lee, G. M., 'Presbyters and Apostles', *ZNW* 62 (1971), 122.

—— 'Eusebius on St. Mark and the Beginnings of Christianity in Egypt', *TU* 115 (1975), 422–31.

Levine, L. I., *Roman Caesarea*. Qedem 2, Jerusalem, 1975.

Lieberman, S., 'The martyrs of Caesarea', *Annuaire de l'institut de philologie et d'histoire orientales et slaves*, 7 (1944), 395–446.

Lightfoot, J. B., *The Apostolic Fathers*, I: *S. Clement of Rome*, I. London, 1890.

—— (and Westcott, B. F.), 'Eusebius of Caesarea', *Dictionary of Christian Biography*, ii (London, 1880), 308–48.

MacMullen, R., 'Roman Bureaucratese', *Traditio*, 18 (1962), 364–78.

MacRae, G., 'Miracle in the *Antiquities* of Josephus', *Miracle*, ed. C. F. D. Moule (London, 1965), 127–47.

Mantel, H., 'The Causes of the Bar Kokba Revolt', *Jewish Quarterly Review*, 58 (1967–8), 224–42, 274–96.

Markus, R. A., 'Church history and early church historians', *The Materials Sources and Methods of Ecclesiastical History*, ed. D. Baker (Oxford, 1975), 1–17.

Martin, C., 'Le "testimonium flavianum": vers une solution définitive?' *Revue Belge de philologie et d'histoire*, 20 (1941), 409–65.

McGiffert, A. C., *Eusebius: Church History*. A Select Library of Nicene and Post-Nicene Fathers, Second Series, I, ed. P. Schaff–H. Wace. New York, 1890.

Méhat, A., *Étude sur les 'Stromates' de Clément d'Alexandrie*. Paris, 1966.

Meinhold, P., *Geschichte der kirchlichen Historiographie*, i. Munich, 1967.

—— 'Polykarpos', *RE* XXI (1952), 1662–93.

Milik, J. T. 'La Topographie de Jérusalem vers la fin de l'époque byzantine', *Mélanges de l'Université Saint Joseph*, 37 (1960–1), 127–89.

Mitteis, L. with U. Wilcken, *Grundzüge und Chrestomathie der Papyrusurkunde*. Berlin–Leipzig, 1912.

Moehring, H. R., 'Rationalization of Miracles in the Writings of Flavius Josephus', *TU* 112 (1973), 376–83.

Momigliano, A. (ed.), *The Conflict Between Paganism and Christianity in the Fourth Century*. Oxford, 1963.

—— *Essays in Ancient and Modern Historiography*. Middletown, Conn., 1977.

—— 'The Historians of the Classical World and their Audiences', *The American Scholar*, 47 (1977/1978), 193–204.

Momigliano, A., 'The Historians of the Classical World and their Audiences: Some Suggestions', *Annali della Scuola normale superiore di Pisa, Classe di lettere e filosofia*, Ser. III, VIII, 1 (1978), 61–75.

Mommsen, T., 'Ueber die Quellen der Chronik des Hieronymus', *Abhandlungen der philologisch-historischer Classe der Königlichen Sächsischen Gesellschaft der Wissenschaften*, 1 (1850), 669–93.

— — 'Zweisprachige Inschrift aus Arykanda', *Archaeologisch-epigraphische Mittheilungen aus Oesterreich–Ungarn*, 16 (1893), 93–102; Nachtrag by O. Benndorf and E. Bormann, 108.

Moreau, J., *Lactance De la mort des persécuteurs*. Paris, 1954.

— — 'Eusèbe de Césarée en Palestine', *Dictionnaire d'histoire et de géographie ecclésiastiques*, xv (Paris, 1964), 1437–60.

— — *Scripta minora. Annales Universitatis Saraviensis*. Reihe: Philosophische Fakultät, Band I. Heidelberg, 1964.

Mosshammer, A. A., *The Chronicle of Eusebius and Greek Chronographic Tradition*. Lewisburg, N. J.–London, 1979.

Mras, K., *Eusebius Werke: Die Praeparatio Evangelica*. Berlin, 1956.

Musurillo, H., *The Acts of the Christian Martyrs*. Oxford, 1972.

— — 'Early Christian Economy: a Reconsideration of P. Amherst 3 (a) (= Wilcken, *Chrest.* 126)', *Chronique d'Egypte*, 31 (1956), 124–34.

— — *St. Methodius: The Symposium*. Westminster, Md., 1958.

Naldini, M., *Il Cristianesimo in Egitto: Lettere private nei papiri dei secoli II–IV. Studi e testi di papirologia*, 3. Florence, 1968.

Nautin, P., *Le dossier d'Hippolyte et de Méliton*. Paris, 1953.

— — *Lettres et écrivains chrétiens des iie et iiie siècles*. Paris, 1961.

— — *Origène sa vie et son œuvre*. Paris, 1977.

Negev, A., 'Inscriptions hébraiques, grecques et latines de Césarée Maritime', *RB* 78 (1971), 247–63.

Nesselhauf, H., 'Das Toleranzgesetz des Licinius', *Historisches Jahrbuch*, 74 (1955), 44–61.

Nestle, W., 'Legenden vom Tod der Gottesverächter', *Archiv für Religionswissenschaft*, 33 (1936), 246–69.

Neusner, J., *A History of the Jews in Babylonia*, iv. Leiden, 1969.

Nigg, W., *Die Kirchengeschichtsschreibung: Grundzüge ihrer historischen Entwicklung*. Munich, 1934.

Noakes, K. W., 'Melito of Sardis and the Jews', *TU* 116 (1975), 244–9.

Opitz, H.–G., 'Die Zeitfolge des arianischen Streites von der Anfängen bis zum Jahre 328', *ZNW* 33 (1934), 131–59.

— — *Urkunden zur Geschichte des arianischer Streites 318–328 = Athanasius Werke*, III. 1. Berlin, 1934/1935.

— — 'Euseb von Caesarea als Theologe', *ZNW* 34 (1935), 1–19.

Paschoud, F., *Zosime: Histoire Nouvelle*, i. Paris, 1971.

Paulsen, H., 'Erwägungen zu Acta Apollonii 14–22', *ZNW* 66 (1975), 117–26.

Peppermüller, R., 'Griechische Papyrusfragmente der Doctrina Addai', *VC* 25 (1971), 289–301.

Perler, O., *Méliton de Sardes Sur la Pâque*. Paris, 1966.

Plümacher, E., *Lukas, als hellenistischer Schriftsteller.* Göttingen, 1972.
Prigent, P., 'L'hérésie asiate et l'église confessante', *VC* 31 (1977), 1-22.
Radford, L. B., *Three Teachers of Alexandria.* Cambridge, 1908.
Richard, M., 'La Question pascale au iie siècle', *L'Orient Syrien,* 6 (1961), 179-212.
—— 'Malchion et Paul de Samosate: Le témoignage d'Eusèbe de Césarée', *ETL* 35 (1959), 325-38.
Richardson, C. C., 'The Condemnation of Origen', *Church History,* 6 (1937), 50-64.
Robert, L., 'Sur les inscriptions d'Éphèse', *Revue de philologie,* 41 (1967), 7-84.
Roller, K., *Die Kaisergeschichte in Laktanz 'de mortibus persecutorum'.* Giessen, 1927.
Routh, M. J., *Reliquiae Sacrae,* Ed. 2. Oxford, 1846.
Saffrey, H. D., 'Un lecteur antique des œuvres de Numénius: Eusebe de Césarée', *Forma Futuri: Studi in onore del cardinale Michele Pellegrino* (Torino, 1975), 145-53.
Scheideweiler, F., 'Zur Kirchengeschichte des Eusebius von Kaisareia', *ZNW* 49 (1958), 123-9.
Schemmel, F., 'Die Schule von Caesarea in Palaestine', *Philologische Wochenschrift,* 45 (1925), 1277-80.
Schmid, W., 'Eusebianum. Adnotatio ad Epistulam Antonini Pii a Christianis factum', *Rheinisches Museum,* 97 (1954), 190-1.
—— 'The Christian Interpretation of the Rescript of Hadrian', *Maia,* 7 (1955), 5-13.
Schoedel, W.R.-Wilken, R.L. (eds.), *Early Christian Literature and the Classical Intellectual Tradition: in honorem Robert M. Grant.* Paris, 1979.
Schreckenberg, H., *Die Flavius-Josephus-Tradition in Antike und Mittelalter.* Leiden, 1972.
Schürer, E., 'Zur Chronologie des Lebens Pauli zugleich ein Beitrag zur Kritik der Chronik des Eusebius', *Zeitschrift für Wissenschaftliche Theologie,* 21 (1898), 21-42.
Schumrick, A., *Observationes ad rem librariam pertinentes de* ΣΥΝΤΑΞΙΣ ΣΥΝΤΑΓΜΑ ΠΡΑΓΜΑΤΕΙΑ ΥΠΟΜΝΗΜΑ *vocabulis.* Marburg, 1909.
Schwartz, E., 'Eusebius von Caesarea', *RE* VI (1909), 1370-1439.
—— *Eusebius: Kirchengeschichte* I-III. Leipzig, 1903/1909.
—— 'Zu Eusebius Kirchengeschichte I. Das Martyrium Jakobus des Gerechten', *ZNW* 4 (1903), 48-61.
—— 'Zu Eusebius Kirchengeschichte II. Zur Abgarlegende', *ZNW* 4 (1903), 61-6.
Sedlacek, I., *Dionysius Bar Salibi in Apocalypsim, Actus et Epistulas catholicas. CSCO, Scriptores Syri,* Series Secunda, CI (versio). Rome, 1910.
Seeberg, E., *Die Synode von Antiochien im Jahre 324/25.* Berlin, 1913.

Seidl, E., *Der Eid in römisch–ägyptischen Provinzialrecht*, i. *Münchener Beiträge zur Papyrusforschung und antiken Rechtgeschichte*, xvii, 1933. 2. Ibid., xxiv, 1935.

Simon, M., 'La migration à Pella: légende ou réalité?' *RSR* 60 (1972), 37–54.

— — *Verus Israël*. Ed. 2. Paris, 1964.

Sirinelli, J., *Les Vues historiques d'Eusèbe de Césarée durant la période prénicéenne*. Université de Dakar, Faculté des lettres et sciences humaines. Publications de la Section de langues et littérature, 10. Dakar–Paris, 1961. See also Harl, M.

Smallwood, E. M., 'Atticus, Legate of Judaea under Trajan', *JRS* 52 (1962), 131–3.

— — 'Palestine c. A. D. 115–118', *Historia*, 11 (1962), 500–10.

— — *The Jews under Roman Rule*. Leiden, 1976.

Smith, M., *Clement of Alexandria and a Secret Gospel of Mark*. Cambridge, Mass., 1973.

Soden, H. von–Campenhausen, H. von, *Urkunden zur Entstehungsgeschichte des Donatismus*. Ed. 2. Berlin, 1950.

Somerville, R. S., 'An Ordering Principle for Book VIII of Eusebius' Ecclesiastical History: A Suggestion', *VC* 20 (1966), 91–7.

Sowers, S. S., 'The Circumstances and Recollection of the Pella Flight', *Theologische Zeitschrift*, 26 (1970), 305–20.

Stauffer, E., 'Zum Kaliphat des Jacobus', *Zeitschrift für Religions- und Geistesgeschichte*, 4 (1952), 193–214.

Stein, E., 'Konstantin d. Gr. gelangt 324 zur Alleinherrschaft', *ZNW* 30 (1931), 177–85.

— — *Histoire du Bas-Empire*, i. Trans. and ed. J.–R. Palanque, Paris, 1959.

Stevenson, J., *Studies in Eusebius*. Cambridge, 1929.

— — 'The Life and Literary Activity of Lactantius', *TU* 63 (1957), 661–77.

Stoop, E. de, *Essai sur la diffusion du manichéisme dans l'empire romain*. Ghent, 1909.

Storch, R. H., 'The "Eusebian Constantine"', *Church History*, 40 (1971), 145–55.

Strack, H. L., *Introduction to the Talmud and Midrash*. Philadelphia, 1931.

Swete, H. B. (ed.), *Essays on the Early History of the Church and the Ministry*. London, 1918.

Syme, R., *Ammianus and the Historia Augusta*. Oxford, 1968.

Taubenschlag, R., 'The Imperial Constitutions in the Papyri', *Journal of Juristic Papyri*, 6 (1952), 121–42.

Telfer, W., 'When did the Arian Controversy Begin?', *JTS* 47 (1946), 129–42.

— — 'Was Hegesippus a Jew?', *HTR* 53 (1960), 143–53.

Thackeray, H. St. J., *Josephus the Man and the Historian*. New York, 1929.

Toynbee, J.–Perkins, J. B. W., *The Shrine of St. Peter*. New York, 1957.

Turner, C. H., 'The Early Episcopal Lists', *JTS* 1 (1899/1900), 181-200; 529-53; 18 (1916/1917), 103-34.

— — 'Apostolic Succession. A. The Original Conception', *Essays on the Early History of the Church and the Ministry*, ed. H. B. Swete (London, 1918), 95-142.

Völker, W., 'Von welchem Tendenzen liess sich Eusebius bei Abfassung seiner "Kirchengeschichte" leiten?', *VC* 4 (1950), 157-80.

Wallace-Hadrill, D. S., 'The Eusebian Chronicle: the Extent and Date of Composition of its Early Editions', *JTS* 6 (1955), 248-53.

— — *Eusebius of Caesarea*. London, 1960.

— — 'Eusebius of Caesarea and the *Testimonium Flavianum* (Josephus, *Antiquities* XVIII. 63f.)', *JEH* 25 (1974), 353-62.

— — 'Eusebius of Caesarea's *Commentary on Luke*: Its Origin and Early History', *HTR* 67 (1974), 55-63.

Walzer, R., *Galen on Jews and Christians*. Oxford, 1949.

Weijenborg, R., 'Die Berichte über Justin und Crescens bei Tatian', *Antonianum*, 47 (1972), 372-90.

Wiesen, D. S., *St. Jerome as a Satirist*. Ithaca, 1964.

Wilcken, U. See Mitteis, L.

Wilken, R. L., *The Myth of Christian Beginnings*. Garden City, N. Y., 1971.

Zahn, T., *Forschungen zur Geschichte des neutestamentliche Kanons und der altchristlichen Literatur*, III. *Supplementum Clementinum*. Erlangen, 1884.

— — 'Der Exeget Ammonius und andere Ammonii', *ZKG* 38 (1920), 1-22; 311-36.

Zernov, N., 'Eusebius and the Paschal Controversy', *Church Quarterly Review*, 116 (1933), 24-41.

Zimmermann, H., *Ecclesia als Objekt der Historiographie. Sitzungsberichte der Oesterreichische Akademie der Wissenschaften zu Wien*, 235, No. 4, 1960.

Zuckschwerdt, E., 'Das Naziräat des Herrenbruders Jakobus nach Hegesipp (Euseb, h. e. II 23, 5-6)', *ZNW* 68 (1977), 276-87.

INDEXES

ANCIENT AUTHORS AND DOCUMENTS

1. Eusebius' works apart from the Church History

2. Other ancient authors and documents

MODERN AUTHORS

PRINCIPAL SUBJECTS